How To Use The Maps And The Photo Finder Feature™

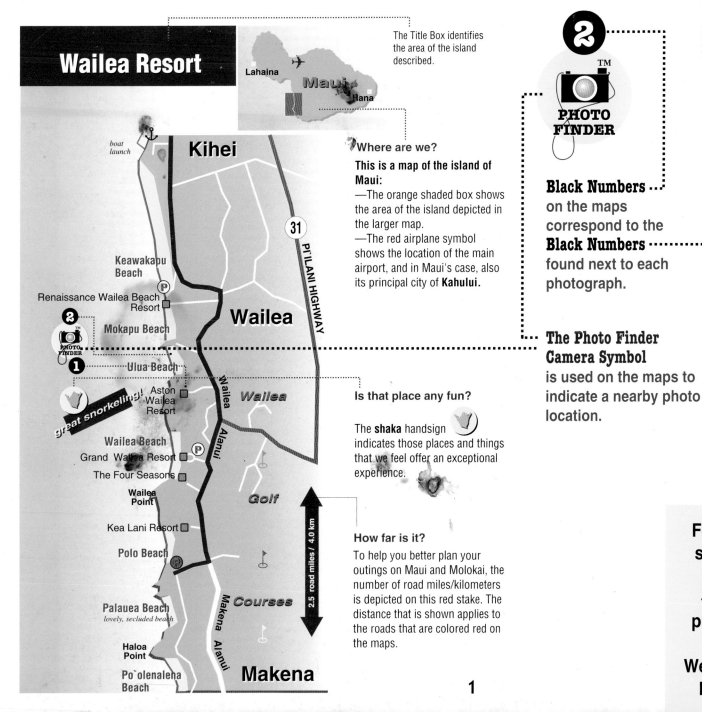

Wailea Resort

The Title Box identifies the area of the island described.

Where are we?

This is a map of the island of Maui:
—The orange shaded box shows the area of the island depicted in the larger map.
—The red airplane symbol shows the location of the main airport, and in Maui's case, also its principal city of **Kahului.**

Is that place any fun?

The **shaka** handsign indicates those places and things that we feel offer an exceptional experience.

How far is it?

To help you better plan your outings on Maui and Molokai, the number of road miles/kilometers is depicted on this red stake. The distance that is shown applies to the roads that are colored red on the maps.

PHOTO FINDER

Black Numbers on the maps correspond to the **Black Numbers** found next to each photograph.

The Photo Finder Camera Symbol is used on the maps to indicate a nearby photo location.

Match the **Black Photo Number** with the **Black Map Number** to pinpoint the exact location on the map where each photo was taken.

For photographers and videocam shooters alike, our revolutionary **Photo Location Guide Feature** –found in no other guidebook– provides a blueprint for unlimited photographic opportunities. We can almost guarantee your best Hawaii photos and videos ever!

D0752316

1

Driving & Discovering Hawaii Books are published by:

Montgomery Ewing Publishers
2290 Silver Ridge Ave.
Los Angeles CA 90039
USA
℡ (323) 662-2289

©2002 Richard Sullivan and
Montgomery Ewing Publishers
All rights reserved

Sullivan, Richard, 1949-
Driving & Discovering Hawaii: Maui and Molokai
Richard Sullivan – 2nd edition
ISBN 09636828-9-X
1. Maui and Molokai (Hawaii) – Description and Travel – Hawaii — Guidebooks – Photography Books

We can produce custom editions of Driving & Discovering Hawaii books to be used for sale, promotion, and premiums. Special editions can be produced with custom covers and inside pages to suit individual needs. For more information, email <editor@discoveringhawaii.com>, call (323) 662-2289, or write to: Montgomery Ewing Publishers, 2290 Silver Ridge Ave., Los Angeles CA 90039

Check for guidebook updates before your visit:

www.discoveringhawaii.com

Also by Richard Sullivan:
Driving & Discovering Hawaii: Oahu

To my parents, Jeanne & Harry Schwartz, for their unending faith, respect and encouragement.

To Elizabeth Baker, my former English teacher at South Park High School in Buffalo NY, for her sincere encouragement and initial push along this rewarding path.

For Denise Takashima, for truly caring, and for sharing the best and worst times of my life, —and for sticking by me no matter what.

And...

Alex del Rosario M.D.
Gordon U. Kai, Budget Rent A Car Hawaii
Amy Kastens, Maui Film Office
Walea Constantinau, Honolulu Film Office

Joan Aronson
Gene Yokoi
Sheila Donnelly-Theroux
Gene Poe
Michael Danahy, E! Television Network
Alessandro Calza
Alex Lopez

Jeannie Heilig
Barbara Sullivan
Donna Merritt
Peggy and Dennis Sullivan

Uncle Larry Kalua
and
Mafumi Enomoto

Although we do offer some recommendations for local shopping, eating and accommodations, you may find that at the time of your visit some businesses may not be open or keep to their posted hours, or certain services or activities may not be offered. These probabilities make writing any travel guide difficult. We have made the decision not to leave out recommendations that the reader may find useful although there's a chance some might not apply at the time of his visit.

All photographs in this book were made with Canon AE1™ cameras and Canon and Vivitar lenses. All photos were made on Kodak films, the majority (95%) with Kodachrome 64™ film. The original text composition was done in Microsoft Word™. This book was designed and composed with Adobe PageMaker™ software. The maps were drawn with Adobe Illustrator™.

Special thanks to **Fonthead Design,** on the web at <www.fonthead.com/main.html> for their font "Good Dog Cool" and to **Sean Cavanaugh** for CombiNumerals 6. Also thanks to **The ChankStore**, at <www.chank.com> for "Mr. Frisky".

Other valuable Maui/Molokai references:
John Clark "**Beaches of Maui County**" (includes Maui, Moloka`i, Lana`i and Kaho`olawe)
Greg Ambrose "**Surfer's Guide To Hawaii**"
Individual island maps by **James A. Bier**
Molokai: An Island In Time by Richard A. Cooke III

Page 3/ painting on left:
"L'an deux Mille", oil on canvas, 72" X 41"

Page 3/ painting on right:
"Year 2000 Orange", oil on canvas, 72" X 41"

Alain-Paul Sevilla's artworks are represented by:

Los Angeles County Museum Of Art
Sales and Rental Gallery
5905 Wilshire Blvd.
Los Angeles CA 90036
[213] 857-6500

Montgomery Ewing Publishers,
2290 N. Silver Ridge Ave.
Los Angeles CA 90039
[323] 662-2289

Dedicated to the memory of

Atop Lyon Hill,
overlooking
Hana, Maui

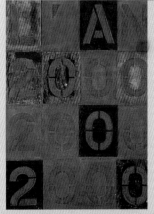

Alain-Paul Sevilla

You were a great artist and the
ultimate friend...
boundlessly gifted,
unceasingly loyal,
astonishingly generous,
completely dependable,
unconditionally loving,
and always, *always* there.
You are irreplaceable
and unforgettable.
And now, Young Marty Jr.,
Maui and Molokai welcome
you home.

3

Contents

MAUI

Paia
Ke`anae
Hana
`Ohe`o 7 Pools
Kaupo

114 INTRODUCTION TO MOLOKAI: The Most Hawaiian Island Of All.

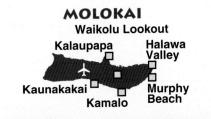

MOLOKAI

Waikolu Lookout
Kalaupapa
Halawa Valley
Kaunakakai
Kamalo
Murphy Beach

116 EAST MOLOKAI Beach Chart

146 WEST MOLOKAI Beach Chart

MOLOKAI

Kaluakoi Resort and Papaohaku Beach
Maunaloa town and Molokai Ranch and Wildlife Park

Just Picture This!

Maui embraces an amazing variety of micro climates ranging from the freezing winds and occasional white snows of Haleakala to the parched and naked hot lava flows of South Makena to the lush rain forests, towering waterfalls and black and red sand beaches of Hana. Maui begs to be captured and cherished on film and videotape.

In April, Upcountry Maui shimmers emerald green due to the generosity of winter and spring rains and in May is blanketed by a blizzard of lavender jacaranda blossoms falling from trees cloaked in beautiful purplish bloom. Eucalyptus vapors fill the air, along with the homey smell of burning logs from stone fireplaces warming chilly high-country homes. Neatly planted pine forests border steep, twisting, narrow roadways that climb into the thousands of feet, right up the side of the dormant volcano. Far below, a neon colored vision of sailboards litters the beach at **Ho'okipa**. Wind riders whiz and zoom over, through, and between ten-foot waves, occasionally somersaulting in precisely executed midair maneuvers to the loud appreciation of fans, casual observers, and us photographers watching from the bluff tops.

Sunsets are unforgettable from **Lahaina Harbor** as the golden orb sinks behind neighbor island Lana'i. Surfers and kayakers just outside the harbor wring a few last rides out of the waves while they can still see. For a full half hour after sunset, the sky glows and deepens in color as dreamy eyed visitors sit at waterside restaurants contemplating a permanent relocation to this wonderful place, absentmindedly twirling the little umbrellas in their Mai Tais and Blue Hawaiians.

Molokai on the other hand is *primeval* Hawaii, the Hawaii of days gone by ...Hawaii as it used to be: unsullied, unspoiled, unpretentious, undeveloped, untouristed, unforgettable.

Astounding vertical 3000' pali walls of green magnificence play with the mists, dance at the edge of the sea, poke their heads into the clouds, glow in the sunlight, and enthrall low flying planes filled with visitors and kama'ainas alike gawking out little windows in wonderment and awe. A ten mile long dirt road climbs through stilled forests to the astonishing isolation, near-perfect silence and enormous vista that is **Waikolu Lookout**. Dozens of waterfalls wash down Waikolu's cliffs, clouds appear from below out of nowhere, and just as suddenly, totally evaporate in midair, right be-

fore your wondering eyes. Picture-perfect, endlessly empty beaches, awash in salty sunlight, devoid of footprints and seldom visited, await your senses, your naked body, and your camera's lens. Ruins of buildings that once housed humans writhing in the misery of leprosy stand near the neat cottages of **Kalaupapa**'s last survivors of this now-arrested disease, on one of earth's most heartbreakingly beautiful peninsulas, protected in isolation.

If you didn't bring a videocam to Hawaii, rent one. If you forgot your camera, stop at the drug store and pick up a few of the single use variety. You cannot

leave Maui and Molokai without commemorating your visit on film. We've said it before and we'll say it again: photographs are small miracles, little portable pieces of time, frozen instants of your own personal history. They are images of wonderful places and people you may never see again, or never see again in the same way...not quite as lovely, not quite as young.

Video's immediacy is sometimes disconcerting. Video is almost real life. Movie film has a texture that is at the same time beautiful and distancing, offering us a diffuse and often prettified reality. But video is crystal clear and raw and in-your-face. Loved ones captured on video will always have a realistic immediacy, seeming to exist in the now. People often regret not taking enough pictures, but rarely do they regret taking too many.

Make sure you have ISO/ASA 100 (or a *lower* ASA number than 100) film for sunny scenes and brilliant

color, and ISO/ASA 400 (or higher) film for dark days, rain forests, shady portraits, fast action, and building interiors. Remember that **the lower the ISO/ASA number, the better the color** and the finer the grain, but the more light or longer exposure you'll need to capture the image. **The higher the ISO/ASA number**, the more apparent the grain and the more subdued the color, but **the less light you will need to capture the image**. But color isn't an absolute necessity...don't ignore the intrinsic beauty of black and white film.

Single use cameras can deliver surprisingly high quality images. Among the many single-use cameras available, one of the most enjoyable and unusual is the three dimensional model made by **ImageTech™**. It is available at many large camera and photo supply stores. These 3-D models truly work best in bright sunlight, and making sure you have an object both in front of and behind your subject takes full advantage of the three dimensional effect. Always use flash, especially when shooting people in bright sunlight...it fills in all the dark shadows but doesn't affect the brightly lit areas.

❶

You will notice that every photograph in **Driving & Discovering Maui & Molokai** is numbered. The same number appears alongside a *Photo Finder logo* on a neighboring map, allowing the traveler to find that location easily, and to duplicate the shot by standing in the exact place that the photographer did. *No other guidebook has ever offered this feature*. The photographs in **Driving & Discovering Books** are not just pretty illustrations, but are *totally integrated with the text*, in order that they might precisely guide the reader to some of this earth's most enthralling sites and sights.

❶ Left: On a dark, colorless, nasty day at Molokai's Murphy Beach Park, this shot was saved by mounting two gradient filters on the lens – a red on top, and a blue on the bottom.

❷ Right: The warm glow of sunrise illuminates Kaunakakai town's Manila Camp on Molokai far below, as well as the airplane's propeller.

❸ Far Right: Orange protea bloom right next to the parking lot at the Sunrise Protea Farm, located on the Haleakala Highway.

No other guidebook series has ever integrated its maps, text and photographs before.

❷ ❸ ➜

Great pictures
can pop up at
unexpected
times:
the sun came
out to turn the
plane propeller
golden in the
light of sunrise.

We stopped for
a sandwich to
take up to
Haleakala
Caldera.
This bush of
stunning orange
protea grew at
the edge of a
parking lot.

Just Picture This!

Maui & Molokai

❶❶ (11)

⓬ (12)

⓭ (13)

❹ Take a shot of your hotel room. We didn't color correct this shot. Its warmth suited the coziness of the room *and* the mood. This is a typical suite at the Hotel Hana Maui.

❺ Kapuaiwa Coconut Grove on Molokai at sunset: to add color, a gradient purple filter shaded the top, and a gradient red shaded the bottom half.

❻ A rainbow hangs above a West Maui sugarcane field.

❼ Detail of a grave marker, Makena, Maui.

❽ ❾ ❿ *Details:* stones on Punalau, one of West Maui's Rugged North Shore beaches; Raindrops on ironwood needles at Pu`u O Hoku Ranch, Molokai; and the door knocker at the Wailuku Congregational church on Maui.

⓫ Serendipitously, a cat poses for a portrait on the seawall at Lahaina Harbor, Maui. Here we were able to capture the essence of Lahaina with the cat adding greatly to the photo's appeal.

⓬ A cowboy at Hana Ranch on Maui stirs up a little day-break dust storm. No filter was used.

⓭ We were happy with both versions of this shot, taken at Kalawao, Kalaupapa Peninsula, Molokai. We took the top shot unfiltered, but added two filters for the bottom version: a purple gradient on top and a blue gradient on the bottom.

⓮ Spike lives at the spectacular Hyatt Regency Maui in Ka`anapali. We waited until he wandered into a place with a natural looking background for this "nature photo" look.

Do Maui & Molokai Have Hawaii's Best Beaches?

Exactly what *makes* a great beach? Clear water? Clean sand? Great views? Well yes, certainly those things. But if they were the only criteria used, then we'd have to say that just about every beach in Hawaii is a great beach. What sets those featured here apart from the rest are a number of differing factors, including islolation [Beau Chien Beach], unusual features [Black Sand and Red Sand Beaches], sheer size [Big Beach], and all-around beauty and safety [Kapalua]. So, choose your favorite size, shape and color, and then be off with you!

KAPALUA BEACH has been rated #1 both by **Sunset** and **Conde Nast Traveler** magazines in their lists of America's Best Beaches. Why? Because Kapalua is visually beautiful.... its sandy shore is ringed by swaying palms and has a beautiful view of the island of Molokai across the channel. Year 'round, Kapalua is the safest swimming beach on this side of Maui, and its protected waters clear the way for great snorkeling. Despite the adjacent imposing hotel properties, Kapalua is open to the public. The parking lot is located at the left end of the beach. **See page 30.**

ULUA BEACH is located in the **Wailea Resort** area, and it too placed high on **Conde Nast Traveler** Magazine's list of Top Ten American Beaches. Actually, all Wailea Beaches are very similar in beauty, quality, views and the amount of sun they receive, so there's no need to be too choosy here. All Wailea Resort beach parks have showers, restrooms and free parking, but be sure to arrive early on weekends, because parking is very limited and fills up fast. **See page 46.**

If its sheer rugged beauty and splendid isolation you're after, **BEAU CHIEN BEACH** in LaPerouse Bay just might be your ticket. You'll have to hike a mile or so along the shore from the end of the paved road, but your reward will be brilliant sunshine, stunningly clear water and nary a soul anywhere in sight. There is very little sand on this black pebble & white coral rubble beach ....and the shore is unprotected by reefs, so it receives the full brunt of offshore weather conditions...but Beau Chien remains one of our favorite leave-me-alone places in all of Hawaii. **See page 48.**

East of Kahului Airport lies one of Maui's great surprises. Spectacular views are the rule at **SPRECKLESVILLE BEACH** along with a pretty little neighborhood to explore —and a lack of weekday crowds. At the end of Kealakai Place, fishermen cast from the rocks, the brilliant red color of the soil is almost surreal, and the coastal vista in both directions is unmatched. Turn makai/seaward from the Hana Highway at mile marker 5 onto NONOHE ST., then makai again on KEALAKAI PL. **See page 57.**

Shimmering red sands contrasted against crystal turquoise waters make **RED SAND BEACH** Maui's most visually spectacular. Located in an almost inaccessible bay, its sheer isolation and treacherous access make it a draw for nude sunbathers. The beach is protected from the open seas by a natural lava rock break water, and snorkeling here is popular. Despite the rough seas, the water stays clear. However, because of the surrounding crumbling cinder cliffs, this is the one beach on Maui that is perhaps better admired from afar. **See page 98.**

Near Hana, at **Waianapanapa State Park**, **BLACK SAND BEACH** is surrounded by jagged bluffs and islets of the same ebony color, all covered in brilliant green naupaka plant. Snorkeling is popular here, with the black sea bottom providing a distinctive and unique visual slant. Don't forget foot covering —black sand gets a lot hotter than the white variety! **See page 95.**

Makena's **BIG BEACH** is one of the island's largest and most enjoyable strands. Its out-of-the-way location limits the numbers of people who use it, but still it is becoming more popular all the time. The shoreline is sandy and drops quickly to overhead depths. The beach is very wide and the water **crystal clear**, providing excellent visibility for snorkelers and divers. Surfers dominate the southeast end of Big Beach, and the cindercone Pu`u Ola`i stands guard at the NW extreme. The trail over the cindercone leads to isolated **LITTLE BEACH.** Little Beach is not only beautiful, but famous for being Maui's most famous **nude beach**. Little Beach is internationally known as a clothing-optional beach and here you're likely to meet people from all over the world. **See page 48.**

left to right: makena's little beach, hana's red sand beach, and wailea's ulua beach.

KAPALUA BEACH

Lahaina

Kahului

SPRECKLESVILLE BEACH

PHOTO FINDER

MAUI

Wailea

ULUA BEACH

BIG & LITTLE BEACH

BEAU CHIEN BEACH

BLACK SAND BEACH

Hana

RED SAND BEACH

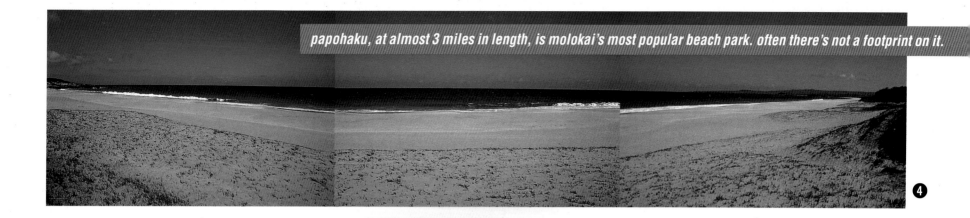

❹

PAPOHAKU BEACH is a three mile long sugar-colored, 100 yard-wide wonder of nature. Washed by transparent tourquoise waters and frothy salt foam, it is not unusual to find that your footprints are the only ones in the sand....and Papohaku is the most popular beach park on the island! Backed by gentle dunes held in place by low grasses, the park also has an attractive shaded picnic area, showers, and restrooms. The seas here at Papohaku and at all West Molokai beaches, are treacherous year `round. Swim at your own risk. **See page 150.**

KAHALEPOHAKU BEACH is as isolated a strand as you will ever find in Hawaii. It is located on Molokai's SW shore. To reach Kahalepohaku Beach, you'll drive a few miles down a well-maintained dirt road from **Maunaloa** town to where it meets the sea and **Kanalukaha Beach**. A right turn puts you on an extremely bumpy "road" which parallels the ocean for a mile or so. The gate most likely will be closed, so you'll have to hike it up and over the next point to **Kapukuwahine Beach**, another exquisite deserted gem. At the end of the road you will have to climb over a bluff of sharp lava boulders. Your efforts will be rewarded when you catch first sight of pristine, perfect, golden, untrammeled **Kahalepohaku Beach**. **See page 151.**

MURPHY BEACH PARK is so South Seas picture perfect that its hard to believe that it used to be the town dump. That is, until the Jaycees came along and transformed Murphy into what is also known as **Jaycees Beach**. This photo was taken from Palalupi Point, just past the park, and shows the long narrow white beach and crystal clear protected waters that make Murphy Beach one of Hawaii's prettiest. Snorkeling is super, and all along this protected, windy coast, windsurfing is superb. The only problem is you'll have to bring your own sailboard —no rentals here. Now, that's what we call **really** unspoiled. **See page 135.**

KAUPOA BEACH is another idyllic sandy shore, but with a twist: a luxury beach camp lies here, all alone and isolated, and is offered for occupancy by Molokai Ranch. Kaupoa is a "rounded-W"-shaped, blindingly white sandy beach in a little private bay. Supremely isolated, sunsets from Kaupoa are a treat to behold, followed by the appearance of the twinkling lights of Oahu, 19 miles and at least a century away. **See page 152.**

There might not be much of a beach here, and when you wade in the water, silt squishes between your toes, but the sunsets at **KIOWEA BEACH PARK** are unmatched, due to the dense coconut groves that grow right to water's edge. Photographers, don't pass this one up. **See page 118.**

❹ **PAPOHAKU BEACH**
■ **Maunaloa** ✈ **Airport** **Kaunakakai**
KAUPOA BEACH
❻ **KAHALEPOHAKU BEACH** ❺ **KIOWEA BEACH PARK**
MOLOKAI
MURPHY BEACH PARK ❼

PHOTO FINDER™

❺ ❻ ❼

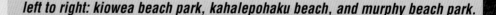

Maui's Best Hikes

Hawaii offers some of the world's most awesome and challenging hiking. But many of Maui and Molokai's best "hikes" are nothing more than short walks off the beaten path. If you want to see some of the islands' most unforgettable sights, but you don't want to get your favorite shoes muddy, bring a pair of old sneakers with you. For dedicated explorers, Maui and Molokai hold wonders unimagined, both challenging and easy to get to. Some of the best hiking can be found right along the road shoulder —walking while facing oncoming traffic for safety, of course. The speed of a car and the attention it takes to drive disguises all kinds of great little discoveries that will be apparent on foot. Arguably, where hiking possibilities are concerned, Maui and Molokai *no ka oi* — they're the best!

The Sierra Club conducts hikes into some of the more remote areas, as does the Haleakala National Park staff. And naturalist Ken Schmitt leads knowledgeable private hikes into more areas than anyone else (see sidebar). If setting out on your own, common sense must prevail, as dozens of visitors are seriously injured each year by underestimating both their abilities and Hawaii's deceptively beautiful terrain.

Rainstorms upslope may occur even while the sun shines brightly on the swimming hole below that you may be enjoying. The placid scene can turn deadly in a few short minutes' time as a flood of water washes down the stream channel from above, turning it into a torrent. Do not attempt to cross even the shallowest stream if it looks like it may be raining upslope: people have been known to become stranded for days. Others who tried to challenge the currents have met grisly deaths, washed over the brinks of waterfalls onto the rocks below.

THE KING'S HIGHWAY still exists in remnants around Maui's perimeter. This ancient trail system was originally constructed to make it easy for the *Ali`i* to get around and collect taxes. The two largest segments include the **Hana-Waianapanapa Trail**, and the **Hoapili Trail**. The **HANA WAIANAPANAPA TRAIL** stretches 3 miles/5k from the Hana Airport past the beautiful *black sand beach* at **Waianapanapa State Park**, ending just before Hana town. For those camping or renting cabins at the park, the trail is a boon for easy coastal explorations. Bring plenty of mosquito repellent. **See page 95. THE HOAPILI TRAIL** follows the southwest coast inland from the ocean's edge, and is paved in unsteady jagged lava. It begins at the end of the paved Makena road, at **La Perouse Bay**. Instead of following the King's Highway from this point, its cooler to start your hike at water's edge, along a lovely seaside trail shaded in spots by ironwood trees, passing the sandy white pocket beaches of crystal clear La Perouse Bay and the black and white rubble shore at **Beau Chien Beach** At this point we rest and then turn around and go back. But for those determined to press on, the trail continues through this beautiful, desolate, hot and thirsty land for 18 grueling miles before rejoining Highway 31 right in the middle of nowhere. Good luck, and don't say we didn't warn you. Bring lots of water, sunscreen and Band Aids. **See page 49.**

POLI POLI SPRINGS is the polar opposite of the Hoapili Trail because its trail system winds through cool, moist high altitude (6000'-7800'/1829m-2377m) forests. Here you will find a cabin for rent, complete with linens and cooking gear, and plenty of cut firewood to keep you warm during Poli Poli's cold nights. There is no electricity, but there is drinking water. Camping spaces are available also. Contact the **Dept. of State Parks at 54 S. High St., Wailuku, Maui, HI 96793.** © **(808) 243-5354** well in advance for information and reservations. **See page 68.**

Haleakala Crater's **SLIDING SANDS TRAIL** (6 miles/9.6 km) begins near the visitor center at the 10,000'/3048m elevation and descends into an other-worldly realm. Three cabins are for rent within the crater itself. Write or call well in advance: **Superintendent, Haleakala National Park, PO Box 369, Makawao HI 96768.** © **(808) 572-9306.** The primitive cabins include bunk beds, cooking utensils, stoves, and firewood. Come prepared for rain and cold weather. Another popular track, **Halemau'u Trail**, challenges hikers and horseback riders as it steeply switchbacks into the crater's west end. Slippery when wet, wear proper hiking boots to safely negotiate it. Once into the crater, it continues across it for another mile to **Holua Cabin**, for a total trail length of 4 miles/ 6.4 km. **HOMSER GROVE** is an easy, cool, shady, very pretty, mosquito-free hike in the woods. The entrance to Homser Grove is just past the Park's ranger station uphill on the left. **See pages 60 and 62.**

ULA`INO ROAD may not be challenging, but it sure is rewarding. This road is described in the Hana Drive Section/Nahiku-Hana, **page 95.** Because the partially unpaved road is not always passable to non-4WD vehicles, hiking its 3 mile length is a good alternative. The road crosses a couple of streams and small falls, passes the **Kahanu Gardens** (© **248-8912**), Hawaii's largest heiau, **Pi`ilanihali Heiau**, and the ruins of **Ula`ino Village**, now overgrown. The real reward is a swim at **Blue Angel Falls and Pool**. Park at/walk to road's end, then walk a few hundred yards down the boulder beach to the left as you face the ocean. The falls cascade gently down a cliff face covered in pink impatiens and into a beautiful pool located right on the boulder beach, close to, but untouched by the ocean's roar.

THE (SEVEN) POOLS AT `OHE`O in Haleakala National Park is an easy seven-to-ten minute hike extending from the roadside parking area to the pools below. **The ocean is deadly here**, so please stay out of it. That goes for the Pools too, if it looks like it is raining upslope. Flash floods aren't uncommon at `Ohe`o Pools, so beware. Upstream from the Pools area the wonders stretch on and on. The **WAIMOKU FALLS TRAIL** is no walk in the park, but its rewards are remarkable... we feel it is the best all-around hiking experience on Maui. The trail begins across the highway from the Park's parking area. Stop in at the ranger station for a trail map and the latest weather advisories, or join **Hike Maui**'s unforgettable `Ohe`o trek. See sidebar. Free guided hikes are offered Saturday mornings at 9 a.m., where park rangers will point out the hidden dangers as well as the smorgasbord of edible treats along the way. The first mile is uphill through hot and thirsty open pasture land, so water is an absolute necessity. **See page 106.**

The views along **WEST MAUI'S RUGGED NORTH SHORE** compare favorably to those in California's venerable Big Sur. Scores of hiking opportunities parallel well-paved, twisting Highway 30. Short grasses make hiking over the expansive bluffs easy. Mosquitoes are no problem here. Be sure to leave nothing visible in your car to entice thieves. You can follow a worn pathway, or else strike out on your own path. With space on top of space, this is an ideal place to bring a panoramic camera. **See page 27.**

❶

❶ West Maui's Rugged Northwest Coast and its grassy, windy bluffs.

❷ Waimoku Falls at `Ohe`o (7 Pools).

❸ Blue Angel Falls and Blue Pool await at Ula`ino.

❹ Sliding Sands trail below Haleakala's summit.

❺ Pristine air and vibrant colors are the rule at Beau Chien Beach, La Perouse Bay.

RUGGED NORTH WEST COAST ❶

Lahaina

IAO VALLEY TRAILS Kahului

MAUI

HALEMAU `U TRAIL

SLIDING SANDS TRAIL ❹

BLUE ANGEL FALLS ❸

HANA-WAIANA-PANAPA TRAIL Hana

POLI POLI SPRINGS

PHOTO FINDER

WAIMOKU FALLS TRAIL ❷

Makena

BEAU CHIEN BEACH ❺

HOAPILI TRAIL

13

Ken Schmitt's Hike Maui

For those of you really interested in seeing the other side of Maui, the hidden, untrammeled and unnamed Maui, then *go take a hike, pal.*

Ken Schmitt will take you where few visitors —or Mauians— have ever gone before. He can lead you through wilderness without trails to waterfalls without names for an experience without parallel. You will wear tabis, two-toed Japanese fishermen's shoes that he provides to allow firm footing in streams and mud, and to inflict minimal impact on the land. The hike will be challenging, the views astounding, the experience unique. Long after you've forgotten what you bought while shopping on Maui, or where you ate, the feelings you experienced on a Hike Maui trek will live on and on. The crystalline waters of a hidden rainforest pool, the magical massage of waterfall-fingers kneading your shoulders, the earthy green scents... they will all come back to you at the oddest moments for years to come. Your memories will provide a relaxing and beautiful refuge for you in times of stress.

We recommend that you join a guided hike led by people who know the terrain and are acquainted with nature's foibles. Both **The Sierra Club** and **The Nature Conservancy Of Hawaii** schedule hikes and trail maintenance work parties on both Molokai and Maui. But for an out-of-the-ordinary encounter with the environment, join one of Ken Schmitt's **Hike Maui** hikes.

Ken Schmitt is an educator. He and his staff provide a nonstop narrative along your route, with fascinating lessons in biology, geology and anthropology. Hikers stop along the way to smell the rose apples and taste any number of edibles, from ginger flower nectar to *'akala*, Hawaii's giant native raspberry. Ken spent three years in Maui's wilderness, living off the land, which qualifies him as an expert in just about anybody's book. He graduated from Valparaiso University with a degree in classical languages and a masters in Oriental philosophy from UC Berkeley. Fully half of Ken's hikers hear about him by word of mouth, and the others find him through guidebooks, activity desks and magazine articles. He does not advertise. He wants to point out that his are not *adventure* treks, they are *nature* treks. His full attention stays on his hikers; he strives to make them aware of the kind of environment they are in, and prod them to see, smell and listen in a new way. The advantages to Ken Schmitt's hikes are many: access to beautiful places (some of which are not indicated on any map), answers to all your questions, and a safe journey.

You can write to Ken for a schedule and prices at Hike Maui, PO Box 330969, Kahului HI 96733. ✆ **(808) 879-5270** .

Other Sources:

The Sierra Club, Hawaii Chapter, 212 Merchant St., Suite 201, Honolulu HI 96813. ✆ **(808) 538-6616**.

The Nature Conservancy of Hawaii, 1116 Smith St., Honolulu HI 96817. ✆ **(808) 537-4508. FAX (808) 545-2019**.

Molokai's Best Hikes

Molokai's Kamehameha V Highway hugs the island's eastern, Maui-facing coastline. Drivers may be treated to some great views as they zoom by, but at their relaxed pace, walkers will notice paths through the trees that drivers don't, paths that lead to beaches and wondrous views hidden from drivers' sight. Walkers get to stop and pet horses tied at roadside, and learn to carry dog biscuits that both friendly horses and barking dogs accept as bribes. They can greet groups of kids on their way to or from school who might reveal locally known swimming holes, hidden waterfalls, eating places, or beaches not found in any guidebook. Simply choose a promising stretch of road, park your car, and get out and walk for awhile facing oncoming traffic.

❶

At the end of the KAMEHAMEHA V HIGHWAY lay Halawa Bay and **HALAWA VALLEY**. **Halawa Beach** is a very pretty gray sand crescent, bisected by Halawa Stream. The waters at the left beach are sheltered, offering the only safe recreational swimming on the entire north shore. Winding up the pali at this end of the beach is a trail/jeep road that can provide a compact amble to the top, or a full day's hike if you'd like to venture farther into the wilds of Molokai's North Shore. Right in front of the little church at the end of the highway you'll see a dirt road leading into the valley beneath a canopy of mango and papaya trees, passing simple houses ablaze with flowers. For those with the time and energy to trek further, this hike to Moa'ula (250') and Hipuapua (500') Falls begins from this road and is an unforgettable way to spend your day. **See page 142 for details.**

For hardcore hikers, the **WAILAU TRAIL** begins near Puko'o, crosses the lofty peaks of the Molokai Forest Reserve, passes through mountain apple forests (and lower down, stands of java plum), and then descends to the mouth of Wailau Stream on Molokai's very remote north shore. *Arduous* would be the perfect word to describe it, and the **Sierra Club** can get you there on one of their infrequent excursions on Molokai. Plan well ahead —give them a call now to see what their schedule is for this and other upcoming Hawaii hikes. ✆ **(808) 538-6616.**

THE KALAUPAPA TRAIL (2 miles long, 1600' elevation loss/gain; hiking permit required) might be the most unique and memorable adventure in the state of Hawaii. Descending the sheer cliffs above the former leper colony, the newly restored trail provides spectacular views of the Kalaupapa Peninsula and Molokai's north coast ramparts. The trail begins in the coolness of **Pala'au State Park** and switchbacks down the cliff wall to **'Awahua Beach**, where you can join a fascinating guided tour of this tragically beautiful place by making previous arrangements with Richard Marks ✆ **567-6171**. Not looking forward to the long climb back up the cliff at the end of the guided tour? Before your hike, you can stop by Molokai's main **Ho`olehua Airport** and buy a ticket for the scheduled afternoon flight from Kalaupapa's tiny airport back to Molokai's main airport. The only hitch will be getting back to your car: the trailhead at Pala`au State Park is 8.5 miles from Ho`olehua Airport. **See page 126.**

THE PEPEOPAE BOG TRAIL begins high in the Molokai Forest Reserve at the 3500'/1050m elevation. Climbing through dense cloud forest, a raised wooden boardwalk leads hikers through the very fragile and deeply muddy bog ecosystem. **The Nature Conservancy** ✆ **(808) 537-4508**, and the **Sierra Club** lead hikes through this unique area. The trail begins just past the fabulous Waikolu Lookout and picnic area. A 4WD vehicle is almost essential for getting up here safely. **See page 124.**

HA`UPU BAY on Molokai's primeval north shore, is accessible only by boat, and only in the relative calm of summer. Astonishing views from points above the bay are other-worldly in their majesty and wonder. Great chunks of profound beauty exist all along the north shore east of the Kalaupapa Peninsula. Check with the Molokai Visitors Office in Kaunakakai for the latest information on those outfits offering excursions to this area. **See photo, page 145.**

MOLOKAI RANCH ✆ **552-2791**, or toll-free from the mainland **[800] 254-8871**, owns vast tracts of the western end of the island, and a public road leads right to a (long, hot, dry) hike to the deserted beaches along the South and West Coasts. If you prefer, you can book one of their mountain bikes for this tour. They'll provide a gourmet picnic lunch, and pick you up at the end of the day so you don't have to bike back uphill. Alternately, the Molokai Ranch Outfitters will saddle you up for a guided trail horseback ride, or put you on a comfortable shuttle for snorkeling or kayaking and a picnic lunch. **See page 150.**

THE KALUAKOI RESORT At the southwest end of Kepuhi Beach, there is a bluff called **Pu'u O Ka-iaka** that separates Kepuhi Beach from 3 mile long **Papohaku Beach**. At the rear of this bluff a short jeep road climbs through the kiawe trees and leads to two fine lookouts. One overlooks the full length of Papohaku Beach and the other surveys the whole west coast from the Kaluakoi Resort all the way to 'Ilio Point. If you are staying at the resort, this is a lovely morning hike for working off the banana-mac pancakes at the Ohia Lodge. Get a coffee to go and bring it up here to enjoy while contemplating the beautiful vistas before you. **See page 148.**

PAPOHAKU BEACH Three miles (4.8 km) long and 90m/100 yard-wide Papohaku Beach is ideal for long romantic or introspective strolls. More often than not, we have been totally alone on this magnificent strand. Although Papohaku is an easily accessible public beach with good facilities, we are always amazed at the number of times we've visited over the years when our footprints were the only ones in the sand. **See Page 150.**

❷

❸

MOLOKAI

Photographs

❶ Far Left: Detail of plumeria blossoms along the Kamehameha V Highway road shoulder.

❷ This pretty path leads from Papohaku Beach's picnic area to its untrammeled, nearly-3-mile-long strand.

❸ A short, one minute-long hike through the woods at the very end of Molokai's Highway 470 rewards in spades: the spectacular, eerily quiet Kalaupapa Overlook.

KALAUPAPA LOOKOUT

PAPOHAKU BEACH PARK

❷

Maunaloa

Airport

Kaunakakai

PHOTO FINDER

MOLOKAI

❸

Halawa Valley

HIPUAPUA AND MOA`ULA FALLS ❼ ❹

WAIKOLU LOOKOUT/ FALLS

❺

❻ Pauwalu

❶

❼

Page 17, clockwise from top:

❹ This roadside panorama is just a prelude to the beauty you'll discover along Halawa Valley's trails.

❺ The Waikolu Lookout is only a few hundred yards from the beginning of the Pepeopae Bog Trail.

❻ At Pauwalu, a hike along the road shoulder of Kam V Highway reveals empty beaches like this one.

❼ In Halawa Valley, Moa`ula is a waterfall in two major installments. The hike to reach it takes about an hour.

❻

Maui & Molokai: Best Waterfalls

Choosing our "Best Waterfalls" —especially on islands as drenched with them as Maui and Molokai are— is a daunting task. So needless to say, our list is downright arbitrary; we decided to choose falls that were both easy to get to and hard to reach, towering and tiny, tame and wild.

Remember: it is always a given that Hawaii's streams and swimming holes are **very slippery**, so be careful getting in and out of pools. We always inch in and out on all fours so if we slip, we don't have far to fall. The one exception here is **Blue Sapphire Pools**, which are crystal clear and ice blue in color, and we've never found them slippery ...but be cautious anyway. It is also a good idea not to stand or swim beneath any cascade, as rocks and other debris can wash over the brink and conk you on the noggin.

Maui

BLUE SAPPHIRE POOLS at **Ke'anae** are *wonderful*. Located right under a Hana Highway bridge, a very narrow rock gorge funnels the stream water into a torrent that empties into the gorgeous crystal clear pool. The accompanying photo was taken from the bridge looking straight down. Kids climbed up the wall of the gorge a few feet, then jumped into the torrent, which propelled them into the pool. Cool! Below the big main pool is a small fall that empties into the **"Swimming Pool"**, a small, deep, sculpted pool that looks Disney-built. The only catch to this one? The mosquitoes can be ravenous. **See page 88.**

PUOHOKAMOA FALLS is located just a few steps from the Hana Highway at mile marker 11. There's a deep slippery pool and **20'/ 8m** waterfall next to a covered picnic shelter (see photo). The pool can get muddy after a good rain, and Puohokamoa *can* become crowded. What most people don't know is that just five minutes upstream there's **another similar waterfall** and pool, where most likely you'll be all alone. Ten minutes downstream, the main fall cascades over a **200'/ 80m** cliff, but its much better and more safely observed from a nearby lookout described on **Page 84.**

200'/61m MAKAHIKU FALLS and **400'/122m WAIMOKU FALLS**, located 1mile/1.6k and 2 miles/ 3.2k, respectively, above the Hana Highway, are the crowning glory of the **'Ohe'o/Haleakala National Park** area. The Park service leads free hikes on Saturday mornings at 9 a.m., or you can pick up a map at the ranger station located near the grassy parking area and do it yourself. *We think this is the best do-it-yourself hike on Maui.* **See page 106.**

Difficult to get to due to private property issues, **HANAWI FALLS** is located in easy-to-miss **Nahiku**. Fed by spring water, it flows into a beautiful gorge even in the driest of weather. **Hanawi Falls** gets our vote for *most picture-perfect Maui waterfall.* **Page 93.**

WAILUA FALLS At **200'/61m** tall, and **located roadside** between Hana Town and Haleakala National Park (and the 'Ohe'o [7] Pools), its easy to reach. This is the kind of cascade that people photograph from their car, because its so visible from the road. But stop and walk to it anyway, because Wailua Falls is a *real* beauty. **See page 104.**

Molokai

Gorgeous **MOA'ULA FALLS** (**250'/76m**) and towering **HIPUAPUA FALLS** (**500'/152m**) are in the same section of Halawa Valley. Moa'ula Falls is a little more than an hour from the trailhead, and Hipuapua Falls is about 25 minutes farther. Hipuapua is pristine and deserted, because nobody seems to know its there, whereby Moa'ula is a steady draw for hikers. We'll show you how to find *both*. **See page 142.**

KAHIWA FALLS (**1750'/533m**) is the tallest waterfall in Hawaii. Located on Molokai's difficult-to-get-to North Shore, its reachable only by sea. On the other hand, nearby **WAILELE FALLS** may be Hawaii's prettiest; the winds catch its falling waters and fan them across the cliff face, turning the lower cascade into a wide bridal veil. Summer access only. **Map page 134.**

WAIKOLU LOOKOUT is a challenge to get to, as it is ten miles up unpaved **Maunahui Road** from the Maunaloa Highway, with potholes two feet deep at times. But if the weather's been dry, you may find it passable. After a rain at Waikolu Lookout, standing at the rail, you'll see dozens of waterfalls rushing down the opposite sheer wall of Waikolu Valley. **See page 124.**

Photographs

1 Left: Moa'ula Falls

2 Hipuapua Falls is so big, we couldn't fit it all into one shot. It is actually *much* taller than it looks here; the wide angle lens optics and our close vantage point flattened the perspective.

3 Puohokamoa's middle fall tumbles to a deep blue pool. There is another falls and pool just a two minute rock-hop to the left in this picture, upstream.

4 Kids ride the wild water chute at Blue Sapphire Pools at Ke'anae, along Maui's Hana Highway.

WAILELE FALLS

KAHIWA FALLS

MOA`ULA & HIPUAPUA FALLS ❶❷

WAIKOLU LOOKOUT

Kalaupapa

Maunaloa Airport

Kaunakakai

MOLOKAI

PHOTO FINDER

❸

❹

❷

❻

❺ Hanawi Falls in Nahiku lies along Maui's Hana Drive, and is surely one of Hawaii's most beautiful. The water comes not from upland rains, but from fresh water springs. *Photo: Ken Schmitt/Hike Maui*

❻ Waimoku Falls towers above bathers in Maui's `Ohe`o district at Haleakala National Park, the crown jewel of the Hana Drive.

Lahaina

Kahului

PUOHOKAMOA FALLS ❸

BLUE SAPPHIRE POOLS ❹

HANAWI FALLS ❺

MAUI Hana

WAILUA FALLS

Makena **WAIMOKU AND MAKAHIKU FALLS** ❻

❺

PHOTO FINDER

"Maui no Ka oi" means "Maui is the best".

You'll often see that phrase when you read about Maui, and you will probably hear it daily throughout your visit, reaffirming what everybody already knows: Maui has no equal. Each of the Hawaiian Islands casts its own unique spell ...but as far as *which* island really is the best, most people agree that the best Hawaiian Island is the one they happen to be on at the moment. But anyone who has ever been here will attest to the fact that Maui really is something extraordinary.

On a Maui winter's day, snow-white tropical beaches shaded by swaying palms can be left behind for a drive skyward, through blindingly green pasture lands, to the infrequent snows of **Mount Haleakala**. A visitor's Christmas Day might be spent sipping Blue Hawaiis on the sand on Maui's sunniest beaches as he tans nut brown in 80°F luxuriance, or snuggling in a rustic cabin nestled high in a redwood forest, sipping a hot chocolate by a blazing log fire at **Poli Poli Springs**, where night time winter temperatures often hover around the freezing point. Visitors can hike the deserted seashore at **La Perouse Bay**, peering far down into the depths of its jewel-like aquamarine waters, amble down its wild and beautiful black pebble/white coral rubble beaches, drink in vistas of volcano, sea and sky, and rejuvenate city-tinged lungs in the freshest air on earth. Visitors can participate in a traditional luau with the people of isolated and historic **Hana town**, or partake in one of the **Wailea Resort** versions, which have a bit of Las Vegas flash and flesh thrown in for good measure.

For the visitor who likes to drive, Maui's roads are excellent and unequaled in beauty and wonder. **OLINDA ROAD**, beautiful and virtually deserted, climbs uphill from the cowboy town of **Makawao** into cooler temperatures through tree tunnels of pungent eucalyptus, past panoramic views, neatly planted pine forests, and sturdy homes with big stone chimneys that warm the chilly nights. **BALDWIN AVE.**, the continuation of OLINDA RD., travels downhill from Makawao to the world windsurfing capitol of **Paia**.

THE **HANA HIGHWAY** has become infamous for its hundreds of curves and dozens of tiny one-lane bridges spanning deep gullies. It veers past every manner of tropical splendor; beaches with sands colored black, red, gray, or white; impenetrable jungles of bamboo, multicolored rainbow-barked eucalyptus

trees, white ginger, sweet guava, orange African Tulip trees; carpets of neon pink impatiens, giant ferns, bizarre star-shaped red mushrooms, tumbling waterfalls and chilly sapphire pools, stunning coastal views stretching for miles and miles, and tiny settlements of native Hawaiians and wealthy rock stars content to hum along in the region's blessed virtual isolation. Flowers and exotic plants that need to be coddled and spoiled in mainland hothouses bloom wherever and whenever they please along the road shoulder: stunning red-yellow-green tri-colored hanging lobster claw heliconia; red, pink, cream and white torch gingers, delicate maidenhair fern, painfully shy sensitive plant, spider lilies, and fabulous specimens of shell ginger. Creamy colored elephant ear flowers hide among the plant's monster-size leaves, and a smorgasbord of edible treats like bananas, breadfruit, mountain apples, berries and papayas awaits.

The **Haleakala Highway**, on the other hand, provides a different kind of motoring adventure as it climbs higher, in a shorter distance, than any paved road on earth. It ascends Mount Haleakala smoothly and confidently through a magically verdant rural world of greener-than-Ireland pastures and rolling countryside. The road ends at **Haleakala National Park** near the 10,000 foot elevation in a treeless red-tinged world that looks, unsettlingly, almost identical to the *Mariner* and *Sojourner* lander images sent back from Mars. Sunrises and sunsets from the lip of the crater are a spiritual, and very popular, experience.

Maui is a shoppers' paradise. Money gobbling temptations abound, running the gamut from upscale shops at the **Wailea and Ka'anapali Resort Hotels**, to the art galleries of **Lahaina**, the dusty antique shops of **Wailuku**, the bustling malls of **Kahului** and the unique offerings at the Maui Crafts Guild in **Paia**. Maui is an eaters' paradise as well, with great restaurants in every price range, from upscale Avalon in Lahaina to delicious and down-to-earth Ming Yuen in Kahului. On Maui you'll feast on wonderful cream puffs at the Komoda Store in upcountry Makawao, slurp superior locally made ice cream at Lappert's in Lahaina, crunch on world famous Maui potato chips, bite into raw sweet Kula onions, and sip local Maui grown and roasted coffees.

But beyond all this, one of the primary draws attract-

ing people irresistibly to Maui is her exquisite beaches. They vibrate in every color and hue, and range in size from tiny pockets just big enough for two, to the unobstructed 3 mile length of sand at **Ma'alaea Bay**. A description of every Maui strand worth a visit is included in this book, and most are pictured in photographs.

When it comes to accommodations, some of Maui's most special are its Bed & Breakfasts located in unheralded parts of the island with names like **Huelo**, **Kipahulu** and **Haiku**. Small cozy hotels like the antique-laden little treasure **Lahaina Inn** or the cool upcountry cottages at the **Kula Lodge** promise romance. The cheapest and most unusual digs are the isolated State-run cabins in eerily beautiful **Haleakala Crater**, the highland redwood forest at **Poli Poli Springs**, and near the shore at **Waianapanapa State Park** with its famous Black Sand Beach. The super resort properties at **Wailea**, **Ka'anapali** and **Kapalua** are pitted against each other in an unceasing competition to outdo each other and attract visitors with glitz, glitter, and superpools of aqua theme park caliber.

During your Hawaii explorations keep in mind that travel and discovery should be fun, not some endurance contest. A travel schedule can rob a vacation of the serenity it was designed to nurture. A rigid plan can stand in the way of *serendipity* ...serendipity being that something wonderful and unexpected that occurs while we're busy doing something else. On the other hand, a travel *routine* is to be encouraged. A travel routine includes anything, no matter how lethargic, that one likes to do while on vacation. If there is nothing more you would rather do than sit at a seaside cafe with a glass of wine watching people come and go, then do *exactly* that. Remember: just because Haleakala is *there* doesn't mean you actually have to go. Just buy a postcard; nobody'll find out.

In *Driving & Discovering Maui and Molokai*, an unprecedented number of photographs, each of which is numbered and indicated on the maps with the **Photo Finder logo**, will make it easy to visit and enjoy the *exact locations* in which they were taken. Please feel free to write and let us know what you think about our books, and if you're so inclined, please share your own discoveries made while visiting the magical islands of Hawaii.

PHOTO FINDER ™

❶

Photographs

❶ Just before sunset, the scene at Maui's Ke'anae Peninsula turns magical in the golden glow that photographers wait all day for. Some of the most beautiful photos you can take will be made with this "sweet light". As you head downhill on Ke'anae Road from the Hana Highway, this view will be immediately ahead. There is a small parking area on the left road shoulder.

❶ Toward sunset, the slanting rays tint the shores of the
Ke`anae Peninsula with a
golden hue. The waning
tradewinds refresh residents,
who, knee-deep in taro patch
mud, hurry to finish their
chores before dark. All the
while, endless waves crash
incessantly onto the jagged
ebony shores.

Ke`anae
Peninsula

19

Doctor's Orders:

Alex del Rosario M.D.
is the former chief
resident at California
Pacific Medical Center
in San Francisco.
Dr. del Rosario is
currently engaged in
private practice in
Los Angeles.

Sun Exposure

For some, the best part of taking a vacation in Hawaii -lying on a beach- can result in a painful sunburn. After all, how can you prove to your friends you've had a fantastic vacation if you don't come back with an enviable tan? Most people overestimate their ability to tolerate Hawaii's tropical sun and slather on the baby oil. What many sun worshippers don't realize is that **sunscreens definitely allow you to achieve a wonderful tan** without the burn, the pain or the ugly peeling.
• Try to limit your sun exposure during the peak hours of 11AM to 3PM and bring body cover for the more intense sun period of the day.
• Use a sun screen containing PABA (5% para-aminobenzoic acid). Normally, the minimum suggested SPF is at least a 15. If you have particular sensitive skin you should use an SPF of at least 30. (You will still tan.)
• Apply the sun screen at least 30-60 minutes before your exposure to the sun to allow the PABA time to bind to your skin so it can do it's job. If you apply it while you are out in the sun, its like being under the sun for 30 minutes without any protection!
If you're one of the few people who have allergic reactions to PABA, look for sunscreen with BENZOPHENONE. Alternately, opaque ZINC OXIDE cream physically prevents ultraviolet rays from reaching the skin. Some zinc oxide formulas come in skin colors and are more cosmetically acceptable.
Apply especially to the most-missed areas such as the tops of feet, ears, and backs of knees. All are thin-skinned areas that can become particularly painful when sunburned. And men, don't forget your bald spots — denial can hurt.
Many medications may make you more susceptible to sunburn. Antibiotics like **Tetracycline** or **Erythromycin** should be discontinued at least a week before heavy sun exposure. ALWAYS consult your personal physician before stopping any medication. Also, perfumes, colognes, deodorants and antiperspirants applied to the skin can cause a rash in combination with sun exposure.

Watersports Safety

By far the most common travel related injury presenting to Hawaii's emergency rooms involves water related injuries. If you're vacationing with children, be especially vigilant. Swim near a lifeguard and inquire about dangerous undercurrents or rip tides. Relatively few beaches outside Waikiki have life guards.

Stinging Marine Life

Although beautiful, Hawaii's waters do harbor a variety of stinging marine life. The stinging devices of many hollow-bodied marine creatures are called *nematocysts*. Treat jellyfish stings as follows:
• First, remove any adherent tentacles that will cause further delivery of venom. The tentacles should be lifted off the skin with a stick to avoid further injury to your fingers, DO NOT scrape them off as this will only discharge more stinging *nematocysts*.
• Next, rinse the affected area with sea water to wash away any adherent nematocysts. DO NOT use fresh water, since this will activate them.
• Nematocysts are inactivated by vinegar (or dilute acetic acid 5-10%). During periods of high jelly fish attacks, beach lifeguards may carry spray bottles of acetic acid. NOTE: If no vinegar is handy, then human urine will do in a pinch. Urine is a dilute acid, and if from a male, is usually considered a sterile fluid.
Symptoms of pain can be treated with topical anesthetics, such as those contained in sunburn preparations. Look for the active ingredients like lidocaine or benzocaine. Persistent redness, inflammation or itchiness can be treated with a topical steroid cream like Hydrocortisone 0.5% cream which can be bought over the counter. If symptoms persist or muscle spasms develop, seek medical attention.

Leptospirosis

Leptospirosis is a bacterial disease. Although an infrequent disease on the mainland, it is much more of a problem in Hawaii where wild pigs and goats in the upcountry contaminate the streams. There are as many cases of leptospirosis in Hawaii in any given year as there are in the rest of the entire United States. Leptospirosis can be contracted by swallowing contaminated stream water. The bacteria can also enter through the intact mucous membrane of the mouth, even if you do not have a cut there. Or it can enter through an open cut on the skin. So, the best thing would be to keep out of streams altogether if you have a cut, or to keep your mouth shut so as not to ingest water while swimming in these places. The symptoms are not immediate, and may take up to 7-12 days to manifest, i.e. you may not feel sick until you get back from your vacation and mainland physicians may not be familiar with the symptoms of leptospirosis.
Of those patients infected with leptospirosis, 90% will have the mild form of the disease, which is heralded by the abrupt onset of flu-like symptoms, i.e. muscle aches, fever and malaise.
Ten percent of a patients infected with leptospirosis will have a more severe form of the disease. Treatment requires antibiotics. **Prevention can be achieved by once weekly dosing of doxycycline 200mg.** If you'll be hiking in remote areas, or plan to do a lot of swimming in streams, it would be prudent to get your doctor to write a prescription for doxycycline and fill it before leaving for Hawaii.

Advice for the Immunocompromised or Ill Traveler

Before leaving on your vacation, consult your personal physician as to any restrictions he/she may advise. Bring medication in the original bottles so if you run out, the local pharmacy won't have to guess by trying to match pills with your description of shape or color. If you require a pill organizer to take your medication, be sure to bring at least two entire lists of your medication with dosages, and entrust one copy to your travel companion to keep safe. Ask your doctor about any interaction that alcohol may have with your medication — over the counter antihistamines and certain antibiotics like metronidazole produce very undesirable side effects when mixed with alcohol. The water supply in Hawaii is generally considered safe, but if you have a weakened immune system use bottle water. Always bring a supply of water with you when hiking or visiting the beach to avoid dehydration. For those on strict medication schedules, keep medicines near your wallet or purse in your hotel room so you'll remember to take them with you when going out for the day. If you need to take your medication with/without food, try to plan your meals in advance. This may take away from some of the spontaneity of your vacation, but in the long run will be well worth the trouble.
If you have a portable phone, bring it with you on vacation. Mobile phones in remote locations are the only way to summon help, and many lives have been saved in recent years in Hawaii because people were carrying portable telephones.

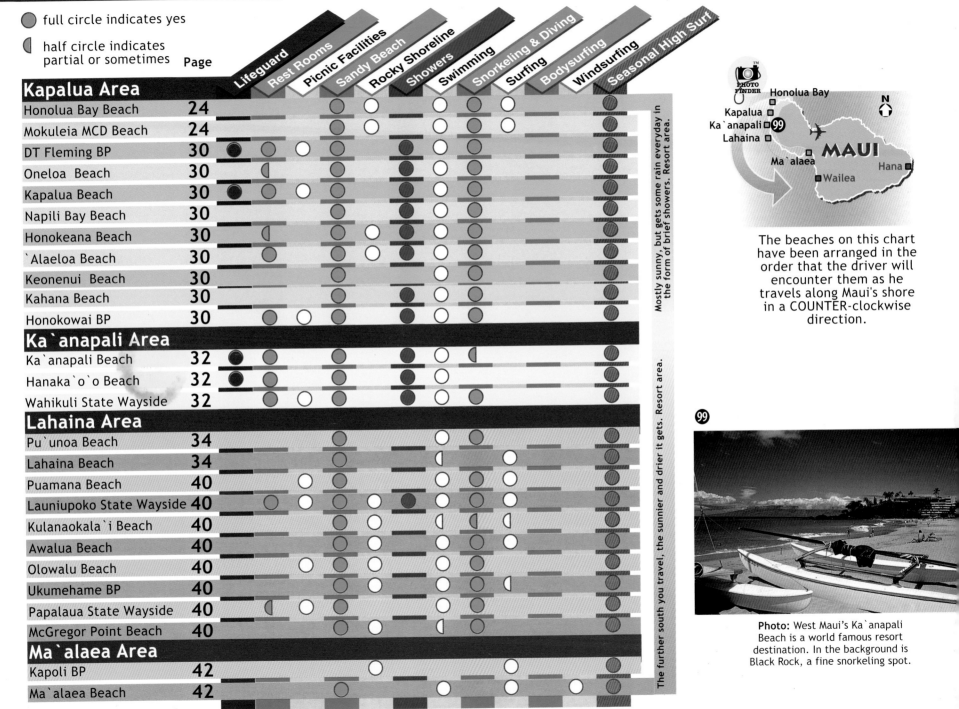

MAUI

West Maui Beaches

Traveling In A Counter-Clockwise Direction

West Maui

- ● full circle indicates yes
- ◐ half circle indicates partial or sometimes

	Page	Lifeguard	Rest Rooms	Picnic Facilities	Sandy Beach	Rocky Shoreline	Showers	Swimming	Snorkeling & Diving	Surfing	Bodysurfing	Windsurfing	Seasonal High Surf
Kapalua Area													
Honolua Bay Beach	24				●	○		●	●	○			●
Mokuleia MCD Beach	24				●	○		○	●	○			●
DT Fleming BP	30	●	◐	○	●		●	○					●
Oneloa Beach	30		◐		●		●	●	●	○			●
Kapalua Beach	30	●	◐	○	●		●	●	●				●
Napili Bay Beach	30		◐		●		●	●	●				●
Honokeana Beach	30		◐		●	○	●	●	●				●
`Alaeloa Beach	30		●		●	○	●	●					●
Keonenui Beach	30				●		●	○					●
Kahana Beach	30				●		◐	○	○				●
Honokowai BP	30		◐	○	●		●	○					●
Ka`anapali Area													
Ka`anapali Beach	32	●	●		●		◐	●	●	◐			●
Hanaka`o`o Beach	32	●	●		●		●	●	○				●
Wahikuli State Wayside	32		●	○	●		●	○	○				●
Lahaina Area													
Pu`unoa Beach	34				●			○	●				●
Lahaina Beach	34				●			◐	●	○			●
Puamana Beach	40			○	●			●	●	○			●
Launiupoko State Wayside	40	○	●	○	●	○	●	●	●	◐			●
Kulanaokala`i Beach	40				●	○		●	◐	◐			●
Awalua Beach	40				●	○		●	●				●
Olowalu Beach	40				●	○		●	●	◐			●
Ukumehame BP	40				●	○		●	●	◐			●
Papalaua State Wayside	40		◐	○	●			●	●				●
McGregor Point Beach	40				●	○		◐	●				●
Ma`alaea Area													
Kapoli BP	42				●			○		○			●
Ma`alaea Beach	42				●			○		○		○	●

Mostly sunny, but gets some rain everyday in the form of brief showers. Resort area.

The further south you travel, the sunnier and drier it gets. Resort area.

The beaches on this chart have been arranged in the order that the driver will encounter them as he travels along Maui's shore in a COUNTER-clockwise direction.

Honolua Bay
Kapalua
Ka`anapali
Lahaina
MAUI
Ma`alaea
Wailea
Hana

Photo: West Maui's Ka`anapali Beach is a world famous resort destination. In the background is Black Rock, a fine snorkeling spot.

This aerial shot of West Maui's Rugged North Shore was taken during the famous Aloha Island Air flight from Molokai to Kahului, Maui. The vistas from this flight are stupendous. Ask the pilot to please fly "viz" (visual) for the best views.

For photo location, see ❶ on the map on page 27.

MAUI

22

exploring west maui's rugged

North Shore

On a rainy day the clouds and haze wrap the tiny and very isolated hamlet of Kahakuloa in a quiet cocoon.

For location, see ❷ on the map on page 27.

MATCH THIS SYMBOL'S MAP NUMBER WITH THE CORRESPONDING PHOTO NUMBER TO LOCATE THE EXACT SPOT WHERE EACH PHOTOGRAPH WAS TAKEN.

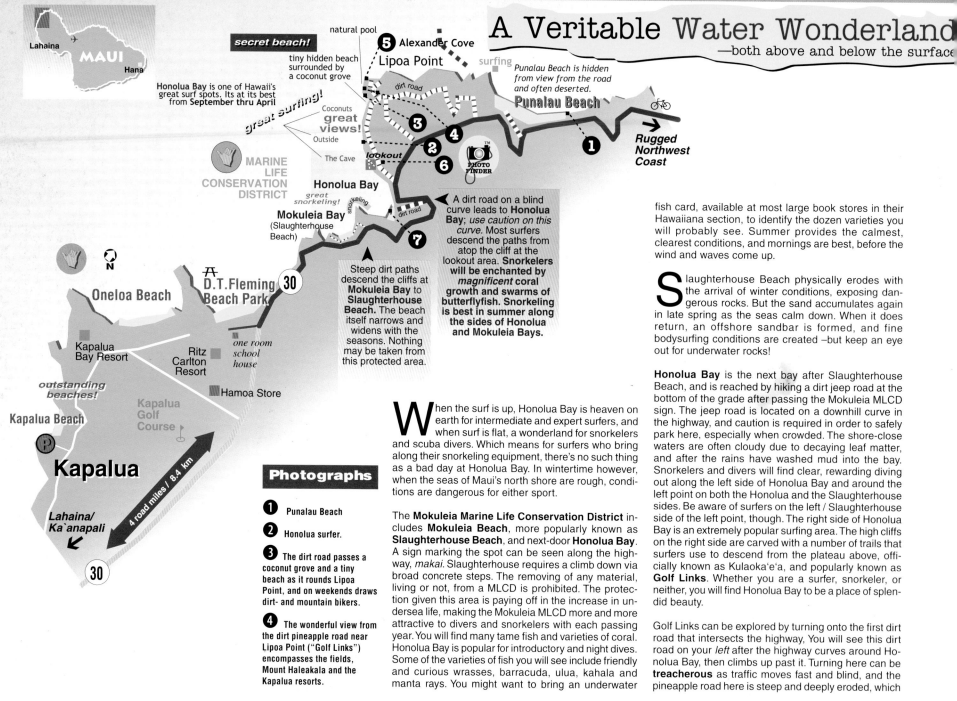

A Veritable Water Wonderland
—both above and below the surface

Map labels:

MAUI — Lahaina — Hana

secret beach!

natural pool

⑤ Alexander Cove

Lipoa Point

surfing

Punalau Beach is hidden from view from the road and often deserted.

Punalau Beach

Honolua Bay is one of Hawaii's great surf spots. Its at its best from **September thru April**

great surfing!

tiny hidden beach surrounded by a coconut grove

dirt road

great views!

Coconuts

Outside

The Cave

③

② ④

⑥ **PHOTO FINDER**

① **Rugged Northwest Coast**

MARINE LIFE CONSERVATION DISTRICT

lookout

Honolua Bay

great snorkeling!

snorkeling

Mokuleia Bay
(Slaughterhouse Beach)

dirt road

⑦

◀ A dirt road on a blind curve leads to **Honolua Bay**; *use caution on this curve*. Most surfers descend the paths from atop the cliff at the lookout area. **Snorkelers will be enchanted by** *magnificent* **coral growth and swarms of butterflyfish. Snorkeling is best in summer along the sides of Honolua and Mokuleia Bays.**

Steep dirt paths descend the cliffs at **Mokuleia Bay** to **Slaughterhouse Beach**. The beach itself narrows and widens with the seasons. Nothing may be taken from this protected area.

Oneloa Beach

N

D.T.Fleming Beach Park

30

one room school house

Kapalua Bay Resort

Ritz Carlton Resort

Hamoa Store

outstanding beaches!

Kapalua Golf Course

Kapalua Beach

Ⓟ

Kapalua

4 road miles / 8.4 km

Lahaina/ Ka'anapali

30

MAUI

Photographs

❶ Punalau Beach

❷ Honolua surfer.

❸ The dirt road passes a coconut grove and a tiny beach as it rounds Lipoa Point, and on weekends draws dirt- and mountain bikers.

❹ The wonderful view from the dirt pineapple road near Lipoa Point ("Golf Links") encompasses the fields, Mount Haleakala and the Kapalua resorts.

When the surf is up, Honolua Bay is heaven on earth for intermediate and expert surfers, and when surf is flat, a wonderland for snorkelers and scuba divers. Which means for surfers who bring along their snorkeling equipment, there's no such thing as a bad day at Honolua Bay. In wintertime however, when the seas of Maui's north shore are rough, conditions are dangerous for either sport.

The **Mokuleia Marine Life Conservation District** includes **Mokuleia Beach**, more popularly known as **Slaughterhouse Beach**, and next-door **Honolua Bay**. A sign marking the spot can be seen along the highway, *makai*. Slaughterhouse requires a climb down via broad concrete steps. The removing of any material, living or not, from a MLCD is prohibited. The protection given this area is paying off in the increase in undersea life, making the Mokuleia MLCD more and more attractive to divers and snorkelers with each passing year. You will find many tame fish and varieties of coral. Honolua Bay is popular for introductory and night dives. Some of the varieties of fish you will see include friendly and curious wrasses, barracuda, ulua, kahala and manta rays. You might want to bring an underwater

fish card, available at most large book stores in their Hawaiiana section, to identify the dozen varieties you will probably see. Summer provides the calmest, clearest conditions, and mornings are best, before the wind and waves come up.

Slaughterhouse Beach physically erodes with the arrival of winter conditions, exposing dangerous rocks. But the sand accumulates again in late spring as the seas calm down. When it does return, an offshore sandbar is formed, and fine bodysurfing conditions are created –but keep an eye out for underwater rocks!

Honolua Bay is the next bay after Slaughterhouse Beach, and is reached by hiking a dirt jeep road at the bottom of the grade after passing the Mokuleia MLCD sign. The jeep road is located on a downhill curve in the highway, and caution is required in order to safely park here, especially when crowded. The shore-close waters are often cloudy due to decaying leaf matter, and after the rains have washed mud into the bay. Snorkelers and divers will find clear, rewarding diving out along the left side of Honolua Bay and around the left point on both the Honolua and the Slaughterhouse sides. Be aware of surfers on the left / Slaughterhouse side of the left point, though. The right side of Honolua Bay is an extremely popular surfing area. The high cliffs on the right side are carved with a number of trails that surfers use to descend from the plateau above, officially known as Kulaoka'e'a, and popularly known as **Golf Links**. Whether you are a surfer, snorkeler, or neither, you will find Honolua Bay to be a place of splendid beauty.

Golf Links can be explored by turning onto the first dirt road that intersects the highway, You will see this dirt road on your *left* after the highway curves around Honolua Bay, then climbs up past it. Turning here can be **treacherous** as traffic moves fast and blind, and the pineapple road here is steep and deeply eroded, which

①

②

③

maui's little-visited rugged north shore awes and surprises with its crystalline beauty.

④

"Golf Links"

could be very bad for your car's undercarriage. This first pineapple road parallels the edge of the cliff, but doesn't come uncomfortably close to the lip. The road is amazingly dusty, and if it has been dry, your car will kick up quite a dust storm. Protect your camera and any electronics. Wherever you see cars parked along here, a steep trail will descend to the surf far, far below. Surfers soon discover that Honolua's world class breakers can become an addiction, spoiling them for anyplace else. Dangerous bugaboos exist for surfers here though –especially the skin-stripping and infamous **Cave**– which is all a part of the challenge, of course. You can't do better than to pick up a copy of Greg Ambrose's **Surfer's Guide To Hawaii**, at most island bookstores and surf shops. This book goes into great detail about what you can expect here, and at all of Hawaii's best surf spots. Its got terrific maps, and to top it all off, the guy is a gifted writer.

The views from the clifftop at Golf Links are wonderful. What is now a neat pineapple field was once the site of the West Maui Golf Course, which closed at the end of W.W.II. The dirt pineapple loop road follows the shape of the peninsula. Along the way are a number of fabulous viewing spots of all the surf and snorkel action below, the adjacent agriculture, and beautiful neighbor island **Molokai** across the channel. A grove of coconut palms with a small, periodically sandy beach was a former picnic spot for golfers and their families. Further up the road, a lava rock wall stands in a Norfolk Pine grove at the site of the old clubhouse. We like to park here on a calm day and walk down the jeep trail to enjoy the coastal views and explore the smooth wave-sculpted boulders at **Lipoa Point**. Best of all, rock hopping along the shore will reveal tiny inlets and **protected crystal-clear pools** for private snorkeling and soaking on calm days. See photo, top right.

little undiscovered coves surrounding lipoa point await the adventurous.

Photographs

See map on page 24 for these photo locations.

5 One of Lipoa Point's wonderful secret snorkeling bays. We call it Alexander Cove, and indicate it as such on the map. You'll have to do some sweaty rock climbing to reach this little beauty. Keep looking and you'll certainly discover others we haven't!

6 Honolua's crystalline baywaters offer one of the best surf and snorkel spots on Maui, and provide beautiful views as well. Here, surfers catch some beautiful sets as they lazily roll in.

7 On a calm summer day, snorkeling in Honolua Bay draws hotel catamarans and individuals alike. The waters close to shore can be murky due to rotting leaf litter on the bottom which your fins will stir up. Swim out to the left along the edge of the bay for the best underwater views and most abundant sealife.

MAUI

MATCH THIS SYMBOL'S **MAP NUMBER** WITH THE CORRESPONDING **PHOTO NUMBER** TO LOCATE THE EXACT SPOT WHERE EACH PHOTOGRAPH WAS TAKEN.

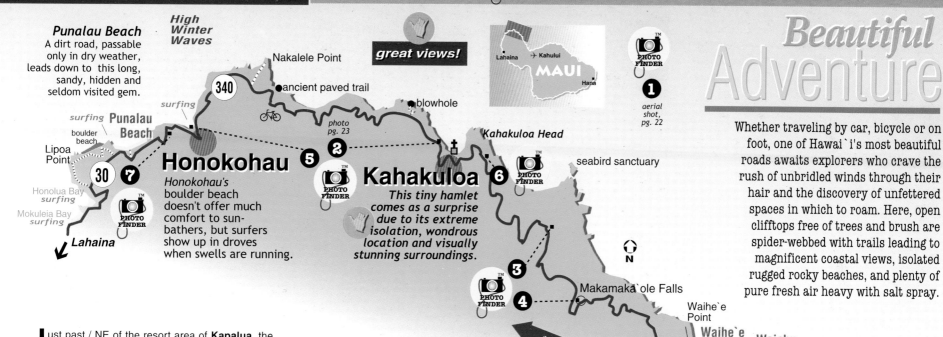

Punalau Beach A dirt road, passable only in dry weather, leads down to this long, sandy, hidden and seldom visited gem.

High Winter Waves

Nakalele Point

great views!

MAUI — Lahaina → Kahului — Hana

aerial shot, pg. 22

ancient paved trail

blowhole

surfing

340

photo pg. 23

Kahakuloa Head

seabird sanctuary

surfing — **Punalau Beach**

boulder beach

Lipoa Point

Honokohau
Honokohau's boulder beach doesn't offer much comfort to sunbathers, but surfers show up in droves when swells are running.

Kahakuloa
This tiny hamlet comes as a surprise due to its extreme isolation, wondrous location and visually stunning surroundings.

Honolua Bay surfing

Mokuleia Bay surfing

Lahaina

30 • 7 • 5 • 2 • 6 • 3 • 4

Makamaka'ole Falls

N

15 road miles / 24 km

Waihe'e Point

Waihe'e Beach Park

Waiehu Beach Park

narrow, steep sandy beaches with great coastal views of east Maui and Mount Haleakaka, little visited by tourists.

Waihe'e

GOLF COURSE

Wailuku & Kahului ↓

Beautiful Adventure

Whether traveling by car, bicycle or on foot, one of Hawai'i's most beautiful roads awaits explorers who crave the rush of unbridled winds through their hair and the discovery of unfettered spaces in which to roam. Here, open clifftops free of trees and brush are spider-webbed with trails leading to magnificent coastal views, isolated rugged rocky beaches, and plenty of pure fresh air heavy with salt spray.

Just past / NE of the resort area of **Kapalua**, the Highway narrows to two lanes. It winds and dips its way along cliff tops with startling views, past pineapple fields and woods of fragrant eucalyptus and needled ironwood. Bands of surfers anxiously cruise the road, stopping at every overlook to size up the wave action below before deciding whether to stay or to keep on searchin'. You may encounter a *legitimate looking* – but *bogus*– sign roadside that officiously proclaims "road closed, residents only". Ignore it: no road in Hawaii that was paved with taxpayer money is off limits, and you became a Hawaii taxpayer the moment your plane landed.

You will approach a little bridge with a sign you *should* pay attention to however: "Yield Right-Of-Way To Oncoming Traffic". Like the Hana Drive, the PI'ILANI HWY. narrows considerably at certain places, so caution is advised. Each turnout must be carefully negotiated as most are located on blind curves along this sinuous and hilly black ribbon of asphalt, and oncoming traffic must be anticipated. You don't have to be afraid, just careful. **West Maui's Rugged North Shore** is just too exquisite to pass up.

You'll understand our cautions better when you feast your darting eyes on the majesty of the surroundings along the PI'ILANI HWY. Locals with their children search the shaded stream beds for wild watercress and other delicacies, while cars loaded with neon colored surfboards glide past. Both wind and

waves crash into solid rock here after enjoying thousands of miles of unbridled freedom. The often sheer, rugged, sun-warmed coastal ramparts face the inviting profile of neighbor island Moloka'i across the channel, and at sunset, the clouds hovering over Moloka'i's Forest Preserve refract the final slanting rays of the sun, projecting an ethereal light show. *Mauka*, the shimmering green flanks of the West Maui Mountains climb skyward as wispy clouds shower the peaks with wet kisses, and in places, the highway edges a little too close to open blue space for comfort. Anticipate cows and their bulls standing nonchalantly in the road around just about any turn. Views grow more enchanting and increasingly rugged as the distinctive landmark **Kahakuloa Head** comes in sight. From rocky bays, light misty fingers reach inland and the distinctive clacking symphony of rocks-hitting-rocks can be heard below as powerful breakers slam stones together on boulder beaches. Faint footpaths littered here and there with cow pie cut across the open and accessible bovine-manicured cliff tops. Solitary homes stand stalwart and cozy and comparatively protected in peaceful cattle-groomed valleys. Everywhere, little man-made towers of rock, their stones balanced atop one other to form a column, sprout like a forest of seedlings from various lichen-covered rocky places along the way.

Some might compare this place to California's Big Sur, which is crisscrossed with fences to keep people corralled at the road shoulder, and which lacks West Maui's enormous, clipped, green clifftop spaces that allow visitors to stand free and run unfettered. Big Sur certainly deserves its fame, but the West Maui Rugged North Coast doesn't deserve its up-til-now obscurity. This drive late in the day allows you to enjoy it in its most beautiful light when traveling from west to east. If traveling east to west, early morning would be best so that you're not driving with the sun in your eyes. Midday sun flattens out the dimensionality and color of the scene and brings the heaviest traffic and most crowded conditions at the lookout areas.

Take advantage of being here to concentrate on capturing what could be some of the most beautiful photographs of your life. Take care and invest effort in composing the shot. For shooting videos, bring out the tripod. We keep ours in the trunk on top of everything else, with legs extended as far as trunk space will allow, for quick and easy access and set up. Walk out on any perfect green bluff, try to find a wind shadow to shelter your equipment from gusts, and use all the camera's capabilities to best advantage. This is the kind of place your miracle machine was invented for. Pan slowly and widely to allow the scene to unfold for the viewer; zoom in on waves crashing into rocks, on the road as it picturesquely winds past boulders and through pasture lands in the distance, and on the rainbows and light effects created on the mountain slopes above by passing clouds. Get close-ups of fence posts trailing into the distance, of the little rock towers, of lichen patterns on the rocks, of roadside memorials to accident victims and of tiny wildflowers hovering close to the ground for protection from the incessant wind. Ask your companion to wander through the scene in the middle distance paying no mind to the camera, remaining silent to allow your videocam's microphone to pick up the solitary sound of the wind. If you are as enchanted with this area as we are, and you're staying in West Maui, you can easily come back again and again at different times of the day and in different weather conditions and make this area a significant personal photo project.

The West Maui North Coast is a wonderful place to be alone, but an equally wonderful place to share with someone special.

As the road meanders around obstacles, and numerous lookout points present themselves, stop and savor. As mammoth Kahakuloa rears its pretty Head, the drive gets lovelier and lonelier, and just when you would least like it to, the road shrinks to one single scary little lane around a curve on a steep grade that descends to the tiny town of **Kahakuloa**. There is a tiny lookout above the pretty little town, with its gorgeous valley location, pebble beach and lovely wooden church. Just past the church we were accosted by an extremely aggressive girl of about 11 with a pidgin accent who brazenly walked in front of the moving car with her hand raised to stop it and commanded us to "buy something". When we politely refused she began spouting a volley of obscenities that even a stevedore wouldn't repeat, and then picked up a rock to hurl at our car. Hopefully she is now residing in juvenile hall.

As the impossibly narrow road climbs out of Kahakuloa, it precipitously hugs the cliff with no guardrail of any kind, and, white knuckled, we pray for no oncoming traffic. It's hard enough to drive *up* this stretch of the road without having to attempt *backing down* it.

Once past the valley where the little town nestles, the road widens again and the views reach their sublime zenith. From one side of the photogenic, fence post-lined road, the town lies far below, and opposite, startlingly green pastures dotted with grazing black cows roll downward toward the indigo sea. All too soon, houses, placed in the most dramatic fashion, begin to dot the landscape here and there, and power lines mar the perfection. Two deep gorges force the road to head inland, and at the larger gorge, because we were traveling slowly in silence, we heard the unmistakable rush of a waterfall. We stopped and parted the grasses to look over the edge to see a real beauty, complete with swimming hole, located well below the road.

As the road descended, twisting and winding toward Central Maui, clouds darkened the sky above, but the views of the dreamy far distant Molokai shore continued to bask in late afternoon sunshine. Just past the little town of **Waiheʻe**, a pretty stretch of beach, narrow and little used on weekdays, fronts the **Waiehu Municipal Golf Course and driving range**. **Waiheʻe Beach County Park** and **Waiehu Beach County Park** both have picnic tables and shade trees seaside, and can be reached by making a *makai* turn from the highway where signs indicate. When the ocean is calm, reef-protected Waiheʻe provides good swimming and fair snorkeling grounds.

Photographs

See map on page 27 for these photo locations.

❸ Although sunny weather is preferred for exploring Maui, a rainy day provides its own special atmosphere for scenics.

❹ This waterfall is hidden beneath Highway 30: we heard it before we saw it.

❺ Another of Maui's very special surfing spots, Honoko-hau gets surprisingly crowded when surf's up. Don't expect to find any sand here.

❻ At the site of a traffic accident, a homemade memorial tops a fence.

❼ Highway 30 provides a wonderful ride, especially late in the day when other cars will be scarce.

❸

❹

❺

MAUI

28

⑦

The Kahekili Highway

usually the only sound you'll hear is that of your nerves unfrazzling.

⑥

MATCH THIS SYMBOL'S MAP NUMBER WITH THE CORRESPONDING PHOTO NUMBER TO LOCATE THE EXACT SPOT WHERE EACH PHOTOGRAPH WAS TAKEN.

D.T.Fleming
Beach Park

Lahaina
MAUI
Hana

Ritz
Carlton
Hotel

one room
school
house

Oneloa Beach

Hamoa
Store

4

Kapalua
Bay
Hotel

2

5

1

PHOTO
FINDER

N

Kapalua Beach

Napili Beach

Kapalua

Kapalua
Golf Course

As determined by both Sunset and Conde Nast Traveler magazines, Kapalua was named America's Best Beach. Conde Nast Traveler magazine's study was conducted by the Laboratory For Coastal research at the University of Maryland.

Napili

Keonenui
Beach

America's Best Beach

Honokowai

Honokowai
Beach Park

30

West
Maui
Airport

If you are staying on this side of the island, you may save hours of travel time to and from other islands by using the West Maui Airport.

7.5 road miles / 12 km

*Embassy
Suites
Resort*

3

HONOAPI'ILANI HWY.

Lower Honoapi'ilani Road

sugar cane train

Ka`anapali

*snorkelers should
be aware of
strong currents
around Black Rock*

Lahaina

Black
Rock

Photographs

1 Poinsettias front a Kapalua church.

2 At Kapalua's one room schoolhouse, shoes are left outside.

3 Our pick for the best area hotel? The Embassy Suites Resort in Honokowai has the largest accommodations and terrific amenities.

4 The last rays of sun bathe Kapalua Beach in a beautiful golden light.

5 The views from the world famous Kapalua Golf Course are truly unparalleled. The island of Molokai beckons from across the channel as pineapple growers prepare the soil that borders the golf course for a new planting.

The communities of **Honokowai, Kahana and Napili** include an area of sandy beaches and nonstop condominiums catering to both Americans and Canadians who prefer comfortable, homelike accommodations that they can really settle into. The condos stretch from the northern edge of the Ka'anapali Resort all the way to the Kapalua Resort, and although this area is not as "upscale" (we're being very picky here) as the resort areas of Ka'anapali and Kapalua which flank it, it's very attractive and a good moderately-priced choice for families. Numerous convenience stores, restaurants and shops dot the area, advantageous for people who are weary of driving. If you are staying in this area, or anywhere in West Maui, and are arriving from Honolulu or a neighbor island, consider flying into **West Maui Airport**, which is located right here, just across HIGHWAY 30. You will save two or more hours of travel time —hours better spent on a beach than sitting in an airport lounge or stuck somewhere in island traffic. From the West Maui airport parking lot you can even see whales spouting right offshore during the season. Other advantages to staying on this part of the island include its proximity to two world class resort areas —and all the amenities they offer— as well as Lahaina town and West Maui 's rugged, majestic and unforgettable North Coast.

You can book accommodations in this area through one of the agencies that specialize in interisland tourism which advertise in the free visitor magazines.

A terrific choice for lodging is the **Embassy Suites Hotel,** located right at the southwest end of this resort area. Included in your rate is a free, cooked to order, all-you-can-eat breakfast, as well as complimentary cocktails in late afternoon. The one- and two bedroom suites are enormous in size and handsomely furnished. The bathrooms are bigger even than some hotel rooms we've stayed in elsewhere. The suite amenities include a 35 inch direct view color TV, VCR, stereo receiver and tape deck, as well as a second TV in the bedroom. The Embassy Suites is quite popular with families, what with so much to keep the kids occupied, including a one acre super pool with 24' waterslide. All this in mind, it is surprisingly quiet. Guest privileges include access to a nearby 18 hole golf course, on-site health club/spa, and four tennis courts. The Embassy Suites is located right on the beach and there are wonderful West Maui views from the lanais —which are set up for dining alfresco— no matter which direction yours may face. This is one of the most comfortable hotels we've ever stayed in, anywhere. We highly recommend it. **The Embassy Suites Hotel is located at 104 Ka`anapali Shores Pl., Lahaina HI 96761. ✆ (808) 661-2000 or toll-free (800) 462-6284; FAX (808) 667-5821.**

1

For the most part, the beaches in this region are safe for swimming when the weather and seas are calm. Be aware that the shore bottom can quickly drop off to overhead depths. Children must always be closely supervised. The popular snorkeling grounds of the **Mokuleia Marine Life Conservation District** are only a few minutes up the coast, just past neighboring **Kapalua Resort**.

The Kapalua area itself is home to the luxury resorts Kapalua Bay Hotel and Villas, and the Ritz Carlton Hotel. **Kapalua Beach** is a crescent shaped, sandy white, palm tree lined treasure; its waters are protected by a coral reef that also provides delightful and easily accessible snorkeling. It has a sandy shore bottom that gently slopes to deeper waters, a convenient public right of way, paved parking, and lovely views of Molokai.....it does sound like the perfect beach, yeah? Snorkeling is good for beginners here, and a handy beach kiosk rents all kinds of recreational equipment. The Kapalua Resort property also includes the Honolua convenience store, uphill from the beach and just *makai/downhill* of Highway 30.

MAUI

Climbing the mountain flanks behind Kapalua is one of the world's most beautiful golf courses, where keeping your eye on the ball is made all the more difficult by the astonishing vistas. Bordered by working pineapple fields, this stunning course is dotted with mini forests of perfectly shaped towering Norfolk Pine. Their symmetrical branches frame dreamlike land- and seascapes, including distant whale pods breaching in the sea, and the south and east shores of neighbor isle

❷

Molokai shimmering across the channel.

Back on Highway 30, one mile past the Kapalua Resort entrance you will see FLEMING BEACH RD., *makai*, just next door to the Ritz Carlton property. This road leads down **D.T. Fleming Beach Park** (which should not be confused with Fleming's Beach, the alternate name for nearby Kapalua Beach). This beach is very popular with residents and visitors, and offers barbecue grills, picnic tables, restrooms and paved

❸

parking. Sea currents can be dangerous and unpredictable here, and the beach has a steep slope which creates a potentially dangerous backwash, even when seas are relatively calm. Notice the little one-room schoolhouse across the road from the parking lot with its neatly placed rows of children's shoes outside. Although they will politely tell you its not necessary, you will gain big aloha points by removing your shoes before entering anyone's house or apartment in Hawaii.

❹

❺

MATCH THIS SYMBOL'S MAP NUMBER WITH THE CORRESPONDING PHOTO NUMBER TO LOCATE THE EXACT SPOT WHERE EACH PHOTOGRAPH WAS TAKEN.

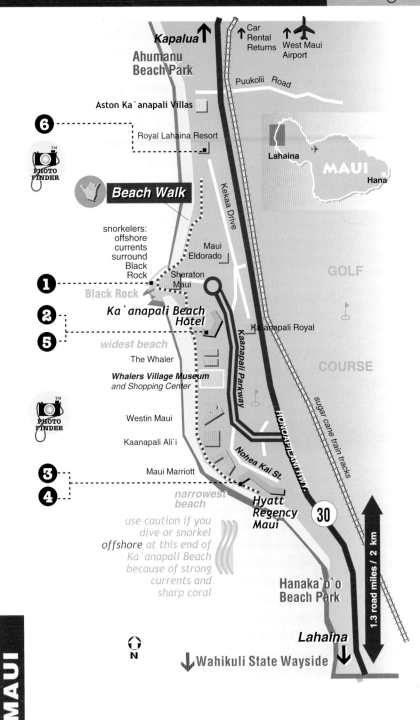

K a'anapali was created from pineapple fields in the 1960s as Hawaii's first planned resort destination. The designers wanted to avoid the untamed and confused growth that had overtaken Waikiki, and to this day Ka'anapali remains a beautiful, successful and mostly harmonious destination. Its ultimate success, though, is directly attributable to its superb setting and splendid beaches.

The shorebreak all along Ka'anapali can be rough, so be aware as you enter and leave the water, and keep an eye on children. Strong currents sometimes exist offshore, especially outside Black Rock (Pu'u Keka'a), the terrific, normally calm snorkeling spot in front of the Sheraton Maui Hotel (snorkeling equipment is available for rent at the beach shacks at the Sheraton and next door [south] at the Ka'anapali Beach Hotel). There is no protecting offshore reef at Ka'anapali, leaving the beach vulnerable to offshore weather conditions and occasional high surf.

Ka'anapali itself, to describe it simply, consists of a string of hotel properties organized along the shore, each offering its own attractions, restaurants and amenities, and one of the world's more attractive outdoor shopping centers, **Whalers' Village**. The hotels, especially at the southern end of Ka'anapali, are continuously trying to outdo each other in the form of such attractions as super swimming pools (which are actually more like compact aqua theme parks), exotic and rare animal menageries (including penguins!), priceless antiques and art in public spaces, and shopping malls. Touring Ka'anapali hotels is great recreation anytime, but its an especially welcome activity on inclement days. A paved sidewalk runs along the beach for just about the entire length of Ka'anapali, from Hanakao'o Beach Park at the south end, all the way to Kahekili Beach Park on the north. Strollers are not only welcome, but encouraged to enter the various properties along its route to look around, eat and shop. Its a really fun way to spend a few hours, or even an entire day.

At approximately the halfway point, Whalers' Village offers great shopping in a truly gorgeous setting, right next to the spectacular Pacific. The free visitor magazines usually contain a coupon for free parking here. Whalers' Village presents a free hula show on Wednesdays and Sundays at 1 pm. The crowning glory of the Whalers' Village is the beautifully outfitted **Whaling Museum** complex located on the 3rd level.

Whale watching has mushroomed in recent years to become a wildly popular visitor activity, as well as having assumed a new and undeniable economic importance to the visitor industry. Taking a whale watching cruise usually leaves the visitor wanting more; more information, more knowledge about the animals themselves and of the history of whaling in Hawaii. The south museum building, called **Hale Kohola**, or House of the Whale, is devoted to the physical aspects of whales. Hale Kohola contains a great **museum shop**, as also does the north museum building, with its wonderfully lit and displayed exhibits of scrimshaw, ship models and whaling artifacts. It is so handsome that it makes you want to move in permanently. Admission is, as of this writing, still free. Open from 9:30 a.m. until 10 p.m.

T he **Lahaina, Ka'anapali & Pacific Railroad** steams along through 12 miles of sugar cane fields and ocean views, the only remaining vestige of an island-wide system of narrow-gauge trains that were the iron workhorses of the sugar cane industry. The railroad makes six daily round trips between Lahaina and Ka'anapali. ℂ (808) **667-6851**

There are three forms of public transportation in the Ka'anapali area: first, the **Whalers' Village Shuttle** is a free shuttle service operated daily throughout the Ka'anapali Beach Resort. Second, the **West Maui Shopping Express** operates from the Ka'anapali Beach Resort, hourly, and will take you south into the town of Lahaina or north to Kapalua for a small fee. Third, the **South Maui Shopping Express** with 8 daily departures will take you to the Wailea Resort on South Maui with stops at many hotels, condominiums, attractions and beaches along the way, round trip for $10.

Golf is another major reason for the popularity of Ka'anapali; the Royal Ka'anapali North Course was designed by Robert Trent Jones Sr., and the South Course by Arthur Jack Snyder.

MAUI

32

Ka'anapali makes a great home base on Maui and the choices of accommodations are varied and wide. **The Ka'anapali Beach Hotel** © [800] 657-7700], conveniently located a stone's throw from Whalers' Village, is a particular favorite and attracts an enthusiastic and loyal following. The Ka'anapali Beach Hotel has allowed its enormous beachfront plumeria blossom-carpeted lawn area to remain a sprawling oasis of loveliness and calm on this oftentimes rambunctious stretch of coast. The real Hawaii is alive and well and celebrated daily at the Ka'anapali Beach Hotel. We have seen returning guests welcomed as family, and have witnessed dozens of hotel employees gather all teary-eyed in the lobby with ukeleles and armloads of fresh leis to serenade favorite guests as they depart!

The gorgeous **Hyatt Regency Maui Hotel** has created its own private world in Ka'anapali. Wild flightless birds roam amidst lush vegetation (meet our buddy *Spike* on page 8). A 150 foot waterslide jet-propels guests into the sparkling super pool, while above, the less adventurous watch from a rustic rope- and-wooden bridge (see photo, *right*). One of the Hyatt's seven major waterfalls pours into the pool here: swim through it into a mysterious grotto, and you'll end up at a fully stocked bar where you can sit in the cool water while sipping a refreshing Blue Hawaiian. Architecturally the hotel is stunning, being one of Chris Hemmeter's earlier ground breaking projects. The nine story hotel completely encloses a central atrium which is open to the sky and filled with greenery, fountains, streams and stunning artworks and sculptures from throughout Asia and the Pacific. The Hyatt Regency Maui is located in the Ka'anapali Resort at **200 Nohea Kai Drive**. Call direct [808] **661-1234**, or via the toll free number **[800] 233-1234** for reservations .

The Hyatt's signature restaurant, the candle-lit **Swan Court,** is open on one entire side to cooling breezes and ocean and pool views. As you descend the grand staircase you will see tables sitting astride a low wall which retains the Hyatt Lagoon's waters, in effect bringing the lagoon right into the room, allowing beautiful swans to swim by at arm's length. *Lifestyles Of The Rich And Famous* called the Swan Court "one of the most romantic restaurants in the world". The menu combines Asian and European flavors and cooking methods to create an intercultural melding of the highest culinary order. Evening resort wear, i.e. no T shirts, is required for dinner. Call 661-4420 for reservations.

One of our **favorite things** to do in Ka'anapali is to wake early, make a cup of morning coffee, and meander down to the beach. We sit in silence and sip as the golden rising sun lights up the mountain slopes of distant, cloud-topped neighboring islands of Lanai and Molokai across the channels. At this time, and in this place, all is right with the world.

For a preview of many of West Maui's dining and entertainment offerings, tune in to the Maui Visitor's Channel on your hotel room TV.

Photographs

❶ At Black Point, snorkeling is the area's best.

❷ The staff at the Ka'anapali Beach Hotel has a well deserved reputation for their spirit of `ohana.

❸❹ A sculpture by the beach at the Hyatt Regency Maui, and the Hyatt's famous sparkling super-pool.

❺ Sunrise lights the island of Lanai across the channel, as seen from the Ka'anapali Beach Hotel's beach.

❻ Ka`anapali from the north end reveals the beauty of the entire region. The island of Lanai is visible across the water.

❷

❸❻

❹

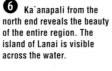

❺

Lahaina town

MATCH THIS SYMBOL'S **MAP NUMBER** WITH THE CORRESPONDING **PHOTO NUMBER** TO LOCATE THE EXACT SPOT WHERE EACH PHOTOGRAPH WAS TAKEN.

Stunning Sunsets

❶

If you are lucky enough to view **Lahaina** for the very first time from offshore, then you will feel like you have sailed right into a South Seas novel. This historic whaling town has more than a few ribald tales to tell, and despite its tremendous popularity, it maintains a unique atmosphere not at all unlike that described by Mark Twain and Robert Louis Stevenson in their observations of the Hawaii of 100 years ago. The town is gorgeously situated against the backdrop of the West Maui Mountains, whose emerald slopes and deep mysterious cloud-canopied valleys enfold pristine beauty and tropical island mystique. Lahaina town nestles, tiny and welcoming, at the foot of this beautiful verdant range. The false fronted wooden buildings along the main drag that is FRONT STREET, the distinctive green and white lanais of the old **Pioneer Inn**, the bobbing masts and rigging of the authentically restored brig Carthaginian, the lethargic and languid wave of coconut palms in Lahaina's late afternoon heat, are all proof enough that we're not in Kansas anymore. The English translation of **Lahaina** is *cruel sun*, and if you happen to be walking down Front St. around 3 pm,

you'll understand just how appropriately named this town is.

Parking? One good area is the **free public lot** across FRONT ST. from the Kamehameha III School at PRISON ST. We often find street parking along here as well, but you'll have a few blocks to walk. The shopping centers, including the New England style **505 Front St.** offer free parking for shoppers. Also, look for free parking coupons in the free visitor magazines. See map for lot locations.

Sunset is probably the optimum time to experience Lahaina. At the harbor, commercial sailing catamarans stocked with beer and snacks fill up with tourists heading out for a sunset sail. What awaits them will undoubtedly prove to be one of their most indelible memories, created as the sun slips all too quickly behind the island of **Lana'i**. If you take a sunset sail, bring a sweater. No matter how hot it is in Lahaina, it can get surprisingly chilly out on the open water. From the sea view, the patchwork fields of sugarcane create an orderly

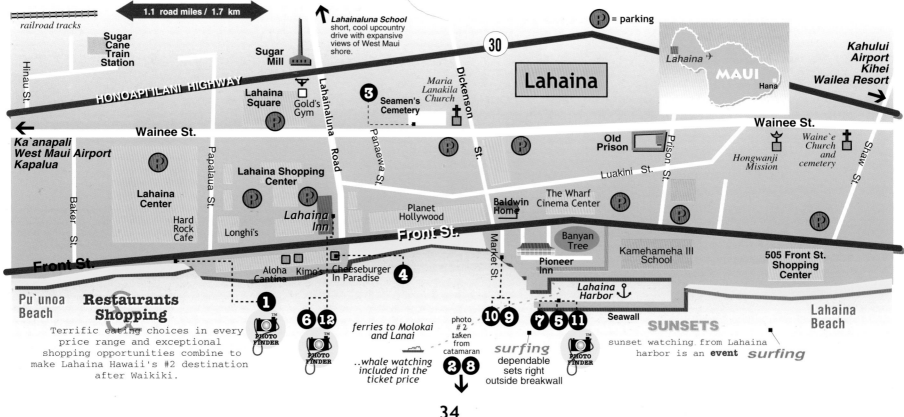

railroad tracks

1.1 road miles / 1.7 km

Ⓟ = parking

Lahainaluna School
short, cool upcountry drive with expansive views of West Maui shore.

Sugar Cane Train Station

Sugar Mill

30

Lahaina

MAUI
Lahaina · Hana · Kahului · Wailea

Kahului Airport Kihei Wailea Resort

HONOAPIILANI HIGHWAY

Lahaina Square

Gold's Gym

❸ Seamen's Cemetery

Maria Lanakila Church

Dickenson St.

Wainee St.

Old Prison

Wainee St.

Waine'e Church and cemetery

Ka'anapali West Maui Airport Kapalua

Wainee St.

Papalaua St.

Lahainaluna Road

Panaewa St.

Luakini St.

Prison St.

Hongwanji Mission

Shaw St.

Lahaina Center

Lahaina Shopping Center

Hard Rock Cafe

Longhi's

Lahaina Inn

Planet Hollywood

Baldwin Home

The Wharf Cinema Center

Banyan Tree

Kamehameha III School

505 Front St. Shopping Center

Baker St.

Front St.

Aloha Cantina

Kimo's

Cheeseburger In Paradise ❹

Pioneer Inn

Front St.

Market St.

Lahaina Harbor ⚓

Seawall

SUNSETS

surfing

Lahaina Beach

Pu'unoa Beach

Restaurants Shopping

Terrific eating choices in every price range and exceptional shopping opportunities combine to make Lahaina Hawaii's #2 destination after Waikiki.

❶

❻ ❶❷

ferries to Molokai and Lanai

..whale watching included in the ticket price

photo #2 taken from catamaran

❷❽

❿❾ ❼❺❶❶

surfing
dependable sets right outside breakwall

sunset watching from Lahaina harbor is an **event** *surfing*

34

❷

Lahaina *viewed from the sea.*

Previous page:

❶ Lahaina's Front Street attracts throngs of sunset watchers.

❷ The best views of Lahaina are from the water right before sunset, when this shot was taken. If you are planning a sunset cruise while in Hawaii, we think Lahaina is the best place to do it.

This page:

❸ This is the seaman's cemetery at the Maria Lanakila Church in Lahaina.

❹ Lahaina's Front St., taken from the stairway at Cheeseburger In Paradise.

❺ Surfers floating off Lahaina Harbor's seawall try to catch the last waves before the sun sets behind the island of Lana`i.

❻ In front of the Lahaina Inn on Lahainaluna St., a salty old sea dog tries to figure out just what the woman across the street could have possibly been thinking of when she put that outfit together.

❼ A surfer surveys conditions from Lahaina Harbor, bustling at late day with sunset cruise traffic.

MAUI

❼

a surfer peers into the setting sun at *Lahaina Harbor* sizing up the last waves of the day.

grid pattern on Maui's mountain slopes, wispy clouds turn golden in the setting sun as they bounce silently off jagged peaks, and the giant **L** laid out high on a slope above the town by the students of historic **Lahainaluna School** is visible for miles offshore.

Sunset viewing from the harbor is a natural. People wander the dock area or sit on the seawall in silence, drinking it all in. The sails of distant craft glide by silhouetted surfers and kayakers who paddle out from the dock for the day's last challenge against Lahaina Harbor's dependable little breakers. Even if it's flat everywhere else in West Maui, the surf's usually up here practically any day of the year. As the sun sinks lower across the 'Au'au Channel, it plays hide and seek among the late day clouds that caress the island of Lana'i, scattering its golden rays into distant streaks and tightly focused beams.

Here at Lahaina Harbor you can catch the **Maui Princess** for a ferry trip to the neighbor island of **Molokai, (808) 667-6165** or call toll free from the mainland **(800) 275-6969**. **Expeditions** makes five trips a day to the neighbor island of **Lana'i**; phone **875-0556** or call toll free from the mainland: **877-464-6284**

The ferry to **Lana'i** docks just a ten minute walk to palm-fringed **Hulopoe Beach's great snorkeling.** Commercial boats also daytrip to Lana'i, providing lunch, drinks, and snorkeling equipment. Check the visitor magazines or the Maui Visitors' Channel on TV for their ads.

Lahaina's sidewalks take on renewed life as the sky anticipates vivid shades of orange and violet. In the vicinity of the **Great Banyan Tree**, next to the harbor-adjacent **Pioneer Inn**, a raucous and shrill cacophony rises from the thousands of birds that congregate here every day at this time, celebrating the sunset in their own brash way. Scores of people, alone and in pairs, gravitate to the harbor in front of the Inn to watch nature's light show. A lucky few end up with railing-side tables at **Kimo's**, the Front St. restaurant where the unobstructed views are sublime. A fresh regiment of insatiable shoppers descends on the town as the sun dips toward the horizon, searching for the perfect souvenir, the most colorful Maui T- shirt, or that skimpy nothing of a bathing suit they wouldn't be caught dead in back home, but will brazenly parade around in here.

Maui changes people. Problems diminish, hang-ups loosen their stranglehold, and the junk that drove them crazy just last week at home doesn't seem worth a passing thought anymore.

There's no shortage of places to spend your money in Lahaina. Besides all the stores catering to visitors that are located along and adjacent to FRONT ST., check out the **Lahaina Shopping Center** (behind Longhi's), the **Lahaina Center** (home of Hard Rock Cafe, across

the street from Longhi's), and one block inland, **Lahaina Square**, for all the necessities; supermarkets, hardware stores and the like. If you're partial to malls, the cool and attractive **Lahaina Cannery Mall** is a half mile north of town center between FRONT ST. and HWY. 30 (see these locations on map).

Lahaina's fascinating human parade is best enjoyed from a table overlooking the streets and walkways. Restaurants in every price range offer this entertaining public service; some are situated right on the sidewalk and others right above it. Some are tucked away, like **Gerard's** (French-Hawaiian; 174 Lahainaluna; <**www.maui.net/~gerard/gerards_main.html**> or David Paul's Lahaina Grill, 127 Lahainaluna Rd. <**www.lahainagrill.com**>. Both incidentally are the deserved darlings of foodies and top gourmet critics from New York to San Francisco. Others, like **Moose McGillycuddy's** (budget American food; upstairs, 844 Front St.), Hard Rock Cafe (900 Front St.), and the efficiently managed **Cheeseburger In Paradise** (street level and upstairs, 811 Front St.) provide dependably satisfying eats at prices that don't break the budget.

Longhi's (888 Front St., ✆ **667-2288**) is one of our longtime favorites for breakfast. Their warm-from-the-oven coffee cakes, sticky buns and küchens are superb –and the coffee's terrific. Longhi's' own thick-cut, crunchy-chewy sourdough toast smothered in butter and preserves is by itself enough reason to come here, but enjoy it along with a fresh vegetable frittata, and you'll have the perfect beginning to a Maui day. Tables are placed in breezy french doorways next to window boxes brimming with flowers, with all the lively street action just a few feet away and views of the Pacific just across the street. We have experienced some quality problems during recent breakfast visits when items were served old, cold and/or burnt, so never hesitate to send things back if the quality does not live up to the high prices. Menus available at <**www.longhi-maui.com**>

A popular breakfast choice for the surfing crowd is the tiny **Sunrise Cafe** on Market St., around the corner from Front St. and **Lappert's Ice Cream** (693 Front St.). The baked goods are great, the crowd very interesting.

Kimo's (845 Front St. ✆ **661-4811**) continues to be our favorite hangout for dinner, and a superb choice for sunset watching. If you want a sunset perch, arrive at 5 p.m. for an upstairs table by the rail, have a glass of wine, kick back and drink in the wondrous mid Pacific view. No trendy gourmet wizardry here, just really good, dependable favorites. Try not to ruin your appetite by filling up on the carrot muffins, though: we watched as a lady at the next table opened her purse and brazenly dumped in an entire basket load, and then handed the basket back to the waiter, demanding a refill. If you have any room left after dinner, try a

towering chunk of Kimo's Hula Pie for dessert.

Friday nights mean open house at Lahaina's numerous **art galleries**, most of which are situated along FRONT ST. Often complimentary wine and *pupus* [snacks] are set out and everyone is invited to join the party. No strong-arm sales pitches here, though. Just stop by, meet the artist, have a drink and enjoy the work on display.

The Lahaina Inn is a terrific choice for lodging in the heart of Lahaina town. Located right off Front St. just a few dozen steps from little Lahaina Beach and all the shopping action, and quite reasonably priced, this small, lovingly restored hotel has earned rave reviews. The Lahaina Inn successfully recreates the feel of 1890s Lahaina, with a luxurious twist. The 12 rooms are individually decorated with antique wood wardrobe closets, ceiling fans, beveled mirrors, and decorator fabrics. The sheets and pillowcases are some of the finest we've ever slept on in any hotel. The bathrooms are well appointed with clear glass stall showers, great water pressure, hair dryers and fine toiletries. The rooms are air conditioned, and even streetside rooms are surprisingly quiet, since Lahaina rolls up the sidewalks early. A free continental breakfast of fresh baked croissants and banana bread, fruit and juice, and wonderful Kona coffee is served from a sideboard at the end of the handsome skylit hallway, for transport back to your room or verandah. The verandah, or lanai, is furnished with rocking chairs and a little table and overlooks the early morning street activity with views of the rainbows that arch above the valleys of the West Maui mountains. Next door, **David Paul's Lahaina Grill**, ✆ **667-5117**, is the kind of linen-tablecloth, dressy but casual kind of place one expects to find in Paris, bustling and alive with laughter and conversation, with attentive well- dressed waiters and fabulous New American cuisine. <**www.lahainagrill.com**>. The restaurant and hotel compliment each other beautifully. Both are located at 127 Lahainaluna Rd. Inn reservations and Information ✆ **(800) 669-3444** or **661-0577**. <**www.lahainainn.com**>

Lahaina is a historic town shaded by mango trees and brimming with handsomely restored structures and countless photo possibilities. For a break from the hustle and bustle, Lahaina's back streets are quieter and shadier and provide a very enjoyable way to walk off a meal. On WAINEE STREET, one block inland paralleling FRONT ST., you'll find the **old prison**, the **Seaman's Cemetery** and **Maria Lanakila Church**. On FRONT ST., across from the Pioneer Inn, are the most photogenic **Baldwin Home** (c.1834; the oldest building in Lahaina) and the exactly-preserved **Masters' Reading Room**, which is headquarters for the very dedicated **Lahaina Restoration Foundation**. Stop in for a free guide to Lahaina's historical sites, which are all located within easy walking distance. Docked nearby at the harbor, the 120-foot, two masted square rigged

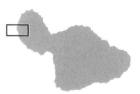

MAUI

38

Lahaina

⑧

⑨

⑩

⑪

 ⑫

brig **Carthaginian II** contains a floating museum of whaling paraphernalia and an AV presentation on Hawaiian sea life.

A *mauka* turn off HWY. 30 (which parallels FRONT ST. a few blocks inland) onto LAHAINALUNA ROAD will take you past the sugar mill's smokestack and uphill for two miles through waving cane fields and ever expanding coastal views to **Lahainaluna School**. Opened in 1831, its the oldest school in the US west of the Rocky Mountains. Visit **Hale Pa'i**, the printing house which published Hawaii's first newspaper and the first Hawaiian language dictionary. If school is in session, they request that you sign in at the principal's office first.

South of Lahaina, HIGHWAY 30 skirts rocky shores and public beaches. This road is **Maui's Blood Alley. Keep an eye on that rearview mirror** as you scope out the scenery, as impatient drivers –both visitors and locals– have a tendency to *really* speed and take stupid chances along here.

All of the following beaches are at, or very close to, roadside:

Puamana Beach Park has a narrow white sand beach and normally calm swimming conditions, a grassy park area with picnic tables, and lovely Lana`i island views.

Launiupoko State Wayside Park has a large, man-made, wave- protected wading pool for kids, beachside. As a picnic spot, it offers good views of the neighbor islands Kaho`olawe and Lanai.

Kulanaokala`i Beach and roadside **Awalua Beach** are both popular with locals and visitors. Awalua Beach also attracts surfers, and both beaches offer a sandy shore bottom and a gentle slope to deeper waters.

Olowalu Beach is a favorite with **snorkelers and scuba divers** because of its offshore reefs, as is **Ukumehame Beach** further down the Highway. **Olowalu** is located at **mile marker 14**, six miles south of Lahaina, with good snorkeling extending all the way to the 16 mile marker. Very popular on weekends with local families, Olowalu's inner reef is protected and shallow, but usually turbid, while the outer reef, 50-100 feet from shore, boasts many kind of fish, turtles, and large coral heads. **Olowalu is considered one of the best snorkeling and diving spots on Maui** for underwater scenery and variety of marine creatures. Picnic supplies can be purchased at the Olowalu General Store at the 15 mile marker.

Papalaua State Wayside Park is a great place to have a late-day cookout and watch the sunset. It has a long, narrow, and pretty *kiawe* tree-lined beach and lovely neighbor island views. The offshore bottom is rocky but shallow, and is equally attractive to swimmers and snorkelers.

In the area of the road tunnel, a glance down the cliff, *makai*, will reveal numerous commercial craft bringing snorkelers to these exquisitely transparent aquamarine waters for some of Maui's finest underwater sightseeing. Then, past the tunnel, after the Highway twists and turns a bit, you'll see a sign indicating a **scenic lookout**, *makai*. This is a prime spot for winter **whale watching** and cinemascopic **views** of neighbor island **Kaho`olawe**, the Kihei Coast, and Mt. Haleakala. **0.8 mile past the lookout**, a sharp *right turn* on a rocky road leads to the lighthouse. Little bays in both directions here offer good snorkeling on calm days. Small deserted golden beaches, invisible from the highway, await to the *left/NE* of the MacGregor Point lighthouse.

MAUI

Lahaina

Lao Needle

Iao Valley

Kahului

Wailuku

WEST

Lahaina

MAUI

Hana

surfing

Puamana Beach Park

Launiupoko State Wayside

Kulanaokala`i Beach
dark sand beach
Awalua Beach

MAUI MOUNTAINS

16 road miles / 25 km

mile marker 14

great snorkeling! reachable from shore

Olowalu Beach

30

boulder beaches

Ukumehame Beach Park
Papalaua State Wayside

great snorkeling! safely reachable only by boat-contact commercial outfitters

Papawai Lookout

tunnel

Be alert for dangerous drivers here!

dangerous intersection

Ma`alaea Harbor

Ma`alaea Beach

tiny pocket beaches reachable via steep dirt side roads makai of highway

McGregor Point Lighthouse

Kihei

Terrific Vantage Point For **Whale Watching**

38

30

350

32

❶

❶

Photographs

❶ From roadside, just east of the tunnel, terrific snorkeling grounds attract underwater explorers to these crystalline waters.

❷ The sun sets behind Lana`i in this wonderful view from Papalaua State Wayside Park, located on the Lahaina side of the Highway 30 tunnel.

❸ This view from the whale lookout at Papawai Point takes in a lot of territory, including Mount Haleakala and the Kihei Resort area, as well as the islands of Kaho`olawe, Molokini and Lana`i (not visible in this photo).

Papalaua

Ma`alaea Harbor and Beach

MATCH THIS SYMBOL'S MAP NUMBER WITH THE CORRESPONDING PHOTO NUMBER TO LOCATE THE EXACT SPOT WHERE EACH PHOTOGRAPH WAS TAKEN.

Photographs

❶ Maalaea Harbor provides berth for many of the excursion craft that shuttle snorkelers and whale watchers to their destinations. It also boasts some fine seafood eateries, great surfing at "Buzz's", a surf break located just outside the seawall, and a relaxing atmosphere.

❷ (Facing page) Almost 3 miles long, Ma`alaea Beach is a popular place for jogging because of its hard-packed sand. Whale watching in winter is super, and the surfing and windsurfing are often terrific. Never crowded, the only drawback is for sunbathers; Ma`alaea has windy conditions along the eastern half.

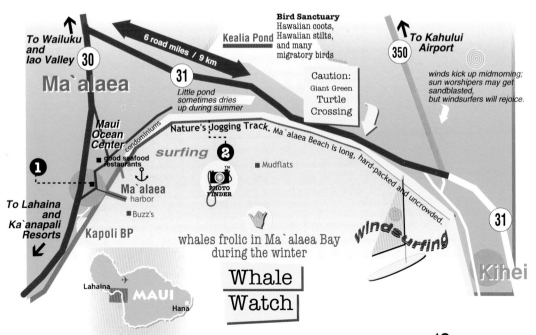

❶

The Ma'alaea District of Maui is located on the south shore of the island's isthmus. Beautiful and nearly deserted, **Ma'alaea Beach** stretches for nearly three miles, and even on weekends, there's plenty of room to be alone here. The beach is anchored on the west end by Ma'alaea Harbor, on the north by the wild and protected **Kealia National Wildlife Refuge**, and on the east by **Sugar Beach**.

On Highway 30 at the 5 mile marker, a *mauka* turn reveals signs in the pineapple fields indicating the **Lahaina Pali Trailhead**. This strenuous 5.5 mile hike ascends 1600'/ 488m Kealaloloa Ridge for stunning views of Maui and neighbor islands. It descends to **Olowalu** on the Lahaina Coast, where a shady snorkeling beach awaits to cool your weary bones.

Ma'alaea Harbor is picturesque and quite busy. Because of traffic, early mornings should be avoided for your casual visit unless you are taking a commercial fishing, snorkeling or diving excursion. Most trips to the very popular offshore diving wonderland of **Molokini** Island depart from here at daybreak, and at that time, the buses which bring passengers from the resort areas effectively clog up tiny Ma'alaea. Check out the free visitor magazines for those companies running excursions. For meals, there's a **Buzz's Steakhouse** at the westernmost end of the harbor, while at **The Ma`alaea Waterfront** restaurant at water's edge, chef Ron Smith buys seafood right off the fishing boats as they dock at the harbor... and you can't get much fresher than that.

Surfers are attracted to the harbor breakwater, due to the incoming breakers' **lightning fast right slide**. Adjacent to the harbor, heading eastward, a string of condominiums indicates the increasing popularity of this area as a destination for visitors. From here, the views looking down the three mile extension of sand, with **Mount Haleakala** looming impressively in the distance, is quite beautiful. The sand for the entire length is relatively hard packed along shore, making Ma'alaea a **favorite for joggers** and those who love a long, easy, uninterrupted walk. Ma'alaea Beach often becomes windy by mid morning, attracting windsurfers but discouraging sunbathers. In winter it's a favorite playground for whales, many of whom venture surprisingly close to shore as they enjoy the warm sheltered bay waters. The shore bottom is sandy but slopes steeply to deep waters, so keep an eye on small children. Happily, under normal conditions there are no currents to worry about. There is wide open beach access from the road along much of the shore length, and sand dunes between the road provide privacy and a buffer against traffic noise. Drive cautiously to avoid endangered **giant sea turtles** crossing the road to lay their eggs. Close to the center of the beach, surfers catch the breakers at a spot known as **Mudflats**. Roomy Ma'alaea Beach is one of the best spots on Maui for a long barefoot sunset walk; the winds die down by late afternoon, the slopes of Haleakala turn golden in the waning sunlight, and the only company you will have will be scattered far and wide and consist of other joggers and walkers and a few people walking their dogs.

Just across Ma`alaea Road from the harbor you'll find the **Maui Ocean Center**. It's **Underwater Journey** exhibit allows visitors to walk through a 57 foot long clear acrylic tunnel traversing a 2,500,000 liter open tank to wander among the fishes, which include tiger sharks and tuna. Other exhibits include **The Living Reef**, **Touch Pool**, **Turtle Lagoon**, and **Graceful Stingrays**. The Center is open from 9 a.m. to 5p.m. daily. Visit their website at <www.coralworld.com/moc> for a preview. Admission charge.

To Wailuku and Iao Valley — **30**

6 road miles / 9 km

Bird Sanctuary
Hawaiian coots, Hawaiian stilts, and many migratory birds

Kealia Pond

350 To Kahului Airport

Ma`alaea

31

Little pond sometimes dries up during summer

Caution: Giant Green Turtle Crossing

winds kick up midmorning; sun worshipers may get sandblasted, but windsurfers will rejoice.

Maui Ocean Center

condominiums

good seafood restaurants

surfing

Nature's Jogging Track. Ma`alaea Beach is long, hard-packed and uncrowded.

❷

Mudflats

❶

Ma`alaea harbor

PHOTO FINDER

To Lahaina and Ka`anapali Resorts

Buzz's

Kapoli BP

whales frolic in Ma`alaea Bay during the winter

Windsurfing

31

Kihei

Whale Watch

MAUI
Lahaina
Hana

Legend:
- ● full circle indicates yes
- ◐ half circle indicates partial or sometimes

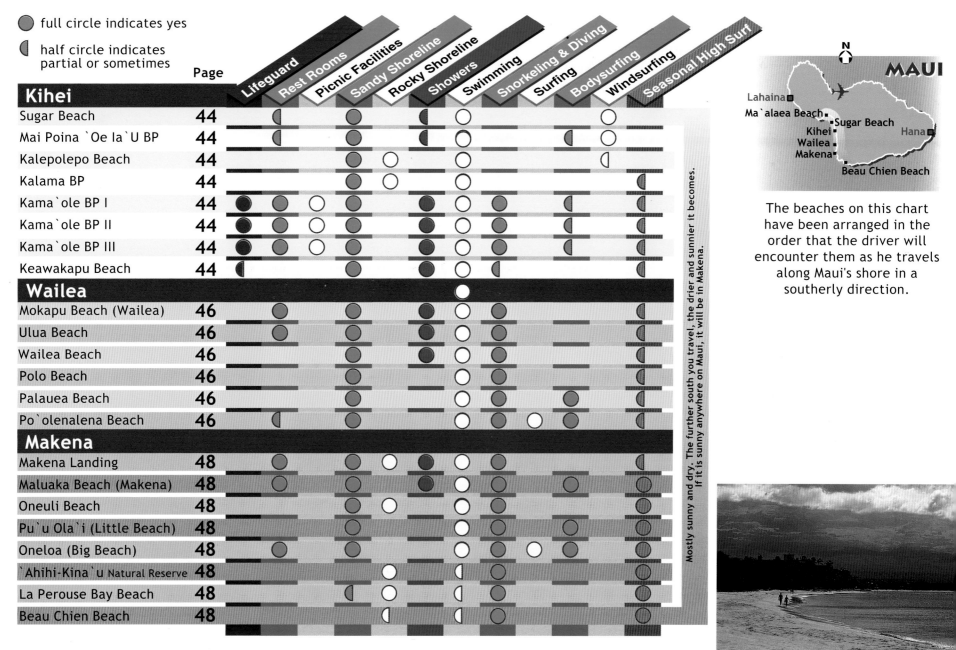

	Page	Lifeguard	Rest Rooms	Picnic Facilities	Sandy Shoreline	Rocky Shoreline	Showers	Swimming	Snorkeling & Diving	Surfing	Bodysurfing	Windsurfing	Seasonal High Surf
Kihei													
Sugar Beach	44		◐		●			○				○	
Mai Poina `Oe Ia`U BP	44		◐		●			○			◐	○	
Kalepolepo Beach	44			●	○			○				◐	
Kalama BP	44			●	○			○				◐	
Kama`ole BP I	44	●	●	○	●		●	●	●		◐	◐	
Kama`ole BP II	44	●	●	○	●		●	○	●		◐	◐	
Kama`ole BP III	44	●	●	○	●		●	○	●		◐	◐	
Keawakapu Beach	44	◐		●		●	○	◐				◐	
Wailea							●						
Mokapu Beach (Wailea)	46		○		●	○	●						◐
Ulua Beach	46		○		●	○	●						◐
Wailea Beach	46		○		●	○	●						◐
Polo Beach	46			●	○	●							◐
Palauea Beach	46			●	○	●			●				◐
Po`olenalena Beach	46	◐		●	○	●	○	●					◐
Makena													
Makena Landing	48		○		○	●	○						◐
Maluaka Beach (Makena)	48		○		●	●							◐
Oneuli Beach	48			●	○	○							◐
Pu`u Ola`i (Little Beach)	48				●	○	●						◐
Oneloa (Big Beach)	48	◐		●		○	●	○	●				◐
`Ahihi-Kina`u Natural Reserve	48			○	●	◐							◐
La Perouse Bay Beach	48			◐	○	◐	●						◐
Beau Chien Beach	48			◐		◐	●						◐

MAUI

- Lahaina
- Ma`alaea Beach
- Sugar Beach
- Kihei
- Wailea
- Makena
- Hana
- Beau Chien Beach

The beaches on this chart have been arranged in the order that the driver will encounter them as he travels along Maui's shore in a southerly direction.

Mostly sunny and dry. The further south you travel, the drier and sunnier it becomes. If it is sunny anywhere on Maui, it will be in Makena.

❷

Kihei

MATCH THIS SYMBOL'S **MAP NUMBER** WITH THE CORRESPONDING *PHOTO NUMBER* TO LOCATE THE EXACT SPOT WHERE EACH PHOTOGRAPH WAS TAKEN.

PHOTO FINDER

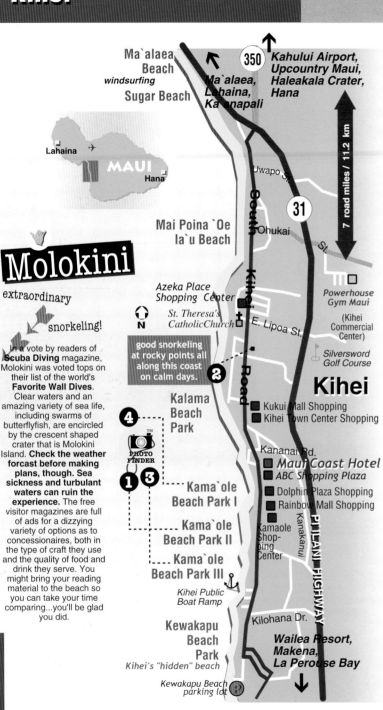

Ma`alaea Beach
windsurfing
Sugar Beach

350 *Kahului Airport, Upcountry Maui, Haleakala Crater, Hana*

Ma`alaea, Lahaina, Ka`anapali

Lahaina

MAUI

Hana

Uwapo St.

31

7 road miles / 11.2 km

Ohukai

Mai Poina `Oe la`u Beach

Molokini

extraordinary

snorkeling!

In a vote by readers of **Scuba Diving** magazine, Molokini was voted tops on their list of the world's **Favorite Wall Dives**. Clear waters and an amazing variety of sea life, including swarms of butterflyfish, are encircled by the crescent shaped crater that is Molokini Island. **Check the weather forcast before making plans, though. Sea sickness and turbulant waters can ruin the experience.** The free visitor magazines are full of ads for a dizzying variety of options as to concessionaires, both in the type of craft they use and the quality of food and drink they serve. You might bring your reading material to the beach so you can take your time comparing...you'll be glad you did.

Azeka Place Shopping Center

St. Theresa's Catholic Church

E. Lipoa St.

N

good snorkeling at rocky points all along this coast on calm days.

Powerhouse Gym Maui

(Kihei Commercial Center)

Silversword Golf Course

Kihei

Kalama Beach Park

■ Kukui Mall Shopping
■ Kihei Town Center Shopping

Kananai Rd.

4

PHOTO FINDER

1 3

Kama`ole Beach Park I

Kama`ole Beach Park II

Maui Coast Hotel
■ ABC Shopping Plaza
■ Dolphin Plaza Shopping
■ Rainbow Mall Shopping

Kamaole Shopping Center

Kanakanui

Kama`ole Beach Park III

Kihei Public Boat Ramp

Kilohana Dr.

PIILANI HIGHWAY

Kewakapu Beach Park
Kihei's "hidden" beach

Wailea Resort, Makena, La Perouse Bay

Kewakapu Beach parking lot

MAUI

When your idea of the ideal vacation spot includes lots of sun, end-to-end beautiful sandy beaches, and good, reasonably priced food and accommodations, then your quest ends in **Kihei**. With condos aplenty lining the shore, Kihei attracts family groups who like to settle into home-like accommodations with meal preparation and laundry facilities.

For those people who don't want anything to do with a kitchen during their vacation, we recommend the handsome, affordably priced **Maui Coast Hotel**. Accommodations at the Maui Coast are *spacious* —unusual for a new hotel these days. Rooms and suites are very attractive. Air conditioning *and* ceiling fans cool each room. The bathrooms are large in size, with beautiful thick towels, hair dryers, double sinks, quality amenities, and *Lordy, Lordy, bless my achin' bones* —Whirlpool Jet bathtubs in all Alcove and Deluxe suites. Sinking into one of these babies after a day of too much sun and endless climbing in and out of a rental car is true luxury. The Maui Coast boasts a laundry room with *complimentary* machines on floors 2, 4 and 6; it has private night-lit tennis courts and both a heated swimming pool and a childrens' wading pool. It is located only five minutes from fabulous world-class golf. And the Maui Coast Hotel has that luxurious something otherwise missing in Kihei...*service*. Call toll free **(800) 426-0670 in the US & Canada; or (800) 895-6284 interisland.**

Kihei is a long narrow oceanside strip community, brimming with great condominium accommodations, often times bargain priced, and lots of eating and shopping choices —and is lined from end to end with *beautiful white sand beaches*. From **Sugar Beach** on the north to **Keawakapu Beach** on the south, the long sandy expanse between is only broken here and there by rocky points. With its location on Maui's sunniest, driest coast, a great Kihei tan can be virtually assured. As a rule, if the sun isn't shining here, its not shining anywhere on Maui. Keep this in mind if you are staying in another part of Maui. It can be clouded over in Ka'anapali but

at the same time perfectly clear in Kihei, so if you feel the need to lie on the beach on any given day, Kihei might just be your best bet.

At the very northern end of Kihei, **Mai Poina Oe Lau Beach Park**, better known as **Sugar Beach**, often gets very windy by noon, offering complimentary dermabrasion treatments for sun worshippers, and a great sporting environment for windsurfers —which can number from 50–100 or more under ideal conditions. A little further south, across the road from the **Canoe Club**, near the **Suda Store** at **61 S. Kihei Rd.**, the **Farmer's Market of Maui** offers the best produce from Maui and Molokai for reasonable prices on **Monday, Wednesday and Friday from 1:30 p.m. to 5:30 p.m.** Here you'll find luscious fruits and gorgeous tropical flowers like king protea and heliconia pendulums to decorate your room at bargain prices. You will notice that KIHEI RD. is lined with strip malls, so if you enjoy shopping, you'll find no shortage of opportunities here.

Arguably the best of the best beaches are the triplet **Kama'ole Sands Beach I, II & III**. According to **John R. K. Clark**'s impressively detailed and indispensable book *The Beaches Of Maui County*, kama'ole in Hawaiian means *childless*... pretty ironic considering that due to the excellent swimming conditions here, these beaches attract legions of families. But be aware that the sandy shore bottom quickly slopes to overhead depths, so watch your kids carefully and swim near a lifeguard tower. Each Kama'ole Beach Park has lifeguards, restrooms, barbecue grills and showers. **Sunset watching is a major event here**, with friendly people informally congregating to enjoy the nightly spectacle together. Notwithstanding all the wonderful experiences we have had over the years on Maui, sunset watching with like-minded people at Kama'ole has brought us some of our fondest memories and favorite photographs. **Kama'ole BP III** is the most popular of the three beach parks and has the widest and longest beach, as well as playground equipment for kids, a huge tree-shaded grassy area at the south end, and good snorkeling on calm days around the rocky south point. There is also **good snorkeling** in front of the **hotel at 2960 S. Kihei Rd.**, along the rocky shore to the right of the sandy beach.

Kihei is Maui's watersports center. Headquartered here are a number of **kayak** outfitters. If you have never tried **kayaking**, you may be as surprised as we were to discover that paddling your own craft is not only *not a chore*, but in fact the freedom and control you experience piloting your own sleek craft is exhilarating. Kayaks can poke into little nooks and crannies, they're able to beach on any sandy shore, and they are even light

enough to carry over obstacles. You can paddle among a pod of spinner dolphins and peer down through crystalline waters at sea turtle colonies. Check out the free visitor magazine for their listings of kayak outfitters, or check with an activities broker; their storefronts can be found concentrated along Lahaina's Front St. and spread throughout Kihei.

Snorkelers will be happy to find that there are four **Maui Dive Shops** in the Kihei-Wailea area alone. Stop in to see the selection of rental equipment, and ask about their popular diving excursions. They'll give you their free dive guide with *great maps* that will lead you to Maui's hidden and uncrowded dive and snorkel spots.

For breakfast or lunch, Kihei boasts a real find. The **Kihei Caffe (1945 S. Kihei Rd. © (808) 879-2230)** is a tiny place with a few tables inside and a few more out front. They serve great coffee, wonderful baked goods, and Kihei's best sandwiches to eat in, or take out. If you are heading out to **Makena Beach** or a hike to **La Perouse Bay**, or a drive to other parts, stop here first to have them pack you a sandwich. Their raspberry twists, almost a foot long, are a big hit and sell out almost as soon as the tray hits the counter in the morning.

MATCH THIS SYMBOL'S MAP NUMBER WITH THE CORRESPONDING PHOTO NUMBER TO LOCATE THE EXACT SPOT WHERE EACH PHOTOGRAPH WAS TAKEN.

Plush Resorts and Superb Beaches

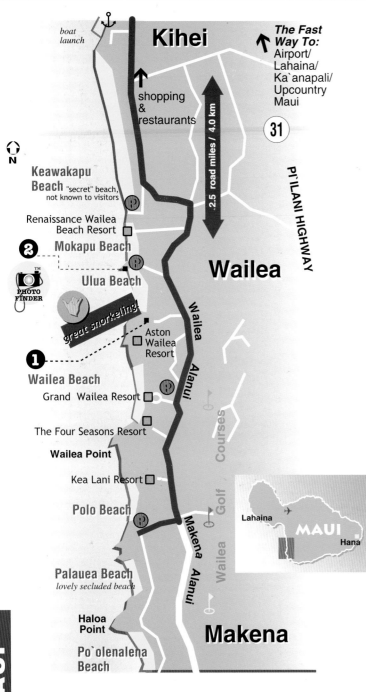

Kihei

shopping & restaurants

The Fast Way To:
Airport/
Lahaina/
Ka`anapali/
Upcountry
Maui

31

N

2.5 road miles / 4.0 km

PI`ILANI HIGHWAY

Keawakapu Beach "secret" beach, not known to visitors

Renaissance Wailea Beach Resort

Mokapu Beach

Ulua Beach

great snorkeling!

Wailea

Aston Wailea Resort

Wailea Alanui

Wailea Beach

Grand Wailea Resort

The Four Seasons Resort

Wailea Point

Golf Courses

Kea Lani Resort

Polo Beach

Makena Alanui

Lahaina

MAUI

Hana

Palauea Beach
lovely secluded beach

Wailea Golf Courses

Haloa Point

Makena

Po`olenalena Beach

MAUI

---

ailea is Beach Heaven. To extol the virtues of one Wailea beach over another is a futile exercise; all are exquisite, with excellent swimming, clear waters perfect for snorkeling, and superb views of the coast and neighbor islands. Depending on where you're standing, the vista may include the islands of Lana'i, Kaho'olawe and/or tiny **Molokini**, the famous offshore snorkel and scuba mecca. For a detailed rundown on history, conditions and the physical attributes of these and all Maui County beaches, including Molokai, Lana'i and even uninhabited Kaho`olawe, pick up a copy of **John R. K. Clark's Beaches of Maui County**. We couldn't do without it.

The Wailea Resort is located south of the sunny Kihei Resort area (see previous page). As you drive along KIHEI RD., the Wailea logo emblazoned on a lava rock wall announces this beautifully designed planned resort. Here, the road segues from KIHEI RD. to WAILEA ALANUI (*Alanui* means road or way). Neat and unobtrusive signage roadside along WAILUA ALANUI directs the driver to individual hotels, shopping and public beaches. There is no town at Wailea, but hotel-hopping to see how each property compares with its neighbors is fine entertainment. The hotels/resorts are extremely competitive and have gone all out in an attempt to out-do each other in grandeur, lushness, architectural boldness, art collections and recreational facilities. Each has, in addition to its expensive showcase restaurants, a relatively inexpensive restaurant choice on property.

If you've got the bucks, there is **unforgettable golf** at each of Wailea Golf Club's 18 hole showcase Blue, Orange and Gold courses. The Gold course is designed by Robert Trent Jones Jr. and opened in 1994. Views from each beautiful course are sublime, so pack your camera or a Kodak Funsaver single use camera in your golf bag, you'll want to show the folks back home what **golf paradise** looks like. Reserve in advance, and check with the course or your hotel about discounts, preferential treatments and free shuttles offered to hotel

guests by some courses. But if you're poor like us, you'll enjoy the nearby **Waiehu Municipal Golf Course** ✆ **(808) 244-5934**. It is an 18 hole course with a pro shop and rentals, a restaurant and putting green.

For tennis aficionados, the **Wailea Tennis Club** boasts 11 **plexi-pave** courts, three of which are night-lighted, as well as three **grass courts** for true Wimbledon-style tennis.

All beaches in Wailea, or in the entire state of Hawaii for that matter, are open to the public. Swimming conditions are usually ideal, except during periods of large surf or heavy kona storms. **The rights of way to each beach are clearly marked roadside by discreet signage**; watch for beach names and **blue** *coastal access* **signs**.

❶

Keawakapu Beach is either Kihei's southernmost beach or Wailea's northernmost beach, depending on who you talked to last. It is reached by going straight ahead on the little *dead end road* where KIHEI ROAD curves to the *left* (just keep to the right of the aforementioned Wailea rock wall with logo). **Keawakapu** is Kihei/Wailea's "secret" beach, fronted by private homes. At the end of the short road is a small parking lot, a shower, and a few concrete steps leading down to the beach. Keawakapu Beach is comparatively narrow in width, and remains tree shaded until about noon.

Mokapu Beach Park fronts the Renaissance Wailea Beach Resort. Mokapu was named for an offshore island and natural bird sanctuary obliterated during W.W.II in the name of artillery practice. **Mokapu Beach** is a wide but short white sandy strand with a mostly sandy shore bottom. There is a tiny park here and a paved parking lot and walkway to the beach, which also leads to...

Ulua Beach. Located right next door to Mokapu Beach, Ulua Beach (pictured, right) is the most popular of Wailea's beaches and was named in the **Top 10 of**

2

America's most beautiful beaches in a University of Maryland study, published in **Conde Nast Traveler** magazine. Bounded by two rocky points, **Ulua Beach** is long and wide, and is bordered on the southern end by the Aston Wailea Resort property. When waves are up, there's often good bodysurfing here, and when its calm, the **snorkeling** along the rocky points is **excellent.** The offshore waters are reported to be Maui's clearest. The water depth around the rocks ranges from 3-20 feet and fish varieties, although less abundant here than other places, include schools of goatfish, wrasses, foot-long puffer fish, trumpet fish, Moorish idols, lemon butterfly fish, and in protected places,

shrimp. But while swimming, be sure to keep an eye out for catamarans launching or landing. You don't want to get whacked in the head.

Wailea Beach comes next. It is long and wide, and *slightly* less picturesque than the others, but remember, we're splitting hairs here. Wailea boasts good swimming, snorkeling —especially along the rocks to the *left*— and gentle bodysurfing when waves are running; **Wailea Beach** fronts the Four Seasons and the Grand Wailea Resorts, and there is paved parking and a nicely landscaped and graded mini park.

Continuing south, **Polo Beach** provides **excellent snorkeling** on calm days around the rocky area. The beach itself is long and wide and is backed by small sand dunes. The shore bottom slopes gradually, making for excellent swimming and bodysurfing. There is paved parking and a mini park at Polo, and the beach is backed by the Kea Lani Resort property. A short walk from Polo's parking lot along the OLD MAKENA RD. passes as yet undeveloped beachfront property. This is **Palauea Beach**, uncrowded and out-of-the-way, the first beach located in the Makena district. See the next page for more about the beaches of **Makena**.

MATCH THIS SYMBOL'S MAP NUMBER WITH THE CORRESPONDING PHOTO NUMBER TO LOCATE THE EXACT SPOT WHERE EACH PHOTOGRAPH WAS TAKEN.

THE NAKED TRUTH: Nudity is "officially illegal" on Maui, but often there are more bodies squeezed onto Little Beach's small crescent than there are on all of neighboring huge Big Beach. Bring plenty of sunscreen.

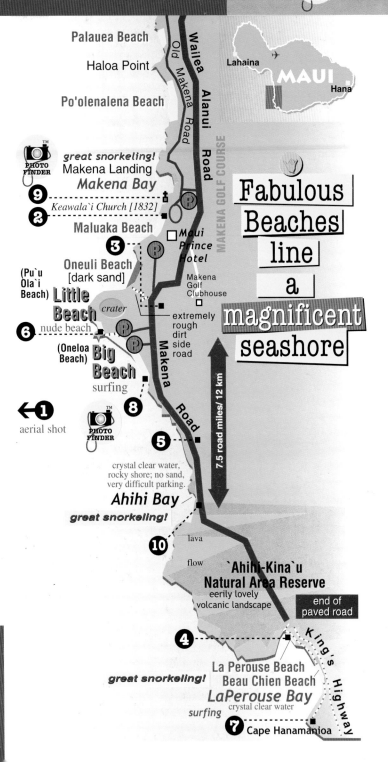

MAUI

Palauea Beach

Haloa Point

Po'olenalena Beach

Wailea Alanui Road

Old Makena Road

MAKENA GOLF COURSE

Lahaina

MAUI

Hana

PHOTO FINDER

great snorkeling!
Makena Landing
Makena Bay
9
Keawala'i Church [1832]
2

Maluaka Beach
3

□ Maui Prince Hotel

Makena Golf Clubhouse □

Oneuli Beach [dark sand]

(Pu'u Ola'i Beach) **Little Beach**
crater
6 *nude beach*

(Oneloa Beach) **Big Beach**
surfing

extremely rough dirt side road

Makena Road

Fabulous Beaches line a magnificent seashore

1 ←
aerial shot

8

PHOTO FINDER

5

7.5 road miles / 12 km

crystal clear water, rocky shore; no sand, very difficult parking.
Ahihi Bay
great snorkeling!

10 lava
flow

'Ahihi-Kina'u Natural Area Reserve
eerily lovely volcanic landscape

end of paved road

4

King's Highway

La Perouse Beach
Beau Chien Beach
great snorkeling!
LaPerouse Bay
crystal clear water
surfing
7 Cape Hanamanioa

From the parking area at **Polo Beach Park**, continue south on narrow OLD MAKENA RD (*not* the Highway). To the *right/ makai* you will see a fenced-off wooded area where pretty, and often deserted, **Palauea Beach** awaits on the other side. There are breaks in the fence for public access. After passing Palauea Beach, **Po'olenalena Beach** appears *makai*. Po'olenalena is undeveloped with an unpaved parking area and porta-potties. Its a good swimming beach with a mostly sandy bottom and gradual slope to deep water.

Leaving Po'olenalena Beach, continue southward. OLD MAKENA RD. passes oceanside homes with enviable views as it rounds a curve and descends steeply toward **Makena Landing/Five Caves**. Here you will find a handsome little park with restrooms and showers, shade trees, blooming oleander and bougainvillea, parking, and a tiny dark sand beach that provides easy entry for exploration of this excellent but lesser known snorkeling and superb kayaking area.

Makena Bay is lovely and photogenic, and makes a nice spot for a picnic, or just a leg stretch. For beginning snorkelers, enter the water at the little sandy beach and swim along the shore to the *left*. For advanced divers, walk along the rocky shore to the *right* from the parking lot until you reach a grave site. Offshore you will find coral heads, caves and **a large green sea turtle colony**.

Makena Landing is also a popular launching site for **kayak** excursions. Under your own paddle power, you can encounter pods of spinner dolphins, sea turtle colonies and in season, humpback whales. Anchored together, a group of kayaks becomes a floating island from which snorkelers can slip beneath the surface to explore Makena Bay's fascinating underwater realm. Check the free visitor magazines to find kayak outfit-

ters. Many of them are located in **Kihei** [page 44].

Continue along OLD MAKENA RD. and you will spot beautifully restored **Keawala'i Church** and its fascinating graveyard, prettily landscaped and bordering a stone beach, and just beyond that, beautiful white sand **Malu'aka Beach**. The road dead ends here at a turnaround that abuts the **Makena Prince Hotel**. The opposite end of Malu'aka Beach can be reached by auto by going back up to the HWY., turning *right/south*, pass-

❶

ing the hotel, and making a very sharp —almost a hairpin— *right turn* (keep an eye out, its easy to miss) through the Makena Golf Course. There is not a lot of parking here, but the views and beach are gorgeous; with a grassy picnic area, clear waters and great coastal and Lana'i views. A very popular fro weddings, beautiful brides can be seen here before sunset almost any day of the week. If a horseback ride sounds good to you right about now, you will see the entrance for **Makena Stables** adjacent to the parking area.

MAKENA ROAD continues, skirting past distinctive **Pu'u 'Ola'i Crater** and an unmarked and very rough, deeply rutted dirt spur road through the trees to **Oneuli Beach**, an dark sand beach with no facilities.

Further along MAKENA RD. you'll see a large paved

parking lot at the northern end of **Big Beach**. There is steep foot trail access to clothing-optional Little Beach from here. **Little Beach** is situated in a beautiful bay a short climb over the bluff at the northern end of Big Beach. Nudity is illegal here, officially, but Little Beach's worldwide fame and secluded location have proven to be an ongoing and lucrative tourist draw. Little Beach is also one of the best beach-access scuba diving spots (depth: 45'/14m) on Maui: enter the water near the *right* end of the beach and swim out. Currents are not a problem unless, as always, seas are stormy. The underwater topography is varied and rewarding. Bodysurfing here can be excellent.

Big Beach, also popularly known as **Makena Beach**, and officially called **Oneloa Beach**, is one of Hawaii's most fabulous strands. At two thirds of a mile long and 100 feet wide, with transparent waters and not a structure in sight, the place is surprisingly popular, considering how out of the way it is. In **Hawaii Magazine**'s anniversary poll, Makena Beach was named the number one favorite among its readers. There are two more parking areas for Big Beach beyond the first one. The third parking area, as of this writing, has been blocked off. This southern part of Big Beach draws **surfers and body boarders**, making for an interesting crowd and some fancy board work in the surf. Big Beach is justifiably famous and well worth a visit.

Continue along MAKENA RD. as it narrows and clings to the very edge of the seashore, winding around tiny **Ahihi Bay**. You may see half a dozen cars parked here as people take advantage of the exceptional snorkeling. Fish and coral abound. The water entry is rocky, but the snorkeling adventure waiting beyond makes it well worth it. Pick up a copy of the **Maui Dive Guide**, available free at all **Maui Dive Shop** locations, for excellent maps of all of Maui's best snorkeling spots.

Just beyond Ahihi Bay, MAKENA RD., narrow but smoothly paved, crosses the eerily barren **'Ahihi-Kina'u Natural Area Reserve**, the site of the most recent (1790) lava flow on Maui. The entire area, including offshore waters, is protected. This protection means any activity not in keeping with preservation, such as fishing, hunting, or removing rock or terrestrial or sea life forms, is forbidden. A great blanket of naked lava has poured down Haleakala's slope here, covering almost everything in its path and creating a beautiful and surreal moonscape uniquely suited to unusual landscape photography. Hiking through this lava field can be hazardous because so much of the material is loose and unstable, making for precarious footing, and all of it is **very sharp** to exposed skin. Unpaved rough jeep trails lead to the seashore. Photographically, this whole area provides beautiful minimalist landscape shots of lava, sea and sky, as well as providing lovely green views up the slopes of **Mount Haleakala**. Through the Reserve, MAKENA RD. smoothly continues on, dipping and climbing until it

comes to an abrupt end at the entrance to stunning and vibrant **La Perouse Bay**.

Just past the homes located beyond the 'Ahihi Kina'u lava flow, you will encounter the unmarked (as of this writing) entrance to **La Perouse Bay**. There is only room for 3 or 4 cars to park here, so to avoid hassles with other people, you may want to double back a few dozen yards and park along MAKENA ROAD.

At the entrance you will have a choice of two very rough unpaved roads to follow —but only on foot. One goes straight ahead, and the other veers to the right toward the ocean. The one that continues straight ahead appears to be an unpaved continuation of MAKENA RD. *but it is not*. It deteriorates even more so from its terrible condition here as it travels over desolate lava flows to become the **King's Highway**, an ancient paved foot trail. There are always "adventurous" visitors who decide to chance the odds and try their luck at driving such "roads", but *forget it* here! For those who are pedestrianly inclined, the King's Trail is a beautiful, **desolate hike** over sharp and wobbly lava rock which roughly follows the coast, but never actually comes down to the water's edge. The hike is a good one for those attracted by desolate and wide open spaces, but if the trade winds stop blowing, you will experience hot and uncomfortable conditions. Bring at least a liter of **drinking water** per person. You must be completely self sufficient if hiking in this area.

The **better choice** for a walk —and the cooler, shadier, prettier and more photogenic choice— is to instead take the unpaved road that heads *makai / seaward* from the end of MAKENA ROAD, toward the ocean. It becomes a shoreline trail in just a few hundred yards, passing tiny white sand pocket beaches made all the more brilliant by the contrast provided by the surrounding jet black lava rock. This seaside trail makes an exquisite hike on a clear day, as there is such a clarity and brilliance here that you can almost feel vibrations from it.

La Perouse Bay is a noteworthy and popular **snorkeling, surfing and fishing** area, and most people seem satisfied venturing no further than the end of the road. Along the *right* side of the bay, fronting the homes, the waters are part of the **marine preserve area**: nothing can be disturbed or taken. If you dive further to the *left* as you face the ocean, you will be safely outside the preserve area. The Bay is rich in marine life and has a white sandy bottom where massive coral heads are prevalent.

The trail meanders in a SE direction closely following the shore and passes under shady native woods where seasonal wildflowers bloom between massive boulders and the impossibly cobalt blue ocean smashes its waves on sun bleached white coral beaches. The hike is wonderful and passes through varied terrain. We met

a solitary woman making this hike in *flip-flops*, believe it or not. Wear sturdy foot protection; lava rock can inflict really nasty cuts, and out here, as they say, no one can hear you scream.

Although the shore does not resemble the classic palm lined Hawaiian scene that the postcards usually depict, **Beau Chien Beach** (Bow-She-"N") emanates a distinctive diamond-sharp beauty. This chunky salt and pepper strand is washed by crystal clear turquoise waters, and is stunning for its unexpected loveliness. It's one of our favorite Hawaiian places to be alone.

The trail leaves the level shoreline just beyond Beau Chien Beach at **Cape Hanamanioa**, climbing over a barren and stark lava cliff toward the lighthouse (not visible from this point). A short climb upwards along the trail will reveal superb views back toward Makena, including the twisting **King's Trail** visible a little ways inland, a building ruin, the emerald green 10,000 foot slopes of Haleakala, endless expanses of sea and sky, and the rugged, beautiful, wooded shore. Looking down into the sea, its unmistakable and foreboding danger is tempered by its inviting, stunningly transparent aquamarine waters.

The King's Trail continues along the south shore for another 12 miles/18 km or so to ultimately join HWY. 31 at Manawainui, which is a place just about as barren and thirsty and as close to the middle of nowhere as you will find on Maui. If you intend to walk the King's Trail, make sure you bring sun protection, food and plenty of water, and let people know where you're going.

❶ This aerial shot plainly shows the situation of Big Beach to the right of the bluff, and Little Beach on the left. The slopes of Mount Haleakala rise up behind these very popular Makena beaches.

❷ Maluaka Beach is a real beauty. The Maui Prince Hotel is the only commercial property on the beach. Parking and a bluff-top picnic area with sublime views are located at the far end of the beach in this photograph.

❷

Photographs

For these photo locations, see the map on page 48.

③ Horses at the roadside, a little south of the Maluaka Beach area.

④ There are not a lot of sandy expanses at La Perouse Bay, but private sandy pocket areas like this provide a place to spread a blanket.

⑤ Parts of Makena Road can be rough, as this not-quite-official traffic sign says.

⑥ Little Beach is secluded and beautiful —and nude. On a calm day it offers fine snorkeling at the far end as seen in this photograph.

⑦ Just past Beau Chien Beach, a foot trail climbs the bluff at Cape Hanamanioa. Looking back, beautiful views of crystal-clear La Perouse Bay, Mount Haleakala, and the winding lava rock-paved King's Highway in the near distance delight the eye.

⑧ These two shots taken at the south end of Makena's Big Beach follows one skim

boarder as he challenges incoming waves. Timing was the key, as was a fast shutter speed to freeze the action.

⑨ Narrow Makena Road skirts around little `Ahihi Bay just a few feet from the water. If you stop to snorkel at this popular spot, pull your car out of the traffic right-of-way.

⑩ The Graveyard at Makena's Keawala`i Church, located just north of/ before Maluaka Beach, has a couple dozen fascinating markers with wonderful old photos of the deceased.

⑪ The bluff at the southerly end of Maluaka Beach is a very popular place for sunset weddings, such as that of Michael and Donna Merritt of Austin, Texas.

⑤

③

④

⑥

MAUI

Makena

❼

❽

❾

❿

⓫

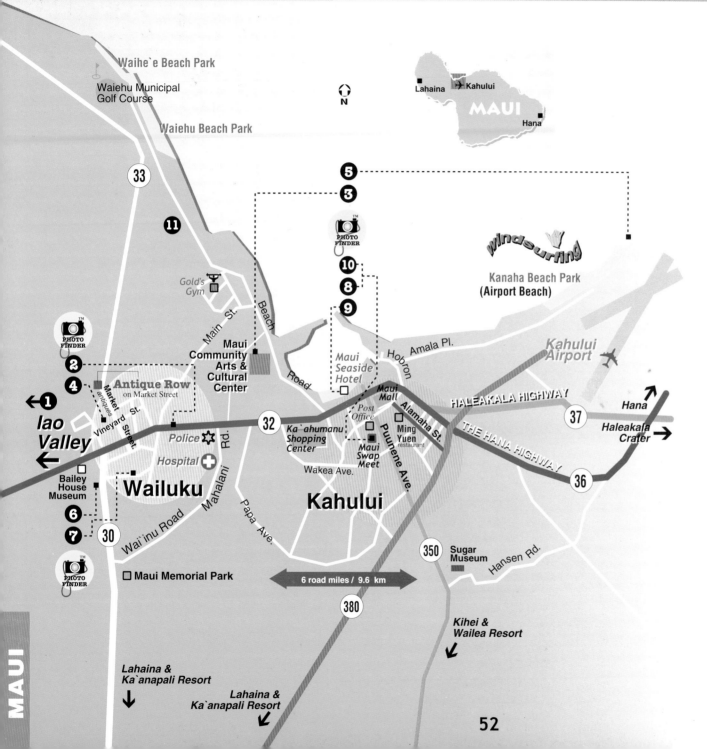

Iao Valley

As you drive the few minutes into Iao Valley via HIGHWAY 32 from downtown Wailuku, you will see The **Heritage Garden** in Kepaniwai Park, designed by Richard C. Tongg. Handsome buildings represent the cultures of Hawaii's many immigrant groups. The park is very pretty and the buildings offer photographers a cornucopia of architectural detail shots representing a wide range of styles from Portuguese villa and garden to a Japanese pagoda. Zoom in on details such as windows, doorways and rooflines to round out your photography efforts on Maui.

The gaping emerald green chasm in the West Maui Mountains that hides **Iao Valley** and provides downtown Wailuku with its dramatic backdrop is like an open gate that welcomes visitors to an exotic vertical world of enfolding sheer-walled peaks spilling delicate white threads of water thousands of feet down their rugged faces. The waters tumble and splash from rock to rock in their single-minded quest to form the tributaries that converge to create **Iao Stream**.

The volume of water that flows between its banks and the unrelenting force of its journey is quite unexpected and exhilarating. The river is accessible from the roadside in Iao Valley, but the going is slippery and where the winds can't reach, **mosquito-rich**. Better to stroll the asphalt pathways that web the footbridge area and lead to prime viewing places. Be sure to bring insect repellent.

Necks craned, its frightening to think of what it must be like to actually stand way up there. Seeing and feeling the presence of such towering, steep-sided mountains in such close proximity is literally dizzying. **Honokohau Falls** drips –or so it deceptively looks from this great distance– from the mysterious cloud topped peaks. The falls drops freely for 1120 feet/341meters. Rains pour eternally up there, a never ending torrent where plants unique in the world thrive undisturbed more than a mile above the sea. 400 inches [10 meters] of rain a year drench a magical world that even few veteran helicopter pilots have ever seen, so relentlessly cloud-enshrouded is this place. Maps show an intriguing and ancient trail that climbs the dangerously crumbling mountainside from the La-

Iao Valley

Wailuku

haina side upward to the great peak, **Pu'u Kukui**, stopping at the edge of the 5788 foot [1765 meter] precipice before its sheer drop to Iao Valley floor. Just thinking about peeking over the edge gives us the willies. The trail begins *mauka* of the West Maui community of Honokowai, north of the Ka'anapali Resort, and roughly parallels Honokowai Stream, then Amalu Stream... and near the brutal and exhausting end passes legendary **Violet Lake** at an altitude of nearly 5,000 feet. The only photos we've seen picturing this cradle of wilderness life forms unique on planet Earth were published in *Islands* magazine in 1997.

The centerpiece of Iao Valley is **Iao Needle**, the distinctively shaped cinder cone, which is a mountain in its own right, towering at 2250 feet [686 m]. The needle provides a beautiful and unique landmark in a place that would still be one-of-a-kind without it. Our view here of Iao Needle is from the bank of the stream that flows beneath the footbridge. Local kids swim in the few protected calm sections of the stream, but **mosquitoes can be relentless** in the more sheltered areas, so if you're the extra-tasty type, wear repellent. On your way out of Iao Valley, visit **Tropical Gardens of Maui**, 200 Iao Valley Road, ✆(808) **244-3085**. The self guided tour through this veritable Garden of Eden is lovely, and amazing plant varieties are for sale in their store.

Wailuku

Wailuku is unexpectedly pretty in the older areas of town. To visitors it is little-known, and to kama'aina, underappreciated. The town is built on the lower slopes of the West Maui Mountains, which form a stunning and ever changing backdrop of constant light and shadow against pinnacled verdant cliffs. Wailuku is home to Maui County government buildings, lots of interesting little restaurants, nearby deserted beaches, historic churches, bargain priced antique shops, very friendly people and a lot of flower-filled front yards.

Wailuku's antique stores offer odd treasures and authentic **Hawaiiana**, little restaurants serve the ubiquitous saimin lunch and ramshackle storefronts await your camera's eye. In the newer section of MARKET ST., near the intersection of MAIN ST., more unusual shops and art galleries await to delight those of us who have grown weary of malls and their generic chain stores. Wailuku is also the place to pick up **camping permits, hiking maps and related literature**, if you haven't already done so by mail at the State Building on **High St. Phone: [808] 243-5354.**

Within walking distance of the intersection of MAIN ST.[HWY. 32] and HIGH ST. [HWY. 30], a number of beautiful historic structures provide photo opportuni-

ties. **Ka'ahumanu Church** photographs best in morning light, but the New England-esque **Courthouse** across the street is better later in the day. **The Bailey House Museum** [admission charge] makes a fascinating stop; the interior is filled with period furnishings and artifacts, the exterior handsome and photogenic, and the museum shop sells **books** of **local interest** at lower prices than most retail bookstores. 2375 Main St. ✆ (808) **244-3326**.

Making Wailuku your home base will give you a central location from which to explore all of Maui. The **Old Wailuku Inn** (✆ 800-305-4899) <www.mauiinn.com> is quite lovely and has 7 rooms with private baths and serves a full breakfast. Many return visitors refuse to pass through Wailuku town without sampling **Chef Long Nguyen**'s delightful fare at the very popular **A Saigon Cafe**,1792 Main, <www.asaigoncafe.com>, or picking up a bento box for a picnic from **Ichiban Okazuya Hawaii**, at 2133 Kaohu St. The long line outside **Sam Sato's**, who specializes in dry mein —not to be confused with fried saimin— attests to the eatery's popularity, which locals would prefer to keep secret. Sam's is located at 1750 Wili Pa Loop in the **Millyard Industrial Park**. Close by you can work off Sam's garlic noodles at **Gold's Gym** at 850 Kolu St., A-3, ✆ **242-6851**, in the heart of Wailuku's industrial section.

A 3 mile/5 km drive up KAHEKILI HWY. [MARKET ST.] from downtown Wailuku will take you past the **golf course** to the **Waihe'e Beach Park** turnoff. Seldom visied by tourists, its coastal views of East Maui and the rare winter snows of Mount Haleakala, it is deserted, tourist-free and reef protected, with good swimming and diving on calm days.

Photographs

❶ Iao Stream rushes through the valley as Iao Needle provides a famous backdrop.

❷ Shot from the overpass spanning Ka'ahumanu Ave., just west of Baldwin High School, downtown Wailuku glows in the earliest rays of morning sun, while the peaks that guard Iao Valley tower behind.

❸ The Maui Community Arts Center Theater. Photo by David Franzen.

❹ Accommodations at rock-bottom prices can be found on this stretch of Vineyard St. in Wailuku.

❺ Windsurfers rule at Kanaha Beach, popularly known as Airport Beach.

❻ The beautiful stained glass window at the Wailuku Union Church, located on High St.

❼ Orchids replace the standard grass lawn in this Wailuku home's front yard.

❸

❹

MAUI

❺

❻❼

Kahului

There are two distinct groups of people who come to Maui: those who want to completely unwind on the beach or by the pool and do absolutely nothing, and those who want to explore the many attractions that the island so richly offers. For explorers, making the Kahului / Wailuku area their home base, instead of the leeward resorts of Ka'anapali and Kihei, makes good sense. Staying in this central area cuts major drive time off the Hana Drive, Ho'okipa Beach's world renowned windsurfing, and cool Upcountry motoring adventures. It is probably best appreciated by those who'd rather not rise as early as 2:30 a.m. to make the sunrise drive to Haleakala Crater, as they would have to do if staying in the Ka'anapali Resort area.

Both Wailuku and Kahului have been included as no more than an afterthought in many guidebooks, but we feel they are full of surprises and have great things to offer the visitor.

Kahului began modern life during WWII when the navy built the supply depot that has since become Kahului Airport. While next door neighbor Wailuku looks every bit like a city, Kahului seems more like a suburban afterthought, constructed in a much faster and less planned fashion. Physically the city is made up mostly of low rise commercial buildings and strip malls, but it is not as unattractive as it might sound.

Things are always changing in Kahului, and the jewel of the city is the **Maui Arts & Cultural Center**, simply known as **The Center**. Located adjacent to **Maui Community College**, the Center is home to the **Maui Philharmonic Society, the Maui Academy of Performing Arts, the Maui Symphony Orchestra and Maui Community Theater.** The Center boasts a first-rate 1200 seat main theater where no seat is more than 100 feet from the stage, and a 4100 square foot visual arts gallery where museum quality shows are held. Architecturally, The Center's buildings pay homage to the classic lines of C.W. Dickey and other traditional island architects. A wonderful addition to Maui's already spectacular assets, The Center is a boon to kama'aina and visitor alike, and firmly establishes Maui as a unique entity, now confidently emerging from the cultural shadow of Oahu. For current program information telephone (808) **242-ARTS**, or write to MACC, One Cameron Way, Kahului, Maui, HI 96732

Kahului's shopping centers and malls, The **Maui Mall, Maui Marketplace, Kahului Shopping Center** and **Ka'ahumanu Shopping Center**, are all located just a short distance from one another. Additional shopping lines Dairy Road and the Hana Highway. The prices in Kahului will be the best you'll find on the island, so this is the place to look for any needed big ticket items. Pick up the daily **Maui News** for current sales at Sears, Walmart, K Mart, Costco, Sports Authority, Borders, Long's Drugs and other Kahului stores.

Dozens of fast food type restaurants are scattered throughout the city, but there is not an over abundance of designer or chef eateries as are found in Lahaina and the resort areas. In the past, famed Hawaii chefs who have opened signature restaurants in Kahului have unfortunately seen them fail. However, Maui being the center of trendiness, especially when it comes to food, new businesses open all the time. Read the local papers and magazines to see what might be new and exciting when you are on island.

When it comes to accommodations, the choice is extremely limited In the Kahului-Wailuku area. There are only three mainstream lodging places in Kahului, and all are much more like motels than hotels. For years, our choice of the three has been the **Maui Seaside Hotel**, located across the street from the **Ka'ahumanu Shopping Center**. Accommodations here are both attractive and budget priced, with color TV and telephones. Groups can arrange for terrific rates. The "Deluxe Tower" rooms are large and a good value. They are air conditioned and have refrigerators. There is a nice little beach [although it is not a great swimming beach] just steps from the pool and the entire property is kept scrupulously clean.

The rooms at the **Maui Seaside Hotel** that surround the handsome pool area are attractive but ceiling fan-cooled. They are not air conditioned and are smaller than rooms in the hotel's satellite buildings. The Maui Seaside staff is most accommodating and we found fellow guests to be extraordinarily pleasant and genuinely friendly. We received some wonderful tips from other guests as this hotel is the favorite of kama'aina who come in from Hana and neighbor islands just for a sale or for special events like the Maui County Fair in October or the Makawao 4th of July Rodeo. Hawaii's residents use the interisland airlines almost like we use taxis, and they *really do* just hop on an interisland flight to go shopping. The Maui Seaside Hotel is located at 100 West Ka'ahumanu Ave. Phone **877-3311**, or call toll free from the US mainland, **(800) 560 5552**.

If you like flea markets you'll want to visit the **Maui Swap Meet** every **Saturday** morning next to the post office on PUUNENE ST. You will find tropical and exotic flowers such as bird of paradise, cattleya orchids, heliconias, anthuriums and torch gingers and more. Fresh sweet pineapple, bananas, sweet sap, mangoes, guavas, jack fruit, lychees, strawberries & juicy oranges and lemons abound, along with fresh vegetables, especially Kula greens, tomatoes and produce. Jewelry, knick knacks, Hawaiian quilts, handmade *tutu* [Hawaiian grandma] dolls and Aloha Teddy bears, homemade Hawaiian tropical fruit preserves, whimsical hand carved wooden furniture and gecko-themed items from Bali and Indonesia abound. You will find some very singular and unique items here. Why purchase overpriced souvenirs in resort areas when so much that is Maui-made is available at the Maui Swap Meet, authentic in origin and craftmanship and inexpensive as well? Don't be afraid to dicker.

❽

And don't forget to check out the delicious specials at the Maui Swap Meet food concession and their famous "Garlic Noodles" with grilled teriyaki chicken or beef, chicken or beef rice bento with chow fun, breakfast bowl of scrambled eggs, teri-beef, spam over steamed rice with furukaki, and much more. If you can swing the 50 cents admission charge, the fun begins at **6:30 a. m.**

At **Kanaha Beach Park** (known locally as **Airport Beach**) in Late May and early June the Maui County Slalom Windsurfing Championships take place with both amateur and professional windsurfers of both sexes. But you can come watch windsurfers here on any day when the winds are constant. At **Puunene** town, The **Alexander & Baldwin Sugar Museum** (admission charge) is located just south of Kahului near the huge sugar mill. The museum is entertaining and has a nice little gift shop. Phone **871-8058**.

❿

⑨

⑪

windsurfing
Kanaha Beach Park
Airport Beach
Sprecklesville Beach
Maui Country Club
Baldwin Beach Park
Ho`okipa Beach
Nonohe St.
Kahului Airport
5 MM
6 MM
Hana Hwy
Paia
4 MM
36
Sprecklesville
Baldwin Ave.
5 road miles / 7.7 km
Lahaina
MAUI
Hana
PHOTO FINDER

Photographs

For photo locations #8-10, see the map on page 52.

❽❾ At the Saturday Maui Swap Meet, near the post office on Pu`unene Street, tremendous bargains can be found on all kinds of goods, including handmade Hawaiian quilts, *Tutu* (the Hawaiian word for *grandmother*) dolls and teddy bears, homegrown produce, and every variety of exotic flower and lei.

❿ The Maui Seaside is one of the most inexpensive hotels on the island. It is centrally located and employs a warm and friendly staff.

Photo location seen on map, above:

⓫ Sprecklesville Beach is popular with those in the neighborhood, but few visitors even know it exists.

Sprecklesville

If you're on a quest for a beautiful **uncrowded** white sandy beach that has gorgeous coastal views, and where tourists are as rare as hens' teeth, then here you go: situated just a few minutes' drive east of busy Kahului Airport, and nestled up against the **Maui Country Club golf course** and the handsome residential enclave of **Sprecklesville**, lies the gem known as **Sprecklesville Beach**.

As you *drive east* from Kahului on the HANA HIGHWAY [36], after passing the airport area keep an eye out *makai/seaward* for MM 4 and **NONOHE ST.**, and *turn left* onto it. Drive around a little to see the homes and beautiful landscaping, then *turn down* **KEALAKAI PL.** toward the ocean and a parking area of brilliant red dirt bordered by naupaka plant-covered dunes. If its a bright sunny day, the contrast in colors among the blue sky, turquoise waters, red dirt and green vegetation is almost psychedelic. Walk out on the point and look west to see the palm lined distant shore curve toward West Maui, and look east past the fishermen on the rocks to see the beautiful beach. Walk down a little ways, stake out your territory, and set up shop. Then, kick back and get Maui-ized.

PHOTO FINDER ™

MATCH THIS SYMBOL'S **MAP NUMBER** WITH THE CORRESPONDING PHOTO NUMBER TO LOCATE THE EXACT SPOT WHERE EACH PHOTOGRAPH WAS TAKEN.

Fabulous, unforgettable views in every direction...uphill, downhill, and sideways too.

Once you have decided on a day to rise from Haleakala, telephone first; call **871-5054** for a weather report. Its a long, dark haul to get up here, and there's no reason to make it if the sunrise will be obscured by bad weather. Check the daily **Maui News** for the time of sunrise/sunset ...people seem to be divided on which is the *more* spectacular experience... and arrive a good half hour beforehand. During the winter, heavy snowfall may close the road, and since snow tires aren't standard on Hawaii's rental cars, you won't be allowed to drive to the top. Bring a jacket and sweater, an extra pair of socks to use as mittens, or else layer whatever light clothes you *do* have for warmth. Reports of **cold** at Haleakala are **no exaggeration**. The first time we ever did the trip, during the month of December, the temperature at the visitor center was 19 degrees F, and bizarre ice formations looking somewhat like sea barnacles grew from the rocky volcanic soil. The slightest breeze sent bone-chilling waves through our bodies.

...view a sun- **572-7749 or**

❶ From the resort areas of Ka'anapali and Kihei, the trip to the summit may take up to **3 hours**. To visit Haleakala directly from Maui resort areas, head toward Kahului (the airport) and HWY. 32. Follow the Haleakala road signs eastward to the HALEAKALA HIGHWAY (HWY. 37), and drive uphill. After passing both the town of Pukalani and the turnoff for HWY 400, make a left turn onto HWY. 377 from HALEAKALA HWY 37.

HWY 377 climbs up through greener-than-Ireland pastures beautifully contrasted in April and May with magnificent shows of **lavender jacaranda trees in full bloom**. Rustic split rail fences, fallen lavender blossoms on the road and grass, weathered barns and other out buildings, isolated woodland patches, rushing streams passing under the highway and fast moving clouds whizzing by just overhead all combine to form a unique, unexpected and idyllic rural haven. You will pass the **Kula Lodge**, with pretty overnight accommodations and a restaurant where you can savor **breakfast** on cold mornings cozily ensconced next to a crackling fireplace. Check out the adjacent rustic flower/gift shop. If you spend the night, you'll be able to sleep an *extra 2 hours* before your early morning trek up the mountain for the Sunrise Spectacular.

A short way past the **Kula Lodge**, HWY. 377 is intersected on the *left/mauka* near the 3200' elevation by HALEAKALA CRATER RD. (HWY 378). *Turn left* onto HWY 378 and prepare for some serious driving. Coming up immediately is the **Sunrise Protea Farm**, on the *left*, where you'll be able to put together a picnic to enjoy at crater's edge. Check out the floral shop where beautiful dried protea wreaths line the walls. If someone special back home is having a birthday or anniversary, you can express-ship a beautiful bunch of assorted protea from either here or the Kula Lodge store that will knock their socks off, at **about half the price** that a similar bouquet would cost at a mainland florist. HWY. 378 climbs **higher in the shortest distance** than any other road on the planet, switchbacking and hairpinning its way to one of earth's most magnificent experiences, Haleakala Crater. A multitude of road shoulder lookouts provide wondrous views as well as launching sites for Maui's **hang glider** enthusiasts.

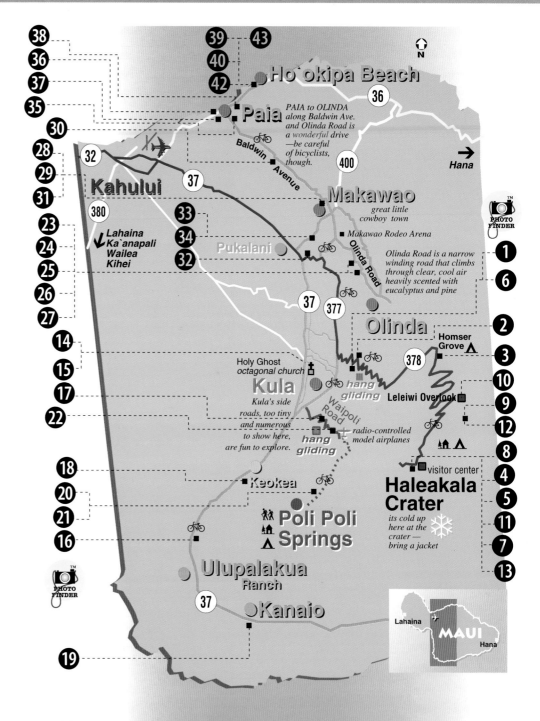

PAIA to OLINDA along Baldwin Ave. and Olinda Road is *a wonderful drive* —be careful of bicyclists, though.

Makawao
great little cowboy town

Makawao Rodeo Arena

Olinda Road is a narrow winding road that climbs through clear, cool air heavily scented with eucalyptus and pine

Olinda

Homser Grove

Holy Ghost *octagonal church*

Kula
Kula's side roads, too tiny and numerous to show here, are fun to explore.

hang gliding

Leleiwi Overlook

radio-controlled model airplanes

visitor center

Haleakala Crater
its cold up here at the crater — bring a jacket

Keokea

Poli Poli Springs

Ulupalakua Ranch

Kanaio

Lahaina
Hana
MAUI

MAUI

Haleakàla *downhill bicycle ride.*

Sunrise at the crater rim is considered a spiritual experience by many, with the most beautiful visual effects occurring before the sun itself becomes visible. Losing one morning's sleep is a small price to pay for a sight you will remember for the rest of your life. Even if you miss the sunrise, early morning is still a good time to make the trip since **often times clouds will move in during late morning**, obscuring the views.

Located near the 6900 foot/2103 meter elevation, **Park Headquarters (open daily, 7:30 a.m. to 4 p.m.)** offers drinking water, restrooms, friendly and helpful rangers, printed literature, a nice collection of books and maps for sale, and a **free hiking trail map**. There are educational exhibits, as well as labeled plants and captive **nene**, the native Hawaiian goose, outside its doors. The nominal charge for a park entry pass is good for an entire week, but if you **arrive before 8 a.m.**, there will be nobody around to ask you for money. Often when the weather is bad you may also drive right in without having to pay. Past the headquarters are two lookouts of note: **Kalahaku Lookout**, with its incredible crater views and unique **Silversword plants**, found nowhere else in the world, and **Lele`iwi Lookout**. Because of their entrance configurations, it might be better and safer to visit these lookouts **on the way back down** the mountain.

On the way up, or down, you may want to visit **Hosmer's Grove** (permit required to camp) near the 6900'/2103m elevation, and its cool, peaceful, chilly upland forest of trees exotic to Hawaii. A **Homser Grove walk is conducted on Fridays at 9 a.m.** and follows a half-mile-long loop trail. The walk takes only an hour and leaves from Homser Grove campground.

A **hike** through the 5,230 acre **Waikamoi Preserve** is scheduled at **9 a.m. Mondays and Thursdays.** Hikers again meet at Hosmer Grove campground. The preserve is one mile by eight miles in size, affording hikers dramatic extremes in ecosystems, topography, climate and terrain, from lush rain forest to cloud forest to desolate volcanic crater. On the Waikamoi Preserve hike you may see some 14 native Hawaiian bird species, eight of which are on the endangered list. In 1992, a nest of the **crested honeycreeper** was found —the first one in 132 years. In 1993, a nest of the critically endangered **Maui Parrotbill** was spotted for the first time ever at Waikamoi. Hundreds of other plants, animals, and insects, as well as the only native Hawaiian mammal, the **Hawaiian Hoary Bat**, found nowhere else on earth, inhabit the Waikamoi Preserve. Only a fraction of the Preserve's insects and land snails have been identified. The Preserve protects some of the state's best remaining forests, essential watershed for Maui. Dress warmly and bring water. Inquire about any changes in the published hike schedule with the visitor center (located just a few hundred yards downhill from Homser Grove Road). Or, call about the **Hawaii Nature Conservancy**'s schedule of hikes and trail

③

maintenance work parties, ℂ **(808) 572-7849**. If you'd like to see Waikamoi Preserve on your own, a permit is required. Write to: **Waikamoi Preserve Manager, PO Box 1716, Makawao HI 96768.** ℂ **(808) 572-7849.**

Photographs

For photo locations, see overall map on page 58 *and* regional map on page 62.

previous pages:

❶ Jacaranda blossoms carpet a pasture along the Haleakala Hwy.

❷ Commercial bicycling outfits lead visitors from the summit of Mount Haleakala all the way down to the sea at Paia. This shot was taken along the Haleakala Highway section.

these pages:

❸ A stream flows through the temperate forest at Homser Grove, a popular, and easy, hiking route near the entrance of Haleakala National Park.

❹ Snowfall covers the ground near the summit of Mount Haleakala, a scene that many might not readily associate with Hawaii. *Haleakala National Park photo.*

❺ The sun rises above the clouds at a 10,000 foot / 3048 meter elevation.

❻ Fallen lavender jacaranda blossoms color a pastoral upcountry scene.

❹

❺

MAUI

jacaranda blossoms carpet a green upcountry pasture.

MATCH THIS SYMBOL'S MAP NUMBER WITH THE CORRESPONDING PHOTO NUMBER TO LOCATE THE EXACT SPOT WHERE EACH PHOTOGRAPH WAS TAKEN.

PHOTO FINDER

Photographs

the following photo locations are also indicated on the map on page 58.

7 At sunrise the Visitor Center at Haleakala Summit glows golden. You can take refuge from the freezing cold in its heated viewing gallery.

8 **11** The walls of Haleakala Caldera, with and without snow. *#8: Haleakala National Park photo.*

10 A silversword plant shot from above in early morning fills the entire frame to emphasize the radial effect.

Be prepared: the temperature at Haleakala's magnificent summit can dip **well below freezing**, and often does. As the colors of dawn begin to paint the sky, visitors wrapped in blankets huddle with each other for warmth in the brightening light. They stand above the cloud tops at the **Haleakala Visitor Center**, but from the volcano rim, the crater itself is still draped in darkness. Slowly the sky brightens and the cloud tops glow with golden luminescence, a precursor to the explosion of sunrays waiting to burst from the horizon.

The event takes place as those assembled stare in awe, lost in their private thoughts and observations. The golden orb rises slowly, lighting the multicolored volcanic ejecta that paints the abyss in reds, siennas and yellows, revealing well worn trails across the desolate landscape that switchback and disappear into the desolate wilderness. The **Big Island of Hawaii**, 80 miles away, floats ethereally in the far distance. **Mauna Kea's winter snows** are tinted rose and peach. This is an exquisitely clear and brilliant day, and the sight distance must be close to 150 miles. Since approximately 1790, the mountain has lain still. That year marks its last eruption, not from the summit itself, but from vents low on the southwestern slope of the mountain above **Makena** (see photo #7 on page 51).

The Park is open 24 hours a day, and the **Haleakala Visitor Center is open from dawn until 3 PM**. The center offers a sheltered, heated, comfortable environment from which to view the wilderness area, with educational exhibits, and books, maps and videos for sale. A 15 minute nature talk takes place daily and **hikes are offered regularly**, beginning at the **Sliding Sands** and **Hosmer Grove** Trailheads. Call **(808) 572-9177** for schedules. Written inquiries may be addressed to: **Superintendent, Haleakala National Park, PO Box 369, Makawao HI 96768.**

Some of those who came to view the sunrise will quickly head back down the hill toward the **Kula Lodge** for morning coffee and a big **breakfast**. Others will hop on their **mountain bikes** for the thrilling downhill 38 mile bike ride all the way to the ocean at the windsurfing town of **Paia**. For **hikers**, the sunrise is just the opening salvo for an adventurous,

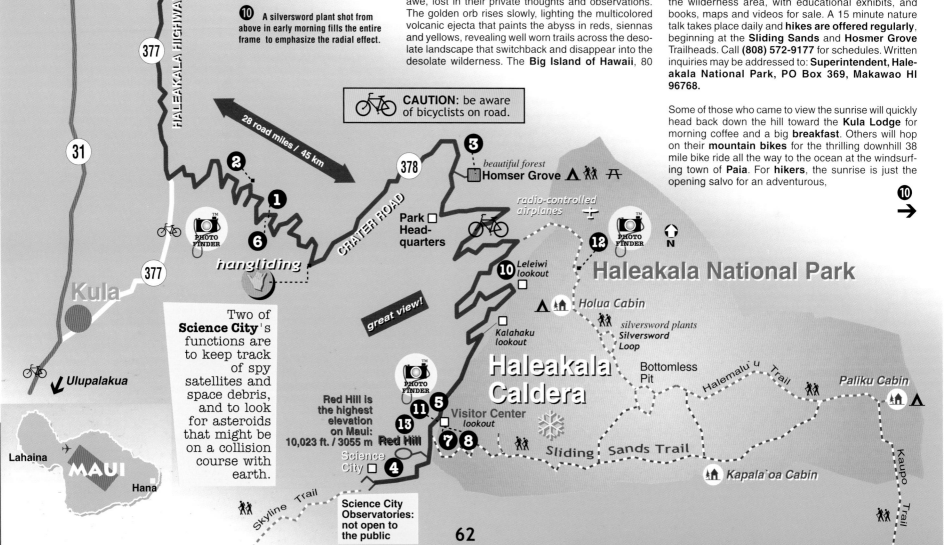

CAUTION: be aware of bicyclists on road.

Two of **Science City**'s functions are to keep track of spy satellites and space debris, and to look for asteroids that might be on a collision course with earth.

28 road miles / 45 km

hanggliding

great view!

beautiful forest **Homser Grove**

radio-controlled airplanes

Park Headquarters

10 Leleiwi lookout

Holua Cabin

silversword plants **Silversword Loop**

Kalahaku lookout

Bottomless Pit

Haleakala Caldera

Haleakala National Park

Red Hill is the highest elevation on Maui: 10,023 ft. / 3055 m

Red Hill

11 **5**
13
7 **8**

Visitor Center lookout

Sliding Sands Trail

Science City

4

Science City Observatories: not open to the public

Skyline Trail

Halemalu'u Trail

Paliku Cabin

Kapala'oa Cabin

Kaupo Trail

Pukalani

37

Kahului

HALEAKALA HIGHWAY

377

31

377

Kula

Ulupalakua

MAUI

Lahaina

Hana

378

CRATER ROAD

PHOTO FINDER

PHOTO FINDER

N

10 →

2
1
6

12

62

don't be fooled just because you're on a tropical island....its often freezing up here!

visually stunning and eerily beautiful descent into a unique, bleak and colorful world. Standing at the rim, astronomy and space buffs will find the area strikingly similar in color and appearance to the photographs that the Voyager, Viking and Mariner spacecraft sent back to earth from Mars, Io and Ganymede. Sadly, a glance at the ground beyond the railing will reveal that thousands of smokers have seen fit to dispose of their cigarette butts in the crater, and streams of photographers have tossed in their photo film packaging for good measure. Please take your `opala to a trash receptacle.

A short hike from the Visitor Center to the top of **White Hill** along a well-traveled uphill trail affords a stunning, 360° view. The trail is only a quarter of a mile in length, but the 10,000' altitude makes the going harder than it looks. Look behind you and notice the white observatory domes of Kolekole, or **Haleakala Observatories**. The facility itself is **not open to the public**. Weather conditions at Haleakala change minute by minute. If its socked in with clouds one moment, it may be clear the next...or maybe not until tomorrow. Normally the clouds disperse late in the day, making sunset viewing just as popular as the sunrise watch.

The most popular Haleakala footfall is **Sliding Sands Trail**, which begins at the Visitor Center and transverses the wilderness area all the way to **Paliku Cabin** at the rainy eastern end of the caldera, 9.8 miles away, passing **Kapalaoa Cabin** along its route at the 5.8 mile mark. **Accommodations** at these cabins, as well as **Holua Cabin** on the Halemau'u Trail, can be yours for a song, but reservations are limited. A lottery for cabin space is held three months in advance. With a little luck, checking at the last minute may produce a canceled reservation. Write to: **Superintendent, Haleakala National Park, PO Box 369, Makawao HI 96768,** ✆ **(808) 572-9306.** The **cabins are primitive** and contain bunk beds, cooking utensils, stoves, and firewood. Campsites are available and capacity is limited to 25 people; come prepared for rain and cold weather. **Earthwalk Press** publishes a good **hiking map** of the park, printed on waterproof paper, for under $10. If you can live with a more compact, non-waterproof version, the **free National Park Service brochure/map (#690-095) is** excellent and tells visitors everything they need to know about Haleakala National Park. Its yours, free for the asking at the visitor center or by writing to the Superintendent (see address above). While hiking, **please don't shout or make other loud noises.** This is a spiritual place for Hawaiians, and in this eerily silent environment, noise drives away the wildlife that you and others came to see.

Check the free visitor magazines for **horseback rides** into the crater, but if you are afraid of heights you may not enjoy this; the switchback trail is very narrow and steep. Our own experience was miserable, as by luck we chose a day that was cold, very damp and cloudy. There was little to see because of the limited sight dis-

tance, and we were already freezing and soaking wet before our less than competent guides decided it was time to unpack the rain slickers. The look on his face, below, says it all.

Keep going past the Visitor Center to **Red Hill Overlook**, the **highest point on Maui** at 10023 ft./3055 m. Here you'll experience a 360° **panorama** that encompasses West Maui and the islands of Lana'i, Moloka'i, Kaho'olawe and Hawai'i. On the way back down the mountain, take the opportunity to stop at **Leleiwi and Kalahaku Overlooks** for fabulous above-the-clouds views of the isthmus and West Maui. At Kalahaku Overlook there is a **Silversword garden and exhibit.** These beautiful plants, a relative of the common sunflower, grow nowhere else on earth but here and the Big Island. For a recorded **weather message** ✆ **871-5054;** for **time of sunrise and program information** ✆ **572-7749. For hiking and camping information** ✆ **572-9177.** For those outside Hawaii, the area code is **(808)**.

For this photo location, see maps on pages 62 and 58.

Photographs

⑫ This page: Soaking wet and looking none too happy, our buddy A-P rides through the crater toward Holua Cabin in the cold rain. Visibility was about 25 feet, and we not only saw nothing on that trip, but we froze our #@*&%!! off. Pay attention to weather reports before booking a horse ride through the crater.

⑫

People with heart problems, high blood pressure and the like may not want to venture up to this altitude. Definitely those people who have been scuba diving within the previous 24 hours should <u>not</u> come here.

Homser Grove
Kahului
Lahaina
Kipahulu Valley
Haleakala National Park
Hana
Haleakala Crater
`Ohe`o/ (The misnamed 7 Pools)
Kaupo Gap

The Ongoing Creation Of A National Park

1916 Haleakala Volcano established as a detached section of Hawai`i National Park.

1951 9,274 acres of the Kipahulu Forest Reserve added.

1961 Effective July 1, Haleakala bestowed separate national park status by Congress.

1964 19,270 acres designated as wilderness under the 1964 Wilderness Act.

1969 The Park's borders extended to include portions of Kipahulu Valley down to the coast.

1976 The Park now has 28,655 acresdesignated as wilderness under the 1974 Wilderness Act.

1980 Haleakala National Park designated an International Biosphere Reserve under the United Nations' Man and the Biosphere Program.

1994 The Nature Conservancy of Hawai`i donates an additional 400 acres of pristine tropical rainforest along the southern boundary of Kipahulu Valley.

MAUI

it looks like haleakala is a lot closer to mars than we previously thought:

earth ⑬

mars

Planet: Earth
Position in the solar system: 3rd planet from the Sun
Region: Haleakala Crater, Hawaii
Evidence of life: Positive

Earth is a planet of extremes in temperature, surface features, and weather conditions. Even though Haleakala is located close to the equator, a typical daytime high temperature may read only 68°F/20°C. For much of the year the atmosphere is relatively calm, with winds clocked at about 5m/sec, or 11 mph. However, violent storms sometimes develop in winter which can sometimes result in wind speeds up to 50m/sec, or 110mph. The clouds seen on the volcano slopes are made up of water, and in the winter, the moisture condenses and freezes, leaving a very thin covering of water ice on the ground about 100 days out of the year.

many people have remarked that maui's haleakala caldera looks like some other-worldly place. apollo astronauts did indeed train here as part of the united states space mission to the moon. but haleakala's similarity to certain regions on mars —based on martian landscape photographs and data gathered by landers on the red planet— is truly uncanny.

Planet: Mars
Position in the solar system: 4th planet from the Sun
Region: Utopia Planitia
Evidence of life: Promising

Mars is a planet of extremes in temperature, surface features, and weather conditions. Even at places located close to the equator, a typical daytime high temperature may read only 68°F/20°C. For much of the year the atmosphere is relatively calm, with winds that can be clocked at about 5m/sec, or 11 mph. However, violent storms sometimes develop in summer which can result in wind speeds close to 50m/sec, or 110mph. The clouds seen on the volcano slopes are made up of water, and in the winter, the moisture condenses and freezes, leaving a very thin covering of water ice on the ground about 100 days out of the year.

Mars photos courtesy of JPL, Pasadena.

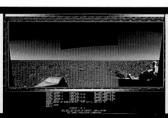

Kula & Ulupalakua

Like the phrase goes, **Its Kooler In Kula**. This sparkling green agricultural community on the upper slopes of Haleakala luxuriates in cool temperatures and shady midday conditions ideal for growing the bizarre and beautiful **protea**, a native of South Africa. The proteas' delicate color is normally subject to bleaching by the sun, but the weather conditions unique to Kula, whereby on most days clouds materialize to shade the area from the sun's strongest rays of the day from about 10 am till 2 pm, help produce a more vibrantly colored Maui protea. These, along with Maui onions, Kula tomatoes, Maui wines, upcountry strawberries and Hawaiian grown herbs have gained an international reputation for quality that has placed Maui solidly on the world's floral and culinary maps.

Kula is a great place to explore Maui's **side roads** and country lanes. Turning up, or down, any one of them will delight, surprise and win your heart...and the **views** from way up here are fabulous. PULEHUIKI ROAD winds prettily past protea farms and citrus orchards, and charming homes with showy gardens, while the next road parallel to it, KAMEHAMEIKI ROAD, is very different —steeper, less manicured and more winding, with lava rock roadside walls and friendly horses and mules whinnying along the way.

Kula town itself just consists of a gas station, general store and deli, and down the road, the newly restored octagonal **Holy Ghost** church. Its 100 year old carved and painted altar is a wonder. On the slopes of the volcano, the **Kula Lodge**, very handsome, rustic and homey, is a wonderful place for an early morning laid-back breakfast. It has a cozy fireplace (mornings can be quite chilly) and superlative views, and a pretty and photogenic little protea crafts and flower shop on the left at the entrance.

The **Kula Botanical Garden** (admission charge ✆ **878-1715**) on ROUTE 377 near the intersection with the KULA HWY. has a minimal flower display, but offers five acres of identified trees and flowering shrubs, and has ponds, streams and picnic tables on the property. Kula is spider-webbed with tiny one lane roads that climb up the slopes of Haleakala, passing pungent huge old eucalyptus stands and productive little farmlets growing Christmas trees, carnations, and vegetables. A tiny and narrow one lane track named ALAE ST. is a good example as it winds steeply up the slope past interesting homes, scattering quail, and profusions of flowers and plants typical of the area. Remember one of our cardinal rules for **Driving & Discovering Hawaii**: explore —don't let dead end roads deter you.

Just *past/west* of the Kula Botanical Garden entrance,

steep, long, winding WAIPOLI RD. heads uphill to the beautiful redwood forest at **Poli Poli Springs** (see our Poli Poli Springs section which follows), and *mauka,* you will see a park with picnic tables, but with few trees to obstruct the view. Its a peaceful and awe-inspiring place for a picnic while taking in the amazing visual tapestry that unfolds in every direction like a cyclorama.

When you reach the KULA HWY., make a *left turn* onto it and continue along to the hamlet of **Keokea**, where you will find a couple of general stores, gas, the Keokea Gallery, and if you're hungry, Grandma's Maui Coffee, where the brew they serve was Maui grown right downslope. **Keokea Park** on the *left/mauka* is another fine picnic spot. The superb views continue unabated as the road pulls past MAKENA ROAD (closed to traffic) and into the **Ulupalakua Ranch** where cattle graze amidst prickly cactus, horses amble beneath April and May-blooming lavender jacaranda trees, and light of sunset colors the rolling landscape with unforgettable orange and golden hues.

The drive from here on through **Ulupalakua** —although not neglected in guidebooks and travel magazine articles— has certainly not been given its due either. We keep looking in our Thesaurus for other words for spectacular, since so much of Hawaii *is* spectacular, and we feel as if we keep repeating ourselves. But the road through Ulupalakua and beyond is just, well, —*spectacular*. It winds and roller-coasters along the slope, with expansive and fabulous views of West Maui, boundless ocean, distant neighbor islands, handsome and sturdy black lava rock walls that sector pastures of green and gold grasses, gangs of cattle crowded beneath huge shade trees to escape the sun, and assemblages of bicyclists who've stopped to take in the wonder of it all –the seasonal wildflowers and a distant examination of Wailea and Makena, way, way down there below. You will probably encounter few other drivers. This is one Maui excursion that may help recall the fun that driving *used* to bring you.

The **Ulupalakua Ranch Store and Deli** has been rebuilt to replace the collapsing structure that preceded it. The store offers good looking caps, polo shirts, T-shirts, belt buckles and cowboy paraphernalia –all emblazoned with the Ulupalakua Ranch logo. The Deli specializes in delicious creative gourmet fare. The rustic store stocks groceries, books, snacks and horse care necessities. Beyond the ranch is Hawaii's only winery, the handsome **Tedeschi Vineyards**. Unscheduled 15 minute tours, followed by a free wine tasting, are conducted as guests arrive.

Ahead, the condition of the road downgrades on the downgrade; the surface transforms from newly paved and smooth to heavily patched asphalt as it descends toward the south shore. The adjacent grasses fade from emerald to gold, the trees all but disappear, the misty rain clears up and the sun blazes down, huge boul-

ders and lava rock stud the landscape, and the views go on and on, unencumbered through the strikingly transparent air. Stop often along here where space and **common sense** permit, and drink in the space, the breeze, and the heat of the sun. Notice how green it is just a thousand feet upslope. Downslope, but not visible from here, there are a number of interesting pocket beaches consisting of white sand, dark sand, and coral rubble, collectively known as **Kanaio Beach**. These beaches are only accessible by 4WD vehicles over ungraded and very rough jeep roads many miles long. You may also hike to Kanaio Beach via the King's Highway foot trail from La Perouse Bay, but it is a long, lonely, thirsty haul. If you try it, bring sunscreen, water and food. There is no shade and *the sun is merciless.*

The bumpy asphalt humps along past the hamlet of **Kanaio** and the holding pens of **Kahikinui Ranch**, roadside, on its way down to sea level. It continues along the unshaded volcanic slope, the vista unobstructed by trees or anything else. **The Big Island** looms eighty miles away across the channel, and on clear days the **snows** atop 14,000 foot **Mauna Loa** shimmer like a mirage. The pavement ends shortly after the gray sand beaches of **Nu'u Bay**. Rental car contracts prohibit driving further, although you will see locals' passenger cars making the drive in dry weather with no problem. The road will be impassable after a heavy rain, but otherwise it is negotiable at slow speeds with a good measure of attention. You will find a description of the rest of this rough road, traveling in the opposite east-to-west direction, in the **Hana Drive/ Kaupo to Ulupalakua** section on page 112.

Photographs

For exact photo locations, refer to map on page 58.

❶❹ The octagonal steeple at Holy Ghost Portuguese Catholic Church...

❶❺ ...and a detail of its richly decorated altar.

❶❻ The Kula Highway winds its way toward the Ulupalakua Ranch Store.

❶❼ Patti Davis packs proteas promptly and proficiently at Poli Poli Protea Farm.

❶❽ Along the Kula Highway, near Keokea, a horse grazes near a blooming jacaranda tree.

❶❾ Near Kanaio, expansive ranchlands radiate gold and green splendor high above the azure sea.

❶❽

❶❾

Poli Poli Springs

Waipoli Road: If you love to drive, then you'll welcome the challenge of this steep, smooth black ribbon of asphalt switchbacking its way up the brilliant green flanks of dormant Mount Haleakala. Overhead, neon-hued hang gliders hook onto rising air currents, and increasingly majestic and humbling views unfold in all directions as the air thins and cools.

WAIPOLI ROAD is paved for half its length, and for those with mountain bikes and non-rental vehicles or 4WDs, very nicely graded the rest of the way to **Poli Poli Springs State Recreation Area**. At the bottom, the road passes a number of upcountry flower and vegetable farms and wooded areas, but once past the cattle guarded entrance, it winds upward steeply through bovine-groomed open pasture lands. As the road ascends you may pass brilliantly colored hang gliders launching from the shoulder and groups of people flying small radio controlled aircraft, while way out there, before your eyes, views exceptional for their beauty and scope include all of the Central Valley and West Maui, both Kahului and Ma'alaea Bays, and the islands of **Molokini, Kaho'olawe, Lanai, Molokai and Oahu**. The shoulder at most places along this road is *usually* wide enough to accommodate a parked car, and the grassy slope makes a terrific site for a picnic, or just a breather. Just be careful you don't go sitting down in a fresh cow pie with your brand new white Levi's on, like ...uhhh...someone we know.

Silence is this area's most outstanding feature. Between an occasional bird's chirp, a fly's buzz and the breeze wafting past your ear, there is nothing but utter silence for long minutes at a time. Human voices speaking at a normal level can be heard for a thousand feet above or below, the words as clear as a bell. Cattle dot the landscape, lilliputian communities group at the edges of huge pineapple and sugarcane fields far, far downslope. Rain showers can be seen over land and water, dumping here and there, while great patches of sunlight dance on the silver seas between them in a checkerboard pattern, and right over your head, Haleakala's clouds whiz by close enough to touch.

The road is, as of this writing, paved until just a few hundred yards short of the **Boundary Trail** trail head. That eerie feeling you experience may take you a while to put your finger on, but Zowee, **there aren't any mosquitoes here!** Blessedly, species of mosquitoes able to survive above a 2500 foot elevation don't exist in Hawaii. The boundary trail descends along the mountain side, so please keep in mind that you will have to return uphill, tough to do at this altitude when you're tired. Or getting old. Notice that the trail looks like some-

one came through it with a plow. This almost unbelievable destruction is the daily unceasing diabolical work of wild pigs, and this tilling sets in motion a heartbreaking chain of erosion and soil depletion that doesn't stop until it washes down and smothers Hawaii 's offshore reefs and chokes off its marine life. This, along with agricultural runoff, is the most serious threat to Hawaii's burgeoning water sports activities industry. This tragic destruction by foreign animals has so far wiped out forever dozens of native Hawaiian bird and plant species. A native of Maui who recently returned after 30 years told me she was shocked to see that the edible **limu** (a seaweed) that once covered the rocks on the Waihe`e shoreline, and was an important part of their local diet, is now totally gone, the victim of this runoff.

Perhaps Poli Poli Springs is most notable for its beautiful mature forests of **redwood** and other trees exotic to Hawaii, like edible plum, and cypress, sugi and ash. If you are coming to hike, gather as much advice and written material as possible because we have found the maps and explanations even in the most popular hiking guides to be woefully unclear and incomplete, and none of us came to Hawaii to end up lost, much less frozen to death (now, how ironic would *that* be?). The ideal solution is to join a **Sierra Club Hike** ✆ **(808) 538-6616**.

Even in summer, on a cloudy day the chill in the air will surprise you. But in winter you'll want to dress the same way you would back home...it often drops **below freezing** at night, and snow flurries aren't at all unusual. If you will be spending Christmas on Maui and you're afraid you'll miss not having mainland Christmas weather and a roaring fire in the hearth, consider reserving the cabin for that time. There is one housekeeping cabin for rent here at the 6200 foot level, fully equipped for all your basic needs. It includes a fireplace and plenty of firewood, but no electricity. The cost is very low. Camping here for up to one week is permissible and the campground is the only place where drinking water is available. Reserve early, or be lucky enough to get a last minute cancellation, by contacting the **Division of State Parks at 54 S. High St., Wailuku, Maui, HI 96793.** ✆ **(808) 243-5354**. Send for their free trail maps and their **Guide To Hawaii's State Parks**. A visit to their office before hiking these trails for in-person info and advice might be in order. But call first to make sure they're open.

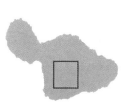

⑳

Photographs

For exact photo locations, refer to map on page 58.

⑳ Views of West Maui from the Boundary Trail are unforgettable. This one is framed by highland forests of fragrant pine.

㉑ This trail looks like someone came through it with a plow. This is a good example of the unchecked destruction that wild pigs cause in Hawaii. The mud that the rains wash down the slope this tilling eventually ends up smothering coral reefs along the coast, greatly diminishing the quality and quantity of sea life, if not destroying it.

㉒ A family group enjoys flying their radio controlled airplanes from the shoulder of Poli Poli's hairpin-curved Waipoli Road.

㉑

㉒
a family launches their radio controlled airplanes at Poli Poli

Olinda Road

OLINDA ROAD, the uphill continuation of BALDWIN AVE., begins in central **Makawao** town and meanders uphill on a wonderful journey through sinus-soothing eucalyptus tree tunnels, open rolling pasture lands, ethereal vistas, small upcountry flower farms, passing clouds, and silent pine forests planted in a grid pattern decades ago by reforestation teams. And for a welcome change, because of the altitude, **mosquitoes are as rare as hens' teeth here**, so at the higher elevations, those above 2500', for once you can forget about the insect repellent.

Olinda is one of those personal favorite hideaways that we half-seriously considered not including in this book because we wanted to selfishly keep it to ourselves. But this place brings us such peace and solitude, and its effect is so contagious, that our enthusiasm to share all that represents the best of Maui won out.

From the center of Makawao town, take OLINDA RD. *uphill*, and *turn right* on HANAMU RD., a lovely mile-long local shortcut road that few visitors see. It climbs, dips and passes through a beautiful, photogenic, and near perfect rural world to connect with the HALE-AKALA HWY (HWY 377). The first downhill/makai road off HANAMU RD. is also very pretty, and it loops around to rejoin HANAMU ROAD at its intersection with HWY. 377. A left turn onto HWY 377 will take you through superb upcountry pasture land to HALEAKALA CRATER ROAD.

Retracing the way back to OLINDA RD., *turn right/up-hill* onto it. OLINDA RD. curves smoothly up through Maui's picture postcard-pretty, eye-popping, ear-popping upper upcountry. Silence is the norm here, save for the winds whooshing through the treetops. Sturdy homes in the shelter of whistling pines sprout big stone chimneys that scent the chilly air with burning wood sap on cold evenings and remind the visitor of Christmas time. Late afternoon's slanting golden sunrays sidelight the peeling bark of the eucalyptus trees that line the road like a towering living fence. Mist and wispy clouds soften the sun's harshness, winds bring a nip to the air, and shadows and light patterns compel the photographer to stop often to try and capture it all on film. From numerous places along the way, the urge to pull over and marvel at the views of rainbows both close by and far below is irresistible. Alternately, vistas include Maui's central plateau and the West Maui Mountains, the breaking waves at **Ho'okipa Beach** far, far below, and everything in between. For photographs, the trees make excellent framing references for distant landscapes, and the colorful peeling bark – and even the bark litter on the ground– make for nice detail shots.

OLINDA RD. continues its climb skyward, and in its upper reaches, pine trees predominate in the landscape. The **Waihou Spring Trailhead** begins roadside on the *right* at the gated entrance of the **Tree Growth Research Area**. OLINDA RD. itself dead ends at the gate for the Forest Preserve located on the mountain slope above.

Returning by the same route will undoubtedly reveal additional sights missed on the way up. Alternately, near the top of OLINDA RD., intersecting PI'IHOLO RD. offers another choice, although one not quite so pretty, for descending the mountain. At the bottom, PI'IHOLO RD. comes out at HWY 400 just a little NW of Makawao town. A left turn from PI'IHOLO RD. onto HWY. 400 will quickly bring us into the center of Makawao town and the intersection of OLINDA RD. again.

㉓

Photographs

For exact photo locations, refer to map on page 58.

㉓   Near the 10 mile marker on Olinda Road, decapitated eucalyptus trees form a roadside fence.

㉔   In the same area, wonderful views over green pasture lands extend all the way to the breaking waves at Ho`okipa Beach.

㉕   Between the 10 and 11 mile markers, this view is framed beautifully by trees and a rustic fence.

㉖   Eucalyptus trees form a tree tunnel along great stretches of twisting, turning Olinda Road.

㉗   A detail of violet colored flowers found along the way.

㉘   In Makawao, a fireplace and heating stove store surprises visitors who never thought it got cold enough in Hawaii to have a fire in the hearth. Or to even *have* a hearth, for that matter. But here in Maui's Upcountry, it certainly does.

㉔

MAUI

SILVER SWORD
STOVES

SILVERSWORD STOVES
AND FIREPLACES
3640

㉕

㉖

㉗

㉘

Makawao to Paia

Our route to **Makawao** goes through Maui's main city of Kahului, past Maui's principal airport, and up HWY 37 (HALEAKALA HWY). As the highway ascends, glorious views unfold on the clouded flanks of the mountain ahead. Behind us, rainbows often hang in the air during the early morning hours and again in late afternoon. To the left of the road, pineapple fields roll back down the hill toward Kahului, and we have repeatedly found great photo opportunities at the road shoulder and from the pineapple field roads.

For those who have not visited Maui in a while, this new section of HWY 37, very wide and excellent from its beginning near the airport, now bypasses central **Pukalani** (Hawaiian for "Hole in the Heavens") **town**. A *left turn* onto HWY. 400 from HWY. 37 will bring you past a perfectly **gorgeous cattle ranch** on your *right* (see photo, opposite page), and into the center of **Makawao** town.

OLINDA RD., located *mauka/uphill* of Hwy. 400 in central Makawao, changes names at the center of Makawao town to become BALDWIN AVE. **Baldwin Ave. travels** *downhill/makai* from here to Paia town. **Olinda Rd. travels** *mauka/uphill* from here through paniolo country and past Makawao's rodeo grounds until it ends miles later near the forested upper reaches of Mount Haleakala.

29 (see the **Olinda Road** section of this book, on the previous page). Keep an eye out for flyers and notices in the daily **Maui News** for local rodeo action, but in any case on just about any Saturday morning you can find *paniolos*, as Hawaiian Cowboys are called, practicing their skills at the rodeo grounds. You can watch the activity for free.

In Makawao town, Old West-style false fronted wooden buildings house trendy shops as well as basic businesses, like a barber shop and general store. This is a delightful place (elevation: 1650'/503m) to be in the cool of the early morning before the upcountry world starts getting busy. **Casanova Deli** offers warm and *wonderful* homemade straight-from-the-oven coffee cakes, muffins, blueberry scones and other delights to be washed down with superior cafe au lait, cappuccino or regular coffee. We feel the Casanova deli ties with the **Peaches and Crumbles Bakery** in Paia for Maui's most incredible baked goods. **Casanova Restaurant** right next door opens later and is famous for good Italian food, infamous for their desserts, and greatly appreciated for bringing top-notch live entertainment to

tiny Makawao. After morning coffee, hightail it a few doors downhill on BALDWIN AVE. to the **Komoda Store** (℄ **572-7261**), and if you didn't phone in an order the day before, hope and pray that they made enough **cream puffs** so you can pick up a few. World class in taste and texture, sensual and heavy with delicious custard, you'll thank us for telling you about them. While you are there, you might want to sample their equally famous cookies. Komoda's is a good general store which can supply many of your basic needs for the road trip. If you're around at lunch time, stop in at **Kitada's**, further downhill one block on BALDWIN AVE., for some of Hawaii's best cheap eats and locally renowned **saimin** (Hawaiian noodle soup). Stroll up and down BALDWIN to see some great shops, including an unexpected-in-Hawaii fireplace and heating stove store.

Early morning, we feel, is the best time to drive downhill to **Paia** on BALDWIN AVENUE, yet another of Maui's many wonderful roads. Keep a watch out for intersecting HALI'IMAILI RD., 2.0 miles downhill from Makawao's center. *Turn left* onto it. It curves and dips prettily through pineapple country and passes one of the Hawaiian Islands' most chic restaurants, **Haliimaile General Store** (℄572-2666). Open for lunch and dinner, the menu is imaginative, the food extraordinary, and the restaurant boasts a master pastry chef. Service *could* be friendlier, but we still enjoy this place.

Continue past the restaurant for a short jaunt around a curve and a great view over the fields toward West Maui, arguably looking its prettiest in the early morning sun. Then *double back again* the way you came to BALDWIN AVE., *turn left* onto it, and *continue downhill*. During the morning hours you will meet groups of **bicycle riders** descending from Haleakala Crater. Be patient. When their leaders realize you are there, and they feel it is safe for all, they will direct their group to the roadside to allow cars to pass. Trust the leaders' judgment; they ride this route every day and are looking to protect both you and their charges. We personally welcome the opportunity to drive slowly anytime on Maui so as to enjoy the superb scenery, especially on BALDWIN AVENUE, so the bikers' speed is just about right for us.

The road gently twists and curves through gorgeous views of sugar and pineapple fields of Maui's Central Valley and the sea. Shower Trees in colorful bloom line the road, showing off their pink, coral, yellow and multicolored puffs of blossoms. When the trades are blowing strong, the winds knock torrents of soft petals from the trees, raining them down on passing cars and tumbling and bouncing colorful natural confetti along the asphalt. Baldwin Ave. passes the entrance of the **Hui No'eau Visual Arts Center (2841 Baldwin Ave., open Tuesday through Sunday** ℄ **572-6560)**. Visitors are encouraged and welcome to view its high quality exhibits. The Center has a *wonderful* crafts shop with

30
31

gorgeous Maui-made jewelry and colorful handmade glass Christmas ornaments in the shapes of dolphins and whales. Lava rock walls line the lower reaches of the road, and finally, after passing the rusting sugar mill paraphernalia in Upper Paia Town, BALDWIN AVE. ends at the HANA HIGHWAY in the center of colorful and lively **Paia town**. Until recently Paia was a near-ghost town but was resurrected from obscurity in the early 1980s by Maui's exploding world famous **windsurfing** scene.

MAUI

(32)

(34)

(33)

Photographs

For exact photo locations, refer to map on page 58.

29 Maui Gift stamps?

30 A Rainbow Shower Tree along Baldwin Avenue, downhill from Hali`imaile Rd., frames a view of Wailuku, Kahului, and Maui's central plain.

31 Downtown Makawao on a sleepy weekday morning.

32 Protea flowers

33 A postcard-beautiful ranch borders Highway 400 between Makawao and Pukalani. This photo was taken from the road shoulder.

34 Plant detail.

Paia to Ho`okipa

Rescued from near ghost town status in the 1980s by an explosion in the popularity of windsurfing, Paia stands newly proud, lively and colorful today. Its Old West style false fronted wood buildings along the HANA HIGHWAY and intersecting BALDWIN AVE. house an interesting mix of clothing and craft stores, galleries, popular restaurants, hair benders and food markets. Brilliantly painted building surfaces abound, much of it making for great photo detail shots. Any time of day is a good time to visit, but as always, we like early morning when the locals are scurrying around trying to get things done before the day trippers arrive. Windsurfers' car rooftops piled high with the tools of the sport ply the streets, and anyplace serving hot morning brew is bustling. Groups of bicyclists coasting down from Haleakala Crater call this the end of the line, and suffering from acute caffeine deprivation, invade the eateries *en masse* for that coffee fix they've been dreaming about of all the way down the mountain. At this time, stores are just opening and uncrowded, parking is easy, people have time to chat, and its just a short stroll to the beach.

If you are on your way to Hana, we highly recommend you fill your gas tank here as there are no more opportunities to do so beyond Paia. Make a stop at **Pic-nics** at 30 Baldwin Ave., open 7 a.m. to 7 p.m. daily. There are dozens of unforgettable picnic spots all along the road to Hana, so you will be glad you stopped to pick up some road food. Pic-nics also has an interesting fact-filled **Guide To Hana** free for the asking. **Café des Amis** at 42 Baldwin Ave. serves outstanding quality world class french crêpes and industrial-strength Lavazza coffee at bargain prices; open 8:30 a.m. to 8:30 p.m.; closed Sundays. Little Paia town is brimming with eating places and shopping options, so park the car and wander around.

Stop in at the **Maui Crafts Guild** at 43 Hana Hwy. for an overview of some of the best handiwork being done on the island today, and some of it at great prices too. For about the price of a Crazy Shirt, you can take home a totally singular made-on-Maui treasure. Everything isn't inexpensive, but its all unique. Paia is brimming with surf shops which we like for both souvenirs and gifts. **Tropix** is a favorite, with it's **Maui Built** logo wear and surfer necklaces and wrist bands.

Just to the west of town, in the direction of the airport, is very popular **H.P. Baldwin Beach County Park**, whose sands and playing fields are really jammin' with locals on weekends. To the east of Paia town is the very picturesque and handsome, shore-situated **Mantokuji Buddhist Temple**, where morning light is best for photographs. Less than five minutes further east at the **9 MM** lies the main reason for all the local color and activity, **Ho`okipa Beach**. Traffic can get a little hairy right along here, so drive defensively. Turn the page for the lowdown on the world's best windsurfing beach.

Photographs

For exact photo locations, refer to map on page 58.

35 On Baldwin Ave. in Paia there are ample opportunities for spending one's money.

36 In Paia, fanciful expressions of individuality and creativity flourish...even on a former gas station's front door.

37 A sculpture of a Hawaiian warrior glares from the window of a Paia art gallery.

38 This small and simple detail shot pretty much sums up what Paia is all about.

39 Windsurfers take to the waters from Paia to close-by Ho`okipa, the windsurfing capitol of the world.

40 Observers watch the windsurfing show from the bluffs above the west end of Ho`okipa Beach.

MAUI

Ho'okipa

Ho`okipa Beach

We always listen to the radio and morning TV to keep abreast of wind and surf conditions on Maui's North Shore so we can time our visit to **Ho`okipa Beach** to coincide with the best action. Many people just stop by for a few minutes on their way to Hana, but **the Makawao-Paia-Ho`okipa Beach area is a terrific day trip all by itself**, one of the really quintessential Maui experiences, so if you have the time, stick around and enjoy this region to its fullest.

We **pay a lot of attention** along the HANA HIGHWAY in this area as we have nearly been killed more than once by any combination of inattentive, suicidal or co-matose local kids *and* adults. Add to that the usual distracted and confused tourists, beautiful scenery, and the road 's blind curves, and you end up with a lot of **good reasons for driving with caution** on this stretch of the HANA HWY.

There is a dirt **viewing area** right *before/west* of Ho`okipa Beach that provides a great place from which to shoot photos of the exciting windsurf and board surfing action below. The unmarked entrance to this vacant lot is **on a curve**, legally -and sanely- accessible only when driving from east to west. The Ho`okipa Beach Park entrance is a little further *on / east* after passing the beach itself. **Ho`okipa Beach Park** has a restroom and showers, picnic tables and barbecue grills, a paved parking lot, and *one-way-only exit and entrance*, not too clearly marked roadside. Again, use caution and **keep an eye on that rearview mirror.** Park your car where you can keep an eye on it.

The entrance to Ho`okipa Beach Park is *past the far end* (*the right-hand end* as you face the water) of the beach. On the bluff *makai* of the descending beach road, you will see a parking and observation area. This is generally the board surfers' domain, where they come to check out the wave action and socialize. There are lots of car break-ins here, so beware. The waters directly below, at the NE end, generally attract board surfers only, while the waters at the other, SW end of the beach are claimed by windsurfers when conditions are right for their sport. On days when the winds aren't right but the surf is up, board surfers use both areas.

If you are here for a swim, the far NE end of the beach, *on the right* as you face the water, is the only *comparatively* safe place to enter the water, but you must be the final judge of whether its safe. On the calmest days you will see many parents with children here.

When conditions are right, the sand at the SW end of the beach, *on the left* as you face the water, is a colorful mosaic of resting and in-preparation windsurfing

boards and sails, with the very narrow water entry point jamming up with traffic at times. Windsurfers dart out to sea to turn around and ride incoming waves at dizzying speeds with admirable skill and control. The area attracts absolutely the best windsurfers in the world, and the acrobatics and midair flips they perform are breathtaking. You won't find better windsurfers anywhere on earth than those here at Ho`okipa Beach. The waves break less than 100 yards offshore, the wind conditions are some of the most consistent anywhere, and waves tower up to 20 feet, with 10 foot swells more common. The Aloha Classic event in the **Pro Windsurfing World Cup Final** takes place here late October/early November. Maui has more than 40 windsurfing shops, and they all offer lessons and rentals. When calling about windsurfing lessons, make it clear you won't tolerate an instructor who is not patient. Plan on investing 6-8 hours before you have your first good ride.

Most of Ho`okipa Beach's length, except sometimes the extreme NE end, is unsafe for recreational swimming, but has a great tidal pool area that at low tide is sheltered by a low barrier reef and is handy for cooling off. The **people-watching** action at Ho`okipa, in the water, on the sand, and in the parking area, is top notch and great fun. Ho`okipa is the north shore's version of *Dig Me Beach*. Groups of surfers and windsurfers congregate to visit and party by their cars or on the lawn. You will also hear more foreign languages and charming accents spoken here than anyplace else on Maui. Scandinavian blondes listen attentively as Irish brogues describe the action Out There, and French girls flirt with much sought after and prized Maui Boys, while Australians, Japanese and South Africans add to the mix. Especially on weekends, its a very popular place for the pretty people to sun and snooze and for everyone to watch everyone else. Considering everything that's going on here, in and out of the water, Ho`okipa Beach gets our vote for one of Hawaii's all around most fun beaches.

Photographs

For exact photo locations, refer to the map on page 58.

42 At Ho`okipa Beach on a fine and windy day, the water is filled with neon colored boards and sails.

43 Ho`okipa Beach's shore reef is a barrier to the surf. Better to enter the water at either end of the beach.

42

43

MAUI

North Shore and Hana Drive Beaches

Traveling In A Clockwise Direction

Maui's Hana Drive

● full circle indicates yes

◖ half circle indicates partial or sometimes

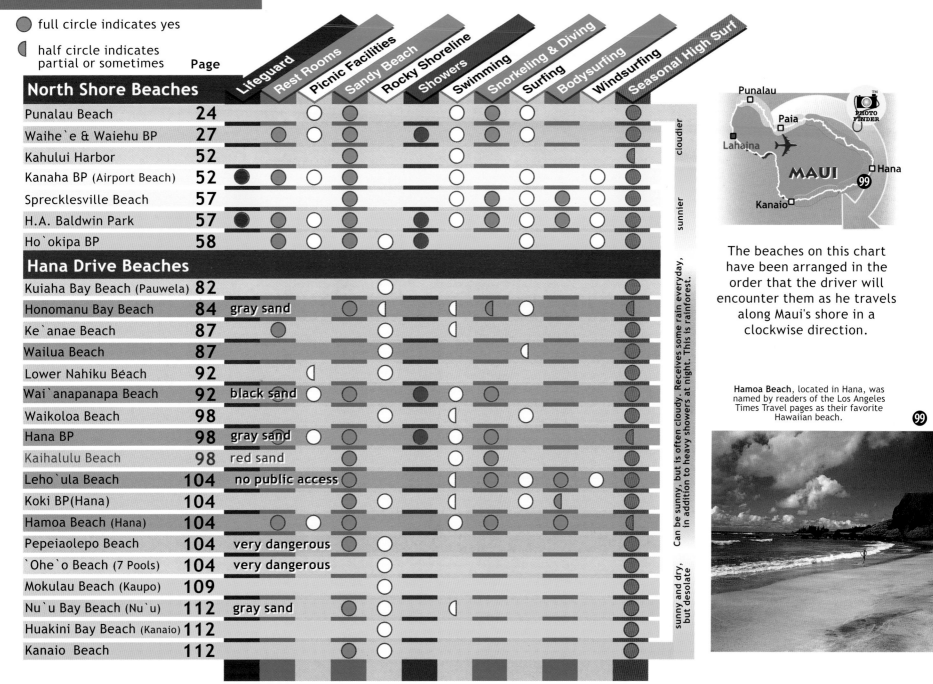

The beaches on this chart have been arranged in the order that the driver will encounter them as he travels along Maui's shore in a clockwise direction.

Hamoa Beach, located in Hana, was named by readers of the Los Angeles Times Travel pages as their favorite Hawaiian beach.

Beach	Page	Lifeguard	Rest Rooms	Picnic Facilities	Sandy Beach	Rocky Shoreline	Showers	Swimming	Snorkeling & Diving	Surfing	Bodysurfing	Windsurfing	Seasonal High Surf
North Shore Beaches													
Punalau Beach	24			○	●			○	◖	●			●
Waihe`e & Waiehu BP	27		●	○	●		●	●	○	◖		○	●
Kahului Harbor	52				●			○					◖
Kanaha BP (Airport Beach)	52	●	●	○	●			○		○		○	●
Sprecklesville Beach	57				●			○	◖	○		●	●
H.A. Baldwin Park	57	●	●	○	●		●	○	○	○	●	○	◖
Ho`okipa BP	58		●	○	●	◖	○	○		●		○	◖
Hana Drive Beaches													
Kuiaha Bay Beach (Pauwela)	82					○							◖
Honomanu Bay Beach	84	gray sand		○	◖	○		◖		◖	○		◖
Ke`anae Beach	87	●			○			◖					◖
Wailua Beach	87				○					◖			◖
Lower Nahiku Béach	92		◖		○								◖
Wai`anapanapa Beach	92	black sand	○	●		●	○	◖					◖
Waikoloa Beach	98				○			◖	○				◖
Hana BP	98	gray sand	○	●		●	○	●					◖
Kaihalulu Beach	98	red sand		●		○	○						◖
Leho`ula Beach	104	no public access			◖	○	○	○	○			◖
Koki BP (Hana)	104			●	○	◖			○	◖		◖
Hamoa Beach (Hana)	104		○	●			●	○		◖		●
Pepeiaolepo Beach	104	very dangerous	●	○								●
`Ohe`o Beach (7 Pools)	104	very dangerous		○								◖
Mokulau Beach (Kaupo)	109				○								◖
Nu`u Bay Beach (Nu`u)	112	gray sand	●	○		◖						●
Huakini Bay Beach (Kanaio)	112				○								●
Kanaio Beach	112			◖	○								●

(Weather note, right margin, top to bottom:) cloudier · sunnier · Can be sunny, but is often cloudy. Receives some rain everyday, in addition to heavy showers at night. This is rainforest. · sunny and dry, but desolate

99

The Road To Hana

Hana... There's no reason to rush to get there, because there is no real *there*. *There* is actually anywhere along *here* that you find yourself. Hana isn't the goal, nor are the 7 Pools at `Ohe`o. What *is* the goal is the kind of experience that can be found and felt as close as Huelo, 15 minutes beyond Ho'okipa's windsurfing beach, or as far away as Kaupo, which you would roll into some four hours later. If its not raining. And if you don't stop. Or, it might be found at any of a hundred places in between. The Hana Drive can be as long or short as you'd like. But just be forewarned: your memories of the experience will last forever.

MAUI

Aloha Ka-ua

The Hana Drive

❼

The infamous Hana Drive can be quite an ordeal, even though the road itself is good. We have driven it about 20 times, and our strong advice is that you must keep *your* eyes on the road — because nobody else does. If it is raining you may want to postpone the trip. Rain will cancel out most of the scenery's vivid color, and driving conditions will demand the driver's total concentration. Heavy rains bring landslides, causing the road to fall away into the sea in places. Visibility will be greatly diminished.

Because most visitors are under the impression that far away Hana town is their goal, they zoom right past some of Maui's most wonderful close-at-hand wonders. **Driving & Discovering Maui and Molokai** will reveal the great rewards that await all along the Hana Highway, no matter how close or far you choose to drive.

❹

You'll want to avoid becoming part of a **caravan** on the road to Hana. Ten minutes may go by without a single car passing along the highway, and then suddenly a group of 10 or 20 vehicles will go by. And then again, after they pass, nothing. If someone is on your bumper, pull over when it is safe to, and let them go by. Don't let a line of cars form behind you, making you move faster than you want to, and preventing you from safely stopping at places you'd like to visit.

Driving straight through from Kahului to Hana will take about three hours or so. From the Ka'anapali Resort area to the 7 Pools, the drive will take four and a half hours. And that's not counting stops to swim beneath waterfalls or explore any of the wonderful side roads. To enjoy the entire Hana Drive to its fullest, you might want to *consider staying overnight* in the Hana area. There are a number of B&Bs [Bed and Breakfasts] along the Hana Drive route, some of them charging as little as $50 per night double. Even if you have already paid for a hotel room in Ka'anapali or Kihei, to be able to truly savor the flavor of the Hana Drive, its really worth it to spend the extra money to stay the night in Hana.

Our usual routine entails staying overnight in or near town, giving us the entire day to dally and explore along the highway before reaching Hana town–keeping in mind that there's no place to buy food after 5 p.m., except the very expensive **Hotel Hana Maui** restaurant. Early next morning, we visit the **7 Pools** before

anyone gets there (the crowds start to arrive about eleven), and drive leisurely through **Kipahulu**, visiting the streams and falls. If it hasn't rained, we'll go past pavement's end and visit one of the most peaceful and beautiful places in all of Hawaii, Kaupo's windswept **Mokulau** ("many islands") **Beach** and superbly situated Hui'aloha Church.

The roads around Hana and environs are positively deserted at dawn, absolute peace abounds, and the slanting golden rays of the morning sun beautifully sidelight the awesome landscape. East-facing waterfalls that most daytrippers see in the afternoon shade now shimmer in the bright morning sunlight. Friendly local residents meander down the middle of mostly trafficless roads, walking their dogs and drinking from their steaming coffee cups.

You'll want to **fill or top off the gas tank** at the beginning of your journey in the windsurfing town of **Paia**, or before, as there are no other gas stations until you reach Hana Town. Pick up some picnic food and drink too, either here or at the wonderful **Pauwela Cafe** uphill from **MM3** (see pg. 83). There are dozens of spectacular spots ahead where a picnic can become an unforgettable addition to your vacation memories.

Ahead of you along the Hana Highway lie the tiny and lovely hidden towns of **Huelo**, **Ke`anae**, **Wailua** and **Nahiku**; forests of bamboo, fern, and eucalyptus; edible treats like guava, mountain apple and mango, abandoned coffee trees and creamy blooming ginger, countless unnamed untamed waterfalls, water chutes, pools and swimming holes. Spectacular overlooks cling to cliff tops, providing distant views of the sinuous road both ahead and behind, carved early in the 20th century with pick and shovel like a jagged scar into the full length of the seaside ramparts. Below the road, vibrant orange African Tulip Tree blossoms contrast vividly with the shimmering sapphire sea, and fluorescent carpets of wild pink and scarlet impatiens line the asphalt. Jungle so primeval that you'd expect to see Tarzan swinging from the tangle of vines beckons you to enter its wet and eerie world of shadows: *Sensitive Plants* recoil their tiny fern-like leaves for protection when you brush against them, bizarre bright red star-shaped fungi, looking like something from outer space, push up through the rotting forest floor litter, and swarms of mosquitoes drink a

crimson toast to your welcome.

Try to keep in mind that you may only get to come this way once, so you'll want to enjoy the region to its fullest. Be aware that the majority of cars taking this drive actually do not stop very often, so even though there may be dozens of cars driving past, many a deserted crystal clear pool and cascading waterfall await hiding only a hundred yards from the road, and they can be all yours just for a short walk. The Hana Drive section of **Driving & Discovering Maui and Molokai** will show you which are the prettiest and most accessible.

Bring along a variety of **film**, from fine-grained ASA/**ISO 64 or 100 for sunny scenes and brilliant colors**, to fast **ASA/ISO 400, or faster, for dark, shady or late-day shots**. Whether shooting stills or video, if you're serious about getting some great shots, bring a tripod. We keep ours in the trunk with legs extended as far as space allows for easy access and fast set up. Placed on top of everything else in the trunk, we can grab it quickly. For photographs of moving water and waterfalls, the tripod allows for long exposures and will keep non-moving details sharp, while allowing the water, clouds and moving leaves to blur into a dreamy visage.

Photographs

6
5
4
7

PHOTO FINDER™

pages 78 & 79:

❶ An abandoned catamaran on the Ke`anae Peninsula.

❷ Detail of 400' Waimoku Falls in Haleakala National Park.

❸ Detail of foliage near the Hana Community Center.

pages 80 & 81:

❹ Wananalua Congregational church in the heart of Hana town.

❺ A horse grazes on the Ke`anae Peninsula, seemingly unaware of the beauty of his surroundings.

❻ An African Tulip Tree growing on a slope beneath the Hana Highway beautifully frames a scene of the Hana Coast on a beautiful day.

❼ Collapsed caldera at Hana.

MAUI

Adventure Awaits

MATCH THIS SYMBOL'S MAP NUMBER WITH THE CORRESPONDING PHOTO NUMBER TO LOCATE THE EXACT SPOT WHERE EACH PHOTOGRAPH WAS TAKEN.

After leaving Ho'okipa Beach, the Hana HWY. dips and climbs and curves through beautiful geometric patterned bluff-top pineapple fields backed by the shimmering azure Pacific. Great photos can be had here from the road shoulder. A telephoto lens can help isolate small areas for an abstract look or to frame a geometric vignette, while a wide angle lens allows the beauty and order of the entire scene to be captured. In the morning and late afternoon, rainbows may add to the unforgettable setting. We are now officially on our way to Hana, but there is a lot of profoundly beautiful country between here and there. A myriad of opportunities exist at road shoulders and lookouts for beautiful slow panning shots with a videocam...if you don't have Electronic Image Stabilization, take the time to mount it on a tripod and make sure the camera is level before you shoot, or the pan will be shaky and tilted, and may end up boring the life out of your viewers. Unfortunately, if you haven't booked a room or B&B, you will have to bypass a lot of beautiful and rewarding sites —that is, if you're determined to make it all the way to the 7 Pools at Haleakala National Park, and return by dark.

After leaving Ho'okipa Beach you will pass a number of roads on the *right/mauka* side that lead uphill to one or more of the upcountry towns: **Haiku**, **Kokomo**, **Makawao**, **Kaupakulua** and others. These roads and their little side roads and country lanes are always fun to drive as they meander by all types of upcountry farms, ranches, mansions, cottages, woodlands, pasture lands and blazing tropical gardens. All of them, as long as you keep heading uphill, will sooner or later converge with the others and eventually deposit you in the Hawaiian cowboy town of **Makawao**.

Pauwela

The tiny hamlet of Pauwela, on the *makai* side of the Hana Highway, is unmarked with a sign, but there *is* a sign announcing the **Pauwela Lighthouse**, located at the intersection of the paved Hana

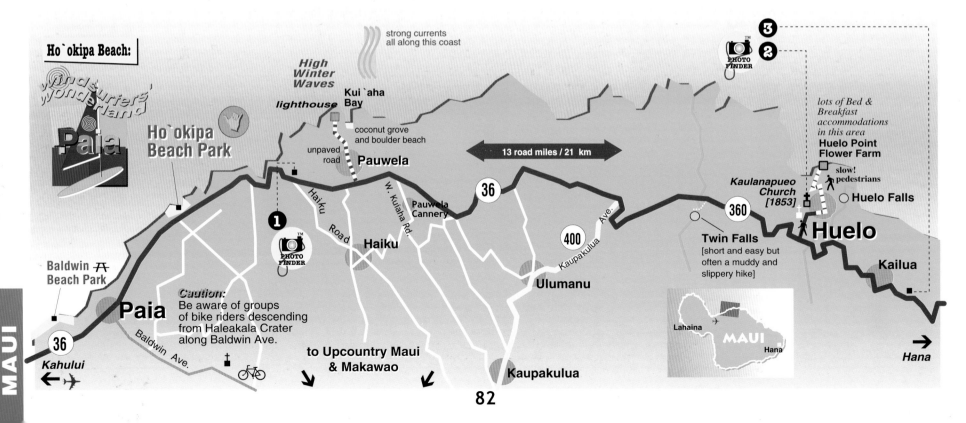

Ho'okipa Beach:

windsurfers' wonderland

Paia

Ho'okipa Beach Park

High Winter Waves

strong currents all along this coast

lighthouse

Kui'aha Bay

coconut grove and boulder beach

unpaved road

Pauwela

13 road miles / 21 km

lots of Bed & Breakfast accommodations in this area

Huelo Point Flower Farm

slow! pedestrians

Kaulanapueo Church [1853]

Huelo Falls

Huelo

Haiku Road

W. Kuiaha Rd.

Pauwela Cannery

36

400

Kaupakulua Ave.

360

Twin Falls [short and easy but often a muddy and slippery hike]

Haiku

Ulumanu

Kailua

Baldwin Beach Park

Paia

Caution: Be aware of groups of bike riders descending from Haleakala Crater along Baldwin Ave.

to Upcountry Maui & Makawao

Kaupakulua

Lahaina

MAUI

Hana

36

Kahului

Baldwin Ave.

MAUI

Hana

Highway and a dirt cane road. Follow this road for five minutes toward the sea to the automated lighthouse in a beautiful bluff top setting. Park your car on the grass, or if you have a mountain bike, continue to ride or walk eastward, up past the lighthouse, for great coastal views and a nice hike/ride down to little **Kui'aha Bay** and its pretty coconut palm-lined boulder beach. From the lighthouse area, this lovely scene is enhanced by the cloud topped heights of Mount Haleakala rising up from the rear of Kui'aha Valley.

Back on the Hana Hwy. at the **3MM**, look for W. KUIAHA ROAD. Turn right/mauka/uphill onto it. At about **0.6 mile** you will see the **Pauwela Cannery** on the left. **The Pauwela Cafe**, one of Maui's best and most creative little restaurants, is located here. Breakfast is a joy, with unusual international items like *pain perdu* and *chilaquiles* on the menu, as well as great coffees. Their *Kalua Turkey* specialty is wrapped in ti leaves and steamed for *ten hours*. The result is the most tender and moist turkey you've ever tasted. Don't miss it! Also at the cannery: **Da Kine** innovative surf designs and **ding repair.**

The last major *mauka*-intersecting side road that you'll pass along the Hana Highway is HWY. 365, KAUPAKALUA RD. **The mile marker [MM] you just passed is MM 16, but for whatever reason, after this point the highway begins its numbering system again at 0, so set your car or bike odometer to 0 and we'll try to keep you on track as we move along here.**

0.2 miles past MM 2 is the Ho'olawa Bridge. There are two sets of **Twin Falls** here. One is a mile uphill through the cow pasture. You will usually see a number of hikers' cars parked right before the bridge here. (See Robert Smith's book *Hiking Maui* for directions), but the other is just a two minute walk from the bridge. We parked beyond the bridge on the *right hand/ mauka* side of the road and walked back toward the bridge. Just before the bridge is a little trail that goes through the trees and descends to the stream that the bridge crosses. We were cautioned that if the stream is raging, forget it and save Twin Falls for another day. If it has been raining upslope, it may be too dangerous to continue. We found the short, easy trail very slippery, and with no strong trees to hold onto in places, we chose our steps carefully. When we reached

the stream, we walked upstream for 100 yards to the lovely little falls and pool. It had been exceptionally dry both times when we were there (and yet, the trail was still slippery) and only one of the two falls was flowing.

Huelo

Just 0.7 miles past MM 3 is a hidden treasure few have seen in their haste to reach Hana. **Huelo** is a beautiful hamlet located on **Waipio Bay** whose

main road is marked at the Hana HWY. only by a faded HVB Warrior marker for the **Kaulanapueo Church**, and a bank of mailboxes on a **blind curve**. It will appear shortly after marked WAIPIO ROAD, *makai*. Due to the blind curves, caution making these *left/makai* turns is extremely essential. Huelo nestles in a resplendent, idyllic and isolated setting...and it is brimming with **Bed & Breakfast accommodations**. Besides a towering 200'/68m unnamed waterfall, ocean vistas, pretty country lanes and a spectacular setting, Huelo boasts two picturesque churches. The aforementioned **Kaulanapueo Church** is absolutely one of Hawaii's finest restored churches. In constant use since **1853**, the simple and beautiful structure is extremely photogenic and lovingly cared for. Its large expanse of mani-

cured lawn is dotted with coconut palms, the tiny graveyard *makai*, is brimming with flowers, and the structure's spare but lovely architectural details make for great photographs. It is situated adjacent to a charming gravel lane and the cobalt blue Pacific provides a soothing backdrop. Drive Huelo's lanes very slowly. **Children are playing**, dogs are snoozing and horses are standing —*all in the middle of the road.*

Some of the most spectacular bed and breakfasts we have ever encountered are here in Huelo, perched magnificently near the edge of the cliff overlooking exquisite Waipio Bay 200' below. Guy Fisher and Doug Self have built a magnificent compound of very private quarters in the midst of his **Huelo Point Flower Farm**. Prices are a bargain, but considering the heavenly surroundings, the wonderful amenities and the sublime isolation, your experience here will be priceless.

Located about 15 minutes from Ho'okipa Beach's windsurfing and Paia town's eating and shopping, **Huelo** is a magnificent find, offering the best of all worlds. Guy and Doug will also point you toward other B&Bs in Huelo if his are full. The same architect, WhiteStar, who built their compound has built other homes and guest gazebos in the area, and since Guy and Doug opened their B&B, Huelo has become home to a number of other B&Bs. One overlooks Huelo Falls, 200' in height, yet not found on any map —just another of Huelo's mysterious treasures. **Huelo Point Flower Farm** can be reached at **(808) 572-1850.** Their address is **PO Box 1195, Paia HI 96779.** Other fine local B&Bs include **Jeff and Sharon Stone's Lookout House**, with its spectacular views all the way up the coast to Hana, and their separate Cottage, both new, bright and sunny and very handsomely decorated. Write/call for a full color brochure: **PO Box 117, Paia HI 96779. PH/FAX (808) 573-0914.** There is a healing center in Huelo called **Hale Akua**, on the beautiful Grace estate, offering accommodations in a range of prices. **Hale Akua** is a clothing optional property, © **(808) 572-9300.**

At one time the Huelo area was the home to more than 75,000 Hawaiians, attesting to its fertile soils and abundant 125 inch annual rainfall. The flora in this region

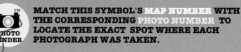

MATCH THIS SYMBOL'S **MAP NUMBER** WITH THE CORRESPONDING PHOTO NUMBER TO LOCATE THE EXACT SPOT WHERE EACH PHOTOGRAPH WAS TAKEN.

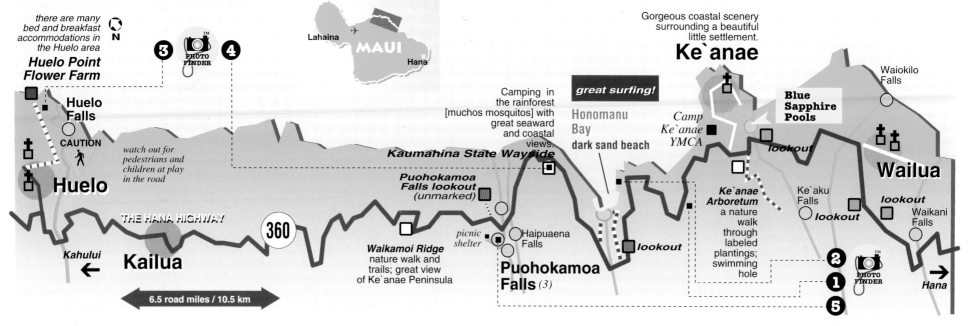

there are many bed and breakfast accommodations in the Huelo area

Huelo Point Flower Farm

Huelo Falls

CAUTION

Huelo

watch out for pedestrians and children at play in the road

THE HANA HIGHWAY

360

Kailua

Kahului ←

6.5 road miles / 10.5 km

MAUI
Lahaina
Hana

Camping in the rainforest [muchos mosquitos] with great seaward and coastal views.

Kaumahina State Wayside

Puohokamoa Falls lookout (unmarked)

picnic shelter

Waikamoi Ridge nature walk and trails; great view of Ke`anae Peninsula

Haipuaena Falls

Puohokamoa Falls (3)

great surfing!

Honomanu Bay

dark sand beach

Gorgeous coastal scenery surrounding a beautiful little settlement.

Ke`anae

Camp Ke`anae YMCA

Ke`anae Arboretum a nature walk through labeled plantings; swimming hole

lookout

lookout

Blue Sapphire Pools

lookout

Waiokilo Falls

Ke`aku Falls

lookout

Wailua

lookout

Waikani Falls

Hana →

varies widely and wildly, often changing its form dramatically from one curve in the highway to the next. You will pass forests of fern-carpeted hillsides, individual stands of towering and fragrant eucalyptus (including painted bark or *rainbow eucalyptus*), beautiful but ecologically disastrous brilliant green waving bamboo stands, huge and sturdy mango and Java plum. Giant variegated philodendron, just a house plant on the mainland, climbs to the very treetops, then lowers its Tarzan vines to the ground, all told extending its reach a couple hundred feet or more.

t **MM 11** look for a bridge with a space right before it only big enough for two cars to park. A pathway leads from here a very short way *mauka* to a wood picnic shelter with one table which overlooks pretty **Puohokamoa Falls and Pool**. The few people who *do* stop here don't realize that this is just the *middle falls*, and that another falls with pool **lies just above it,** in addition to yet another towering 200' ribbon fall **down-**

stream. On our first visits here the weather was rainy and the stream was swollen and muddy, and we thought the place was pretty unremarkable. But afterward we visited when the weather had been dry, the water level low, and numerous exposed boulders provided a dry stream crossing. We crossed the stream and climbed up the trail on the other side. A short way ahead, another falls and pool, out of the sight and the hearing of those below, was a welcome surprise. We've had the luxury of enjoying the upper pool completely to ourselves over the years many times since. After a swim, its possible, when the water level is low, to backtrack by boulder-hopping past the middle falls again and continuing for about 15 minutes downstream until cautiously approaching the lip of **Lower Puohokamoa Falls**. There is no way from this vantage point to really appreciate this falls since you are behind the brink which is disintegrating, and footing is **treacherous**. But there *is* a great view you can take in from above:

*Back on the HANA HIGHWAY, we backtracked toward Kahului a few hundred yards uphill to the first sharp left curve in the road. On the right at this point is a wide shoulder big enough for four or five cars to park. There we found a break in the trees right next to the telephone pole. This path lead under a rail and a few dozen yards along the top of a ridge there was a lookout which pro-*vided a **great view** of the cascading falls and the Hana Highway traffic passing above it.

Moving on, a little past **MM 12** you will see **Kaumahina State Wayside** on the *mauka* side of the road, with its **superb views** of the rugged Hana coast and upcoming **Ke`anae Peninsula**. The Ke`anae Peninsula is home for a lovely and isolated Hawaiian agricultural community. Its land was formed eons ago by a lava flow spilling out of Ke`anae Valley and marks the *halfway point to Hana*. There may or may not be any identifying sign here at Kaumahina Wayside, by the way, due to souvenir hunters.

At **MM 13**, the highway descends toward **Honomanu Valley**, and right after **MM 14** on the *left/makai* side, a short unpaved road leads to **Honomanu Bay**, a gray sand beach where fresh water from Honomanu Stream meets the ocean and hopeful **surfers** peer out to sea. Honomanu Bay offers both short-and longboard surfing, as well as bodyboarding, with breaks happening all year. The waves here are sheltered from the constant offshore winds that destroy their shape in other north shore areas, but there is a scary rip current in the center of the bay eager to drag swimmers out to sea. Refer to **Greg Ambrose's** *Surfer's Guide To Hawaii*, avail-

Photographs

1 Heavy rains turn the Hana Hwy.'s waterfalls into raging torrents —beware.

2 Just past Honomanu Bay, three roadside benches wait for visitors to sit and contemplate the scene.

3 Rainbow Shower Tree blossoms bloom at roadside.

4 From the viewing/picnic area above the Hana Highway, a car zooms by in early evening at Kaumahina State Wayside.

5 Middle Puohokamoa Falls is located just a few steps from roadside. A covered picnic shelter with table makes for a nice lunch spot, but not for the mosquito prone.

MAUI

a deluge can turn the hana highway's normally gentle streams and waterfalls into frightening and deadly torrents.

85

able at most island bookstores, for *great maps and detailed information about surfing* at Honomanu Bay and other great Hawaii surf spots. Short, very bumpy dirt roads lead off the HANA HIGHWAY on each side of the stream toward the beach. After rounding this bay, the HANA HIGHWAY ascends steeply again, and from a dramatic roadside lookout uphill on the *eastern side of the bay,* great shots of this area can be taken (look for the picnic-style benches).

Ke`anae Arboretum

Just **0.8 miles past MM 16, Ke'anae Arboretum** is a popular stop, with picnic tables, hiking trails and a large collection of labeled trees and plantings. The entrance is on a sharp turn in the highway: watch for a large identifying sign and aluminum gate. The arboretum is an interesting blend of both introduced and native plants. It can be either sunny or rainy here, so if you are planning to hike, come prepared for either extreme. If you are particularly interested in the plant life and geology of this area, bring along a copy of **Angela Kay Kepler's** *Maui's Hana Highway: A Visitor's Guide*, available at most island bookstore locations. It is *filled* with color photos identifying all the flowers, plants and trees that thrive along the way, and has a detailed section devoted to the Ke'anae Arboretum.

Photographs

For these photo locations, see map on page 87 (opposite).

1 A Ke`anae resident tends his flooded taro patch.

2 A boy dives into the pool formed at ocean's edge at Ke`anae Beach, as viewed from the roadside lookout.

3 Detail of the facade of Ke`anae's `Ihi`ihi o Iehowa o na Kaua Church (1860).

MAUI

86

The Ke`anae Peninsula
and Wailua

MATCH THIS SYMBOL'S **MAP NUMBER** WITH THE CORRESPONDING **PHOTO NUMBER** TO LOCATE THE EXACT SPOT WHERE EACH PHOTOGRAPH WAS TAKEN.

The Hana Drive

Unless you are paying close attention as you round the curve in the HANA HIGHWAY., you may miss the **sign on the left** indicating **Ke`anae**. The sign is located just about *100 yards past the Ke`anae Arboretum*. Be very careful making this turn as approaching traffic around the curve on the HWY. is **hidden from view**. You will see a left turn at the Ke`anae YMCA camp, but you *don't want to take that one*, unless you have to make a phone call. That public phone is no mirage, as unlikely as its location is so far away from everything else. It sits at a fork in the dirt road, above the camp, with other-worldly views indescribable in mere words. We stopped one day right before sunset, and under the spell of the golden hour, the area's crashing surf and other-worldly beauty, stood in the fading orange and gold sunlight while we called our best friend on the mainland. He couldn't be on Maui for that trip, but knows and *loves* **Ke`anae**. "Hey, Pal, guess *where we're* calling from...?"

After making that left turn from the HANA HIGHWAY onto narrow KEANAE ROAD, you will soon pass a private property on the right that is a natural as a lookout point, but the owners got fed up with tourists tromping their flowers and finally fenced it off. Further down, where the road meets the boulder beach, a classic Maui seascape (see photo on page 19) beckons those with cameras. Unbridled waves wash white on the black boulder beach as distinctively shaped ebony lava heads and waving coconut palms complete the scene. For those staying in the area, Ke`anae is best appreciated in the early morning or in late afternoon near sunset.

The road skirts by a number of little plantation homes, including a tempting vacation rental...some with horses tied to a stake in the front yard to keep them from roaming. In a grove of palms, an abandoned and peeling catamaran overlooks the dramatic coastal vista, and nearby stands the lovely and beautifully situated **'Ihi 'ihio lehowa o na Kaua Church, c.1860**. The church graveyard is interesting for its ceramic photo-illustrated headstones and tropical flowers. Nearby grazing horses blithely tolerate the hitchhiking mynah birds who use their backs as lookout towers to scout for goodies scuttling around in the grass. Coconut palms sway and whoosh in the often times strong trade winds. The primitive parking area at the rugged shoreline opposite the church attracts photographers, fishermen, and Hana daytrippers who recognize a memorable picnic spot when they see one. There's even a public restroom. Ke`anae is a special Hawaiian place where residents are still friendly despite the tourist invasion that has interrupted their peaceful existence. Please don't drive into private-looking places and honor all KAPU (keep out/forbidden) signs.

Continuing to follow the seashore past the parking area, the paved road turns to dirt and curves to the left, and shortly reaches a turn around. No room to park here, so leave your car in the parking area and walk back to this place (2 minutes). Following the shore, we encounter teens diving into the large **pool** formed by the

We confess that we've lost track of where this bridge is located along the Hana Highway.

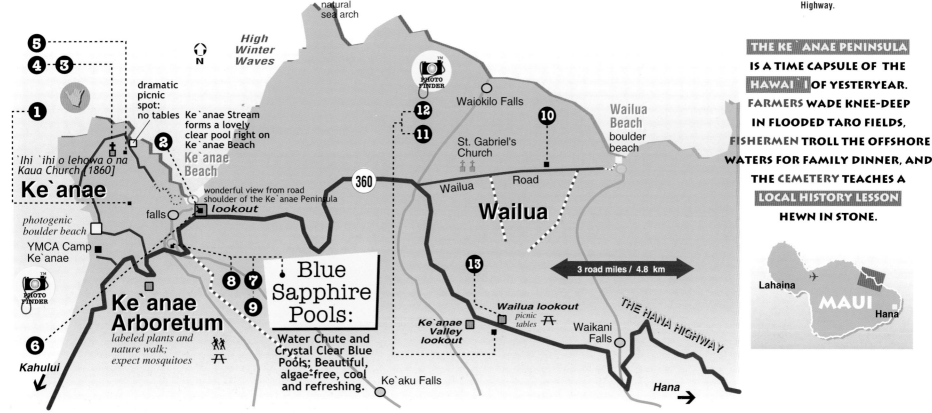

natural sea arch

High Winter Waves

N

5
4 · 3
1

dramatic picnic spot: no tables

Ke`anae Stream forms a lovely clear pool right on Ke`anae Beach

2

`Ihi `ihi o lehowa o na Kaua Church [1860]

Ke`anae

Ke`anae Beach

photogenic boulder beach

YMCA Camp Ke`anae

falls

wonderful view from road shoulder of the Ke`anae Peninsula

lookout

Ke`anae Arboretum
labeled plants and nature walk; expect mosquitoes

6

Kahului

8 · 7
9

Blue Sapphire Pools:
Water Chute and Crystal Clear Blue Pools; Beautiful, algae-free, cool and refreshing.

Ke`aku Falls

360

12
11

Waiokilo Falls

St. Gabriel's Church

Wailua   Road

Wailua

13

Ke`anae Valley lookout

Wailua lookout
picnic tables

10

Wailua Beach
boulder beach

Waikani Falls

THE HANA HIGHWAY

← 3 road miles / 4.8 km →

Hana →

Lahaina

MAUI

Hana

Ke'anae Stream on the Ke'anae boulder beach, while a Hawaiian father and son stand at the mouth of the stream where it meets the sea, casting their blue fishing nets to the wind. We swim upriver and around a bend to discover a lovely little waterfall. Away from the shore, neat plots grow vegetables and flooded terraced rectangles support taro crops. The residents of Ke'anae lead what to some would seem like an enviable existence, isolated and self reliant, in a place of extreme beauty and naked exposure to the elements.

Returning from Ke'anae to the curved HANA HIGHWAY, we make a *careful* *left turn* to continue. In a hundred yards or so, at the next curve, is a bridge. Looking over the edge, we see another pretty little waterfall emptying into a large deep pool. But the pool's walls are high and sheer, and there looks to be no way to safely reach it, much less escape if the water level starts to quickly rise...and anyway, the mosquitoes are ravenous.

That's okay, because at the very next bridge, in another few hundred yards, **Blue Sapphire Pools** are far more welcoming. Traffic is light as we approach. On the right, just before the bridge, a jeep road climbs up past trees into a pasture. There is a **gate** that swings across it, but we have never seen it closed. There is ample room to park around here, *but we wait until we can neither see nor hear any other cars before we scurry across the road and descend the pathway makai of the bridge. We love this place and want to be alone....you will notice that on the Hana Drive, cars will often stop out of curiosity when they see other cars parked, just to see what might be there. We knew if people saw us descending the path to the stream, that they'd stop, follow us ...and discover our secret place.*

We were in luck this time. **Sapphire Pools** was deserted, and the deep, sun-pierced, crystal-clear, algae-free waters reflected the rich blue clarity that gave them their name. In all the years we've been exploring Hawaii's backroads, Sapphire Pools is our all-time favorite swimming place. An absence of algae means that the rocks are not slippery, and the water has remarkable clarity, even when it gets crowded with people (we have been here when its a veritable **zoo,** as well). There is a minuscule beach-like area where we can quickly ease into deeper waters, but we find entering from the rocks is quite easy also. Just downstream, a little waterfall empties into another very lovely, very blue, deep pool, and the mosquitoes *here* are more of a problem. Right below the bridge, the main pool is at its deepest and bluest, and a water chute, cut out of the rock, is formed by the narrow stream banks. One of the photos shows a time when we found the area crowded with people, and kids were having a heyday climbing on the rocks and dropping into the water chute, which quickly zoomed them along for a few yards into the main pool.

Shortly after leaving Sapphire Pools and continuing along the HANA HIGHWAY again, you will see an **unmarked lookout** at **MM 17** with a **superb view** of the peninsula and its emerald green patchwork of taro patches far below. It is located on the *makai/seaward* side of the HWY. **next to a telephone pole** that has a tsunami siren attached. If you're as lucky as we were, you'll witness passing showers caressing rainbows lit by the setting sun as farmers stand knee deep in mud and water, hurrying to finish tending their taro patches before dark. To the left, right over the lip of the embankment —careful!— you can see a little waterfall upstream from the boulder beach swimming hole.

0.2 mile past MM 18 is the turnoff for Ke'anae's neighbor taro-farming peninsula, **Wailua**. Wailua is larger than Ke'anae but lacks its dramatic setting and accessible seashore, and is not quite as charming. WAILUA ROAD descends from the HANA HIGHWAY to the village and passes two churches, including **St. Gabriels',** which until recently was affectionately trimmed with painted red hearts, and interesting graveyards that are usually erupting in a riot of color from tropical flowers. The pavement ends near the unremarkable **Wailea** (boulder) **Beach** at the mouth of a stream where villagers come to launch their fishing boats. Backtracking, look to the *left/mauka* along WAILUA ROAD to see **Waikani Falls** spilling down a cliff below the HANA HIGHWAY on their way to refresh Wailua's taro patches.

Up on the HIGHWAY again, we saw a tiny waterfall gushing down the embankment roadside and climbed up to look for its source. We found there a lovely grouping of flooded taro fields separated by banana trees and looking as perfect as any botanical garden. A lone, handsome, exotic looking Hawaiian man, muscular and tall, stood knee deep in the water next to a wheelbarrow that held his tools. He was spattered with mud, he wore an eye patch and a buzz cut, and told us his name was Gundi. Gundi talked great story, and like most Hawaiians, felt it was important that visitors understand the spirituality beneath the distracting beauty of this place. He explained that he traveled from Kula once a week to work in this taro patch so that as a Hawaiian, he could maintain his spiritual connection with the land.

0.9 mile past MM 18 is the **Ke'anae Valley lookout** on the *right/mauka* side of the HWY., with great views deep into the Ke'anae Valley and on a clear day, all the way up the slopes of Haleakala to the crater rim. Climb the stairs through the hau tree tunnel for a great vantage point above the highway with views in all directions.

Then, **0.2 mile past MM 19** on the *left/makai* side is the **Wailua Peninsula lookout**, where those with telephoto lenses can zoom in for interesting shots of Wailua's churches, little roads, and people tending their pretty geometric maze of taro patches far below. There are picnic tables here. Way upstream and inaccessible,

but visible from a helicopter, is the **Wailua Nui Chain of Pools**, consisting of an impressive series of pools and falls cascading down the slopes. They can be clearly seen from the church area back in Ke'anae after a good rain.

The HWY. soon enters forested country again, and **0.6 mile past MM 22, Pua'a Ka'a State Wayside** usually has quite a few cars in its parking lot adjacent to the restrooms, on the *makai* side. Across the road, a short path leads to the very accessible waterfalls and swimming holes. Many people take advantage of this easy bathing spot due to the shortage of beaches and safe ocean swimming in this region. The Wayside also has picnic tables and grills.

6 →

Photographs

4 In the graveyard at Ke'anae's historic church, a loving remembrance is left on Mother's Day.

5 A horse grazes in the field behind Ke'anae's church.

6 A rainbow scores the partly gray sky just before sunset at Ke'anae Peninsula. This view is from the roadside lookout at MM17, beneath the tsunami siren.

4

5

MAUI

❼

❽

Blue
Sapphire
Pools

❿

❾

90

Wailua

⑪
⑬

Photographs

❼ Swimmers revel in the crystal clear waters at Blue Sapphire Pools. This view was taken from the bridge.

❽ We passed over this bridge many times before realizing Blue Sapphire Pools are right beneath it.

❾ Looking straight down from the bridge, kids ride the whitewater through the narrow gorge into Blue sapphire Pool.

❿ A detail of a red plumeria blossom.

⑪ ⑫ Gundi keeps in touch with his Hawaiian roots in part by working in this Wailua taro field once a week.

⑬ The community of Wailua as viewed from the roadside lookout area / picnic spot.

⑫

Nahiku to Hana

MATCH THIS SYMBOL'S **MAP NUMBER** WITH THE CORRESPONDING **PHOTO NUMBER** TO LOCATE THE EXACT SPOT WHERE EACH PHOTOGRAPH WAS TAKEN.

The Hana Drive

Photographs

❶ At the bottom of Nahiku Road, a parking and picnic area awaits those who venture down its three mile length from the Hana Highway.

❷ Isn't this place incredible? Nahiku's difficult-to-reach Hanawi Falls is a gorgeous spring-fed wonder that is just about as photogenic as a cascade can get.

Hanawi Falls photo by Ken Schmitt of Hike Maui.

The turnoff for the flower-abundant hamlet of **Nahiku** is between **MM 26 and 27**, *left/makai* of the HANA HIGHWAY, immediately after the bridge crossing at Makapipi Stream. This is yet another of Maui's wonderful roads, newly paved and bordered along its entire *very narrow* 3 mile length by a breathtaking Technicolor display of exotic flowers and handsome foliage plants. Its smooth surface undulates as it descends through a veritable Garden of Eden to the seaside, and powerful views of the rugged Hana Coast. The Beatles' George Harrison has a home near here, so the appropriate tape to pop in the deck might be *Sergeant Pepper's Lonely Hearts Club Band*, for the psychedelic theme running throughout delightfully complements the visual multi-hued roadside spectacle. Rusting car hulks, a pervasive eyesore everywhere else in Hawaii, surprise us here with their oddly photogenic corroded beauty and bountiful proliferation of flowers and showy ferns spilling out the windows and sprouting unexpectedly from engines, steering wheels and car seats.

At the turn of the last century, Nahiku was inaugurated as a rubber plantation, and a wharf was built seaside for shipping the product, but the rainfall here, it turned out, was *too bountiful* to accommodate the plants' particular needs. The great volume of rainfall explains the amazing variety of blooms you will see, including pure white ginger, lacy ferns, carpets of fluorescent impatiens, hibiscus, clematis, red ti, lavender morning glory, variegated banana, orange cupped-blossom African Tulip trees, guava, papaya, "Tarzan vines" and even some plants we've never seen before. Roadside fruit and flower stands operating on the honor system provided us with the biggest Solo papaya we've ever seen –the size of a football– for $1, and toward the sea, Nahiku's little church, with its distinctive tiny front porch and its great potential for restoration, welcomes visitors. As the road approaches the church, it curves back and forth prettily past red ti gardens and multi-colored laundry flapping lazily on the line in the trades. Allamanda vines entwine mature trees and telephone poles in garlands of distinctive 5-petaled, brown-throated yellow flowers, and near the church, an enchantingly beautiful little blonde girl dressed up in her mother's fancy clothes stands chatting on the unexpectedly located roadside public phone.

After crossing an old wooden bridge spanning Makapipi Stream, the turnaround at the road terminus provides parking for a few cars. Down to the left on the boulder beach a small waterfall empties into a clear little seaside pool that looks as if local residents have landscaped it, and to the right, where Makapipi Stream flows into the ocean, two young boys frolic in a swimming hole. The views along the coast are dramatic and the area, usually peopled only on weekends, provides a lovely spot for a picnic, or simply for contemplation.

Back on the HANA HIGHWAY, after leaving lower Nahiku, **Ali'i Gardens** Ⓒ **(808) 248-7217**, invites visitors to come in and look around. Ali'i's offerings of exotic flowering plants are unparalleled for their variety, and provide a welcome opportunity, having been dazzled by the local flora, to ship a beautiful living souvenir home to yourself.

Up ahead on the *mauka* side of the highway, at the intersection of KALO STREET, is the **Hana Gardenland Cafe and Nursery**, which serves delicious and creative sandwiches and salads along with its lush collection of tropicals. The Gardenland boasts that they were proud to serve Hillary Clinton every day during her 1993 visit. The Cafe, one of Hana's few eateries, is open from 9 am to 5 pm., 7 days a week. Ⓒ **(808) 248-7340.**

❶❷ →

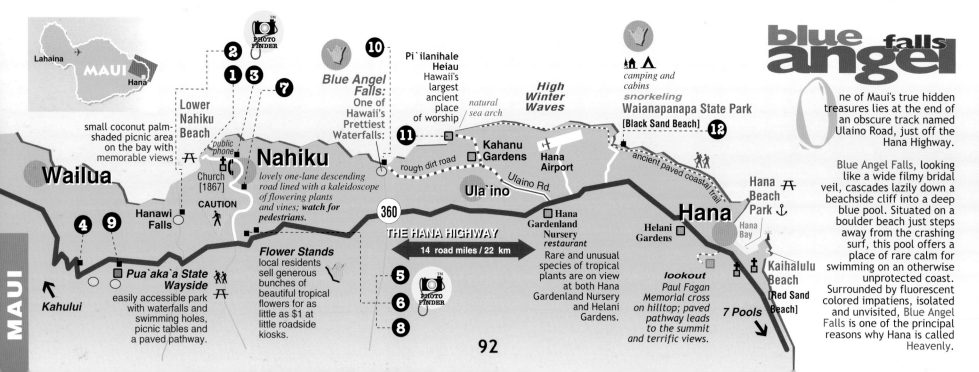

blue angel falls

ne of Maui's true hidden treasures lies at the end of an obscure track named Ulaino Road, just off the Hana Highway.

Blue Angel Falls, looking like a wide filmy bridal veil, cascades lazily down a beachside cliff into a deep blue pool. Situated on a boulder beach just steps away from the crashing surf, this pool offers a place of rare calm for swimming on an otherwise unprotected coast. Surrounded by fluorescent colored impatiens, isolated and unvisited, Blue Angel Falls is one of the principal reasons why Hana is called Heavenly.

Nahiku

Nahiku

MAUI

For a magical experience, keep an eye out for `ULA`INO ROAD, *makai*. It is paved for only the first half of its length, and is "officially" recommended for high riding or 4 wheel drive vehicles, but locals with passenger cars seem to have no trouble as long as they go slow and it hasn't rained recently. Car rental contracts prohibit driving off paved roads. Along its wooded way, you will pass an unmarked (as of this writing) spur road that leads to **Pi'ilanihale Heiau**, the largest of all ancient Hawaiian places of worship. It has been placed on the National Register of Historic Sites and has been lovingly landscaped by the **Pacific Tropical Botanical Garden**. Great views can be had from the heiau's shelter, as well as from the black pebble beach below. You will also pass **Kahanu Gardens** (admission charge; telephone first to see if they're open: **248-8912)**, along whose pebble beach a lovely natural sea arch topped with banyan and naupaka spans the strand.

But the star attraction here is gorgeous, wide, diaphanous **'Ula'ino Falls**, more popularly known as **Blue Angel Falls**, one of the prettiest scenes in all Hawaii. Surrounded by fluorescent colored impatiens, splashing into deep, clear, appropriately named **Blue Pool**, the falls are located right on the boulder beach only a few steps from the roaring sea. We drove to the end of `Ula`ino Rd. and parked in the unimproved parking area, adjacent to which a stream flowed on our *left/west* as we faced the sea. We crossed it and boulder-hopped along the beach for a few hundred yards to the waterfall. Beautiful, cool, clean, virtually mosquito-free, and very slippery, we swam freely, then lay on the huge sun-warmed boulders to dry, totally at peace, alone and undisturbed by neither human nor insect.

You will see few of Maui's gorgeous and unique native birds here, or anywhere else on the island below the 4000' level, for that matter. Wild pigs, in their ongoing unchecked destruction of the environment, are responsible. Their same rooting habit which sends tons of mud into Maui's clear streams and over its waterfalls to eventually settle on and kill the precious offshore coral reefs also creates large bog-like areas in the forests where rainfall puddles and sits. These puddles become prolific mosquito nurseries where millions of the pests emerge and swarm, carrying the deadly **bird malaria** that has wiped out dozens of superb and beautiful varieties of Maui's dwindling native bird species.

1.0 mile beyond 'Ula'ino Rd., the turnoff for 120 acre **Waianapanapa State Park** appears *makai*. Drive very slowly here as local children and pets walk the narrow road. Signs will direct you to the famous and very photo-worthy **black sand beach**, its dramatic and unique setting among black lava cliffs and little ebony islands contrasting against brilliant green beach naupaka and the white sea foam of crashing waves. A footpath here begins just west of the campground and guides us one quarter mile past two black pebble beaches (if you're

barefoot, watch out for stinging Portuguese Man '0' War bladders, looking like little purple-tinged transparent balloons) through the tropical vegetation to Waianapanapa and Waiomao caves. These two seaside **lava tubes** are filled with fresh crystalline waters and are said to be connected. **Honokalani Black Sand Beach** looks out on a natural sea arch out on the point. Here begins the **King's Highway foot trail**, which closely follows the shore for 3 miles/5 km to Hana.

At Waianapanapa you can rent **housekeeping cabins**, which come fully equipped and are some of the cheapest vacation digs anywhere in the world, priced on a sliding scale per person. Other housekeeping cabins similar to these are also located elsewhere on Maui, and on Oahu, Kauai and the Big Island too. Those here consist of units with a kitchen-living room, a bathroom and from one to three bedrooms. Each unit is completely furnished with bedroom and kitchen furniture, electric range, refrigerator, hot shower, bedding, linen, towels, dishes and cooking and eating utensils. Although not needed here, fireplaces or electric heating are provided in cold mountain areas, such as Maui's Poli Poli Springs and Haleakala Crater. It might not be the Hotel Hana Maui, but hey, at about 5% of that hotel's cost, you've got a comfortable place to lay your head. Plan to reserve well in advance and bring plenty of insect repellent. Contact the **Dept. of State Parks at 54 S. High St., Wailuku, Maui, HI 96793. ℂ (808) 243-5354** for information and reservations. Also write to the **Division of Forestry** and Wildlife at the same address for a copy of the **Island Of Maui Recreation Map**.

❽

❾

MAUI

Photographs

For these photo locations, see map on page 92.

⑩ We've given both of these photos the same number as they were taken in the identical location. The smaller photo shows much more water volume in the falls, as it was taken on a rainy day. Blue Angel Falls and Blue Pool occupy a wonderful location just steps from the ocean's roar.

⑪ Offerings of stones wrapped in ti leaves are left by the faithful at the largest heiau in Hawaii, Pi`ilanihali Heiau.

⑫ The black sand beach at Waianapanapa State Park provides one of Maui's most beautiful, and most photographed, sights.

Blue Angel Falls

96

Waianapanapa

black sand beach

⑫

Hana town

MATCH THIS SYMBOL'S **MAP NUMBER** WITH THE CORRESPONDING **PHOTO NUMBER** TO LOCATE THE EXACT SPOT WHERE EACH PHOTOGRAPH WAS TAKEN.

PHOTO FINDER

The Hana Drive

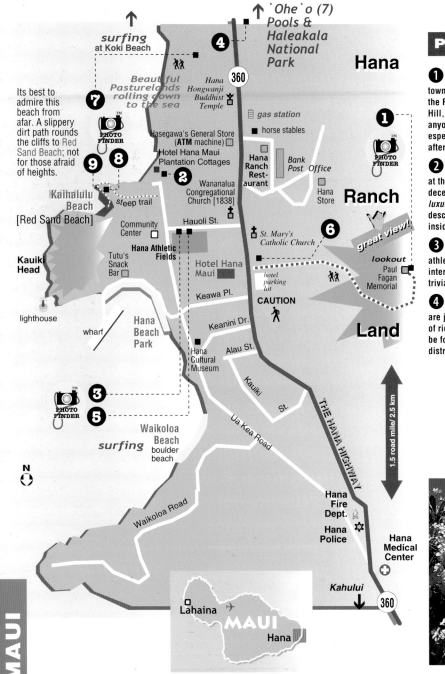

Map labels:

surfing at Koki Beach

`Ohe`o (7) Pools & Haleakala National Park

Hana

Beautiful Pasturelands rolling down to the sea

Its best to admire this beach from afar. A slippery dirt path rounds the cliffs to Red Sand Beach; not for those afraid of heights.

Hana Hongwanji Buddhist Temple

360

gas station

horse stables

Hasegawa's General Store (ATM machine)

Hotel Hana Maui Plantation Cottages

Wananalua Congregational Church [1838]

Hana Ranch Rest-aurant

Bank Post Office

Hana Store

Ranch

PHOTO FINDER

great view!

lookout Paul Fagan Memorial

Kaihalulu Beach [Red Sand Beach]

Steep trail

Community Center

Hauoli St.

St. Mary's Catholic Church

Land

Kauiki Head

Tutu's Snack Bar

Hana Athletic Fields

Hotel Hana Maui

hotel parking lot

CAUTION

lighthouse

wharf

Hana Beach Park

Keawa Pl.

Keanini Dr.

Alau St.

Hana Cultural Museum

Kauiki St.

Ua Kea Road

THE HANA HIGHWAY

1.5 road mile/2.5 km

PHOTO FINDER

Waikoloa Beach

surfing boulder beach

Waikoloa Road

N

Hana Fire Dept.

Hana Police

Hana Medical Center

Kahului

360

Lahaina

MAUI

Hana

MAUI

Photographs

1 The view of the entire town of Hana, as seen from the Fagan Memorial on Lyons Hill, is memorable by anyone's standards, but is especially striking in the afternoon.

2 The Plantation Cottages at the Hotel Hana Maui look deceptively simple, but *luxurious* is the only description for what awaits inside....and oh, those views!

3 This sign at the Hana athletic field reveals an interesting tidbit of baseball trivia.

4 Roadside protea blooms are just one of many varieties of riotously blooming plants to be found thriving in the Hana district…

Hana is a beautifully situated, spotless and very friendly small town populated by many native Hawaiians. People in Hana are disarmingly gracious and generous. In the years that we have been visiting, dozens of lovely individuals have touched our hearts with their kindness and aloha.

It rains a lot in Hana; 89" annually at the little airport and 300" uphill in the Kipahulu Valley, compared to 14" in Lahaina and 19" at Kahului airport. That explains the blinding green color of everything and the stunning variety of tropical flowers.

Hana Beach Park is one of the few safe swimming beaches in east Maui. This gray sand colored is not classically beautiful in the postcard sense, but it is very clean and protected from the open ocean's fury. **The Hana Pier** is located here, and out at the point, there's a small lighthouse on a tiny island separated from the mainland by only a few yards of water. Keep going around the bend, climb over some rocks, and you may find a tiny seasonal white sand beach, with relatively calm waters in summer and good snorkeling.

Hana Beach Park facilities include rest rooms, showers and picnic tables. After leaving the Beach Park, turn right on the first street (UA KEA ROAD) to visit the **Hana Cultural Center**, open from 11 a. m. to 4 p. m. The Center displays beautiful Hawaiian quilts and fascinating historical photographs. Nominal admission fee.

At the center of town is the **Hotel Hana Maui**, a secluded refuge for the upscale traveler, where beautifully decorated quarters include deceptively simple-looking bungalows in the plantation cottage style situated in green pastures rolling gently down to the ocean. Their open front porches catch the salty clean breezes blowing up from the sea, and provide unforgettable sunrise views of offshore Alau Island. If these luxury quarters look like a page out of **Architectural Digest**, it is because the Hotel Hana Maui was featured in a beautiful article in that magazine. Accommodations include king size beds with Hawaiian quilts, overstuffed sofas, wood shuttered windows, furnished private lanais, and bathrooms straight out of WC heaven. The hotel grounds sprawl right through town, with homes, churches, the community center, and playing fields adjacent to or between sections of the beautiful hotel property. To say its lovely and peaceful here sounds trite, but the aura of Hana is quite special: the town is immaculately clean and very quiet, except perhaps during a ball game. You will most likely not see a scrap of paper on the ground anywhere.

The handsome main hotel building contains a beautifully designed dining room and bar, high ceilinged and large, yet cozy and relaxing. Ceiling fans spin overhead, tropical blooms scent the air and fresh breezes waft up from the ocean below. The dining room is open to the public, with prices on the expensive side. Hotel guests are accommodated in the dining room first. If you are not a guest, call ahead & (808) **248-8211** for reservations to avoid disappointment, as the only other eating place in town, The Hana Ranch Restaurant, closes at 3 p.m.

The Hotel Hana Maui offers its guests lots of organized activities, such as horseback rides to secluded swimming holes and luaus on the beach, but few guests seem aware that they have access to virtually the entire Hana Ranch area, so ask about this at the front desk. The ranch property is vast and includes spectacular views and lots of wide open spaces to roam and explore.

Across the road from the Hotel entrance, adjacent to the parking lot, a gated road

4 3 2 →

1

Hana

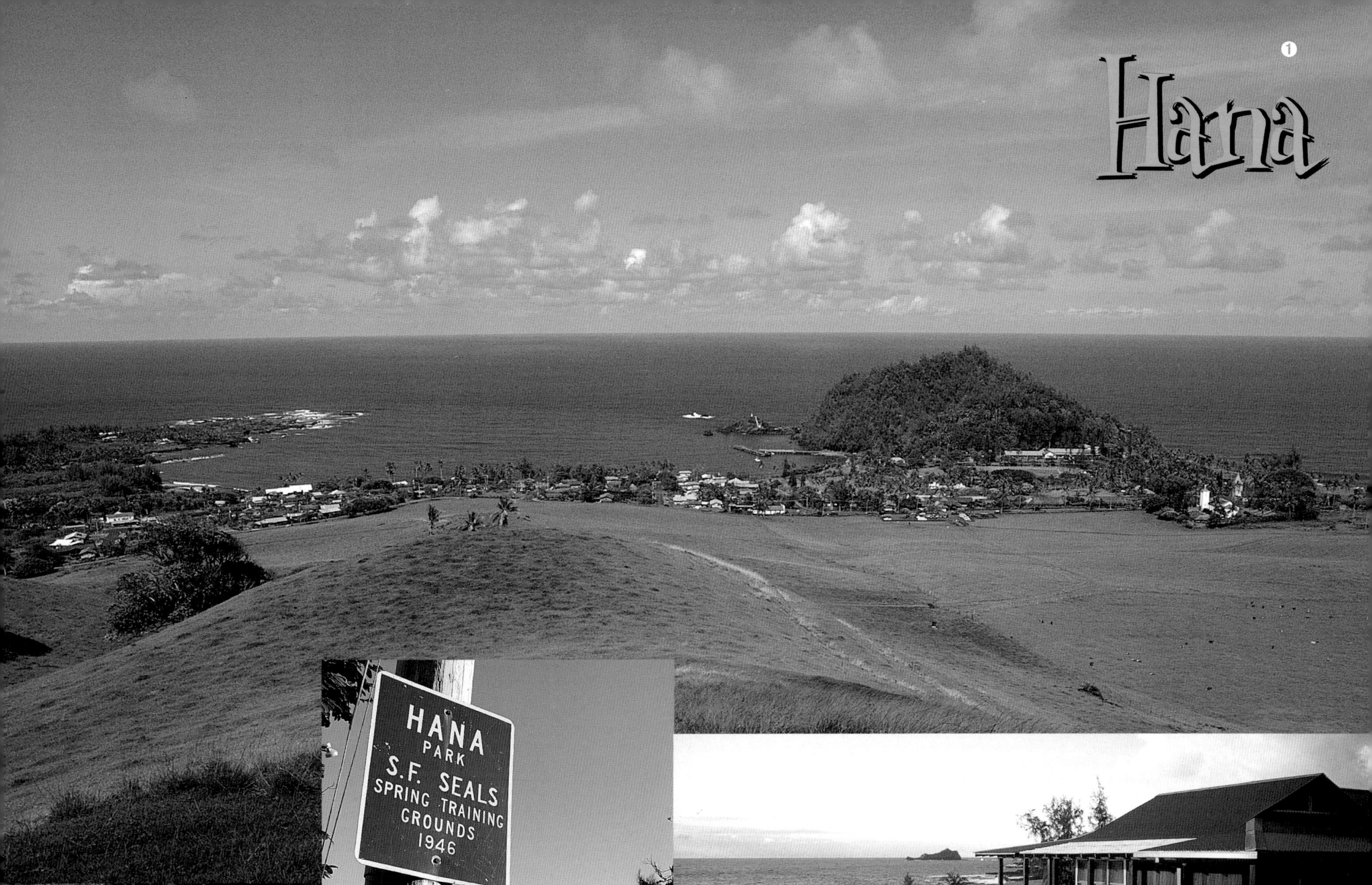

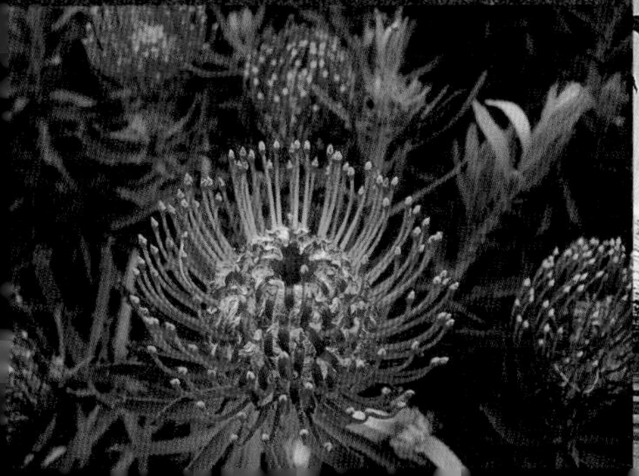

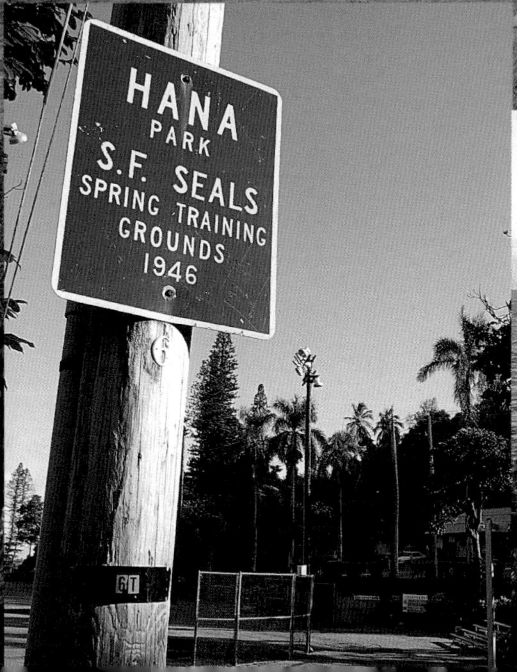
HANA
PARK
S.F. SEALS
SPRING TRAINING
GROUNDS
1946

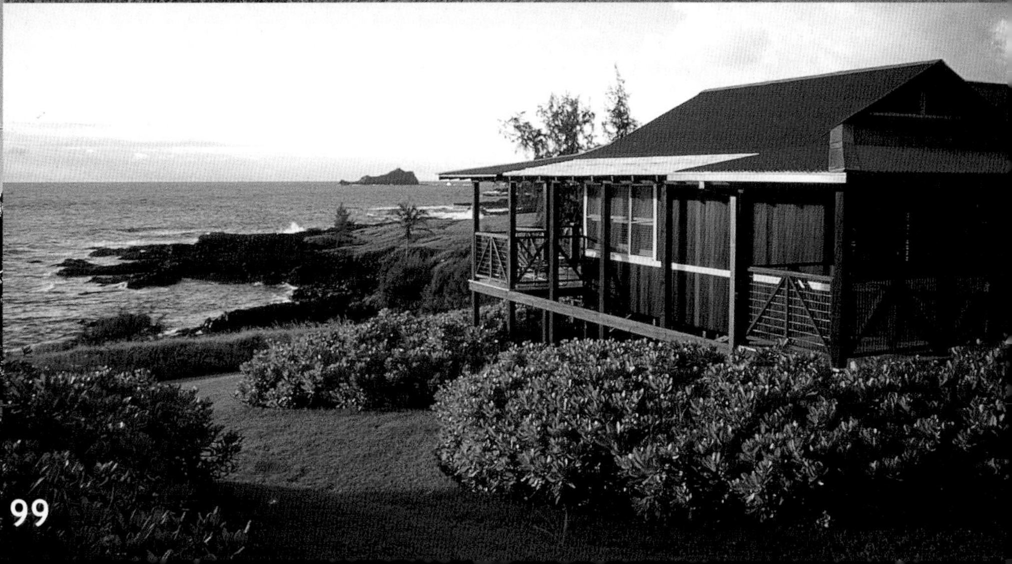

leads up to **Lyons Hill** (Pu'u o Kahaula) and one of Maui's most idyllic views. At the top is a lava-block cross, torch-lit at night, which is a memorial to Paul Fagan, the founder of the hotel and the enormous surrounding ranch. From here, the vista includes thousands of cattle scattered over the emerald green slopes of Haleakala, the picturesque churches of century-and-a-half-old **Wananalua Congregational** and **St. Mary's Catholic Church** below, and stretching out forever beyond the harbor, the cobalt blue Pacific Ocean. For those with a telephoto lens, the possibilities for detail shots from this vantage point are endless, but if you have any kind of camera at all, make the trip up here. Afternoon is best. The gate is next to the gazebo and usually unlocked. If not, ask for the key from the Hotel Hana Maui front desk.

We found a beautiful view of the coast, **Alau Island**, and the Hana Maui plantation cottages from the distinctive monolithic landmark, **Ka'uiki Head**. After passing the community center on UA KEA ROAD, and immediately before the entrance to the hotel's cottages, we walked a trail that follows the fence toward the sea past old Japanese grave markers. The trail forked in three, and we took the easiest route down toward shore; the trail closest to the fence appeared the safest. We experienced slippery walking conditions due to mud, so we watched each step carefully. The trail is quite precipitous as it rounds the point toward **Red Sand Beach**, but we found courage in the knowledge that Hillary Clinton, along with her elderly mother, made this same hike on their visit to Hana. The only difference was, secret service agents went on ahead to ask people on the beach if they'd mind putting their bathing suits back on while the then First Lady was present. Grudgingly, all agreed to do so. Red Sand Beach attracts nude sunbathers, due to its extreme isolation, and snorkelers, because of the clarity of the water. The contrast of the brilliant turquoise and aquamarine-colored sea, set against shimmering bright red sands, is very unique and quite beautiful. The beach itself is protected somewhat from the wild open ocean by an offshore reef that forms a natural sea wall and shields the bay from incoming waves. Swim only within this barrier.

Back on the Hana Hwy., after passing the hotel and churches, you'll see **Hasegawa's General Store** on the *left/makai* side. Hasegawa's carries everything under the sun; from 30 different varieties of machetes and grass knives for all your jungle-clearing needs, to the latest Haagen-Dazs flavors, CD players, and locally grown Kipahulu Estate coffee, Ono Farms organic dried fruit and all manner of groceries. You can also inquire about local activities like horseback riding tours and ocean charters. Hasegawa's has supplied Hana residents since 1910. Across the street *mauka/uphill* you'll find the post office, bank, the **Hana Store** and the **Hana Ranch Restaurant**, which normally closes at 3 PM, except on Pizza Night, Thursdays.

Photographs

5 Wananalua Congregational Church shines in the early morning light. Nightly rain showers are a given. Hana wakes up freshly washed most every morning.

6 The weather vane alongside the paved trail to Lyons Hill makes a good detail shot as well as providing a symbolic welcome to the Hana Ranch.

7 A Hana Ranch *paniolo* (he's from Texas originally) stirs up a little morning dust while separating calves from the herd.

8 Red Sand Beach as viewed from above.

9 The precipitous trail to Red Sand Beach follows the shoreline. Hillary Clinton *and her mother* walked this trail on their visit to Hana.

5

9

Other Hana accommodations include the magical little **Heavenly Hana Inn**, where the apartments look out on verdant Asian style gardens; large screened windows circulate evening breezes, and going to sleep in the arms of someone you love to the sound of rain pittering on the roof overhead will burn warm Hana memories into your heart.

A good source for bed and breakfast accommodations in the Hana area is the internet, at websites like <**www.hanamaui.com**>; or go to a search engine and type in such words as "*Hana Accomodations*", and the like. For those who fall under Hana's spell, a must-have book, beautiful but hard to find, is **On The Hana Coast**, by Carl Lindquist. Carl is a former Hotel Hana Maui manager who aided in the restoration of **Hui Aloha Church** in Kaupo.

Hana

❻

❽

❼

PANIOLO

The Hawaiian Cowboy

The clock barely reads 7 A.M. The galloping horses kick up a small scale dust storm as their pounding hooves careen them tightly around within the cramped confines of the corral. The *paniolos*, as Hawaiian Cowboys are called, work in tandem to separate the calves from the rest of the herd for branding. They sweat in the intense early morning sunlight of Hana Ranch as pampered and sleepy tourists still dream nearby in darkened closed-shuttered rooms at the luxurious Hotel Hana Maui and local B&Bs. Behind this dusty scene, coconut palms move languidly against a cobalt sky in any breeze that can be found. And just below the bluff-top corral area, the Pacific Ocean sparkles intensely silver in the sun's low angle.

One of the paniolos we're watching is originally from Texas, and looks every bit the Marlboro Man. Another is a full blooded Hawaiian and Hana native who prefers a baseball cap to a Stetson, and a T-shirt to a denim collared. Their chaps are bruised and worn, their hands are scarred by otherwise forgotten cuts and rope burns, and their stiff and often aching bodies take a minute or two to completely straighten up once they hop off their horses. These are real, live, honest-to-goodness, sunup-till-sundown cowboys. They toil on one of the world's most beautiful islands, ironically having chosen a difficult and back-breaking profession amidst people of privilege who arrive with the intention of doing absolutely nothing.

In 1832 King Kamehameha III invited a trio of *vaqueros* from Mexico to come and tutor native Hawaiians in the art of cattle management. They called themselves "Españoles", which the natives mispronounced as "paniolos". The word survives to the present day as the term for the Hawaiian Cowboy. Paniolos immediately put their own spin on the vaqueros' style of ridin', ropin' and wearin'. They wove their own cowboy hats from the fronds of the hala tree, redesigned their saddles to include a higher horn and cantle —better to hold a rider on to his steed— and developed ways to more efficiently work cattle on the rugged, hot, and unforgiving volcanic slopes.

One thing that sets the paniolo apart from the mainland cowboy is his Hawaiian love of the lei. Throughout paniolo history, even the rowdiest, roughest and toughest Hawaiian Cowboys wore leis, just for the looks and pure pleasure of it. They selected their lei material primarily for scent, and secondarily for weight. A heavy lei was preferred as it was worn as a hat band and helped keep the hat on the rider's head in the strong trade winds. Flowers, vines and ferns were literally gathered on the run from the horse's back as the paniolos headed home after a long session of hard work. Materials that fluttered in the wind made a showy lei that looked good on a galloping paniolo. "The girls all look at you when you wear a lei", paniolos seem to agree. An extra flour sack would be taken on a roundup to hold unusual local materials gathered from the beach, forest or *kipuka* (an island of green surrounded by a lava flow). Brought back to a wife, mother or a highly regarded lei-maker, the materials were fashioned into a special occasion lei to mark a holiday, birthday, rodeo, or branding.

In 1987 a traveling exhibit sponsored by the National Endowment for the Arts, celebrating Paniolo folk arts and the history of ranching in Hawai`i, brought together a beautiful collection of Hawaiian cowboy regalia. The fascinating catalog from this exhibit is still widely available in larger bookstores: *Na Paniolo o Hawai`i* is published by the Honolulu Academy of Arts. Another fine book, *Aloha Cowboy*, brings alive the history of the paniolo from the introduction of horses in 1803 until the present day. *Aloha Cowboy* is published by the University of Hawaii Press.

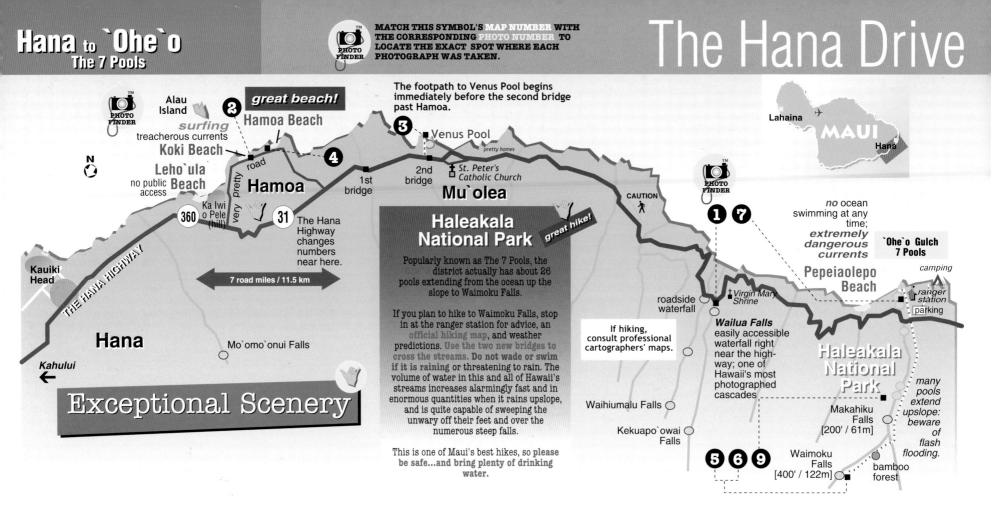

Hana to `Ohe`o
The 7 Pools

MATCH THIS SYMBOL'S MAP NUMBER WITH THE CORRESPONDING PHOTO NUMBER TO LOCATE THE EXACT SPOT WHERE EACH PHOTOGRAPH WAS TAKEN.

The footpath to Venus Pool begins immediately before the second bridge past Hamoa.

Lahaina

MAUI

Hana

Alau Island

surfing
treacherous currents

great beach!
Hamoa Beach

Venus Pool

pretty homes

Koki Beach

Leho`ula Beach
no public access

Hamoa

1st bridge

2nd bridge

St. Peter's Catholic Church

CAUTION

no ocean swimming at any time; *extremely dangerous currents*

`Ohe`o Gulch 7 Pools

360

Ka Iwi o Pele (hill)

very pretty road

31

The Hana Highway changes numbers near here.

Mu`olea

Haleakala National Park

great hike!

Popularly known as The 7 Pools, the district actually has about 26 pools extending from the ocean up the slope to Waimoku Falls.

If you plan to hike to Waimoku Falls, stop in at the ranger station for advice, an official hiking map, and weather predictions. Use the two new bridges to cross the streams. Do not wade or swim if it is raining or threatening to rain. The volume of water in this and all of Hawaii's streams increases alarmingly fast and in enormous quantities when it rains upslope, and is quite capable of sweeping the unwary off their feet and over the numerous steep falls.

This is one of Maui's best hikes, so please be safe...and bring plenty of drinking water.

Pepeiaolepo Beach

camping

ranger station

parking

Kauiki Head

THE HANA HIGHWAY

Kahului ←

Hana

Mo`omo`onui Falls

Exceptional Scenery

7 road miles / 11.5 km

roadside waterfall

If hiking, consult professional cartographers' maps.

Virgin Mary Shrine

Wailua Falls
easily accessible waterfall right near the highway; one of Hawaii's most photographed cascades

Haleakala National Park

many pools extend upslope: beware of flash flooding.

Makahiku Falls [200'/61m]

bamboo forest

Waihiumalu Falls

Kekuapo`owai Falls

Waimoku Falls [400'/122m]

As you leave Hana you'll pass the handsome Hana **Hongwanji Buddhist Temple**, *makai*, and then, open, rolling pasture land. The Highway number now changes from HWY. 36 to HWY. 31, and the mile marker (MM) numbers descend from larger to smaller. *Turn left* at the first street, HANEO'O ROAD This is a **very lovely loop road** that meanders down to the sea through pasture land to **Koki Beach Park** (no facilities). You may meet friendly dogs and surfers crouching in the shade of the trees alongside this pretty road, scouting the wave action. Water currents at Koki are treacherous, and we are warned not to swim here unless conditions are completely calm. The views of the road and coast are beautiful and include a sea arch out near the point to the left. Further along the road is **Hamoa Beach**, a beautiful public strand that is shared with the Hotel Hana Maui, which maintains facilities here. Swimming and bodysurfing at Hamoa are often excellent. In an informal survey, the **Los Angeles Times** found Hamoa Beach to be its readers' favorite

Hawaiian beach. Offshore, little **Alau Island**, you may notice, has a little grove of coconut palms at the top. The story goes that two local brothers, to celebrate and commemorate their safe return to Hana after World War II, paddled out to Alau with sprouting coconuts, clambered to the summit and planted two trees. Since that time, despite extremely exposed conditions, the trees have thrived and multiplied.

Past Hamoa Beach, and back on the HANA HWY., continue along to the **48 mile marker**. Immediately before the bridge, cross over/through the fence and walk through the pasture, following the stream for 5 minutes to its end at a wonderful and isolated find —**Venus Pool**. Scoured out of solid rock, this freshwater pool is adjacent to, but protected from, the ocean's roaring waves.

Continuing on, as the Hana Hwy. enters rainforest again, it resumes its sinuous and twisting nature. A number of beautiful brooks, water chutes and waterfalls appear. Most of these are barely visited, as those

who are intent on reaching 'Ohe'o's 7 Pools are now tired and anxious to get there. **Paihi Falls** is a perfect narrow ribbon cascading into a deep pool immediately roadside at a sharp curve near the big cross. White-knuckled drivers generally don't even notice it. There is a large waterfall right below the road here, but no place to park. **Wailua Falls** appears soon, one of Maui's most photogenic. Recently, locals selling fruit and souvenirs have set up shop here, disturbing the ambiance and creating traffic problems. However, we reached this spot in the early morning before the day trippers arrived and spent 20 minutes here without another car passing by. Wailua Falls comes as close as any to looking exactly like what one would expect a waterfall in paradise to look like. The 200'/61m cascade is a towering, tumbling, diaphanous ribbon of white, gently falling into a natural pool set in a riotous green garden. Red torch ginger and multicolored impatiens are set in just the right place, seemingly on purpose. You might never forgive yourself if you don't bring a camera.

Photographs

❶ **Wailua Falls** is beautiful, and close enough to the road to shoot from the bridge.

❷ A lone surfer and his dogs sit in the early rays of the morning sun, scoping out the waves at Koki Beach.

❸ Located inshore from the boulder beach, Venus Pool reflects the surrounding trees.

❹ Hamoa Beach is beautifully maintained by the Hotel Hana Maui, and open to the public to enjoy.

MAUI

`Ohe`o: The 7 Pools

At long last, ten winding miles after leaving Hana Town, the regulation U.S. National Park Service brown sign with yellow lettering indicating Haleakala National Park appears roadside. This district is officially known as Kipahulu, and the pools, `Ohe`o Gulch Pools. There **is no sign proclaiming "7 Pools"**. The more visited of the `Ohe`o Gulch Pools are located beneath the little concrete bridge that you will cross shortly after passing the brown Haleakala National Park sign. An unpaved parking area is located shortly after the bridge, makai. First-time visitors often miss these clues, and people have been known to drive right by here for many more long miles, not realizing that they had already passed the Pools area because they expected to see a "7 Pools" sign.

Park your car in the unpaved parking lot, and follow the path makai/seaward past the visitor center. The center sells a basic selection of books and maps of the Park area, but you will find a wider selection at larger island bookstores. Ask at the visitor center about any demonstrations or walks they might have scheduled while you are there. Calling beforehand is an even better idea. © (808) 248-8062 or (808) 572-9306. [As of this writing, a guided hike to Waimoku Falls is conducted Saturdays at 9 a.m., but there must be 4 or more people present. So if there aren't enough in your group, grab some strangers. The hike begins at the parking lot and lasts 4 hours. Bring lots of water.]

The path to the "7 Pools" meanders from the parking lot downhill past the visitor center, toward the ocean and across a grassy seaside bluff. Wander the bluff toward the ocean for solitude and spectacular coastal views, but don't enter these extremely dangerous waters.

We have to admit that we traveled through the 7 Pools / `Ohe`o Gulch Pools area at least 5 times before we ever actually explored the "7" Pools themselves. Each time we came this way, the Pools area below the bridge was crowded and very touristy. [We knew that there were many other fabulous Pools —more than two dozen—uphill from the bridge where few visitors ever go, so we explored those instead.] When we finally did wander the "7 Pools" area, we were quite impressed with their beauty and size. Many people walk the path from the parking area just to the bottom pool to take a quick look and go no further, so just because the parking lot is full doesn't mean all these people are swimming. Try to arrive well before noon and usually only a half dozen people will be swimming in the entire area. But by noon a long line of cars might be backed up on the Hana Highway waiting to enter the parking area.

Between noon and 3 p.m., the day tripping throngs arrive, and the pools can get quite crowded with bathers and looky-loos at that time.

The "7 Pools' cascade over waterfalls from pool to pool toward the ocean. Private places can be found, and there are plenty of rocky perches to dry out and sunbathe on. The view of the pools area from the bridge is super, but the road is quite narrow there, and standing on the bridge as cars try to squeeze by is dangerous. Park Rangers are available in the area to answer your questions. Heed their advice, for they have risked their lives on many occasions at 'Ohe`o to save —and sometimes lose—the same people that they had previously tried to caution. Too many people have died here taking foolish chances. It might be a perfectly sunny day at the 7 Pools while upstream it is raining torrents. When this happens, the volume of water in the stream and pools greatly and quickly increases. At the first sign of this happening, here or anywhere else in Hawaii, get out of the water —fast!

Uphill from the "7 Pools", a wonderful world exists for hikers, as two major waterfalls, many beautiful pools, an eerie bamboo forest, and a feast of wild edibles await. This is the same Waimoku Falls hike that park rangers lead on Saturdays, but if you'd like to go it alone, pick up a trail map at the visitor center. Use it in conjunction with Craig Chisholm's book Hawaiian Hiking Trails, published by The Fernglen Press, or one of the other good hiking guides available in Hawaii bookstores. The Park Service has recently built two bridges along this route to make things safer for hikers. The earlier in the day you make the hike, the cooler and more comfortable you will be. That first uphill leg through the pasture can really drain you if you do it under a hot sun. Bring lots of water.

To begin our hike, we passed through a break in the fence directly across the HANA HWY. from the visitor center's unpaved parking area. This is the trailhead. We walked up through the pasture, keeping 'Ohe`o Stream on our right. The open pasture segment of the hike has about a 500'/150m altitude gain. At a point that Chisholm's hiking guide book said was 800 paces from the trailhead, the trail forks. The right fork is a short path to the lip of 200'/61m Makahiku Falls. Stop and take a careful look. Further on, back on the main trail, the trail leads to the bridge crossings at `Ohe`o Stream. Before crossing, we hiked along the stream to explore. Peering carefully over a drop off, we saw the confluence of two waterfalls into a deep pool. The stream, when rain-swollen, can be swift and powerful enough to sweep the unwary over that edge. As tempting as it looks to jump in the deep-appearing pool on a calm, hot day, the park rangers told us that any recent submerged rock slides could make that adventure a deadly one. The locals always check out the depth before jumping in.

After crossing the bridges, you will soon enter the bamboo forest. It may be the bane of environmentalists due to its aggressive invasiveness, but the not-native-to-Hawaii bamboo forest is really quite beautiful. Over 30'/9m tall, this exotic forest is cool and dark and quite spooky. There is a raised wooden walkway to keep hikers from sinking in the mud. The winds that funnel up from the sea cause the leafy tops of the bamboo to sway, and as the poles below knock together in the gloom they produce sounds both beautiful and eerie, like primitive music. The different thicknesses of bamboo produce tones of differing pitch, which ring out staccato-like. And when the bamboo trunks scrape and rub against each other, the screeching and whistling mimic the sound of Tarzan movie jungle creatures.

After the bamboo forest, the trail continues through abandoned taro patches from farming days long past, now covered in Wandering Jew. During the day, mosquitoes won't land on you as long as you keep moving –or so they say– but we always bring repellent anyway, because as far as mosquitoes are concerned, we're a gourmet feast.

The trail, after the bamboo forest onward, is a veritable Garden of Eden of edibles, so banish any fear you have of starving to death. Bright red thimbleberries, similar to raspberries, are everywhere. So are guavas, which unlike mangoes, produce edible fruit year round; and mountain apples, passion fruit, yellow breadfruit, strawberry guavas (they look like cherry tomatoes and grow on a small tree), wild bananas, papayas, coconuts, avocados.... even edible, and delicious, fern tips, which taste something like asparagus. During the summer when the yellow ginger blooms, pick the flower, bite off the base where it joins the stem, and suck out the sweet nectar.

Soon, a glimpse of 400'/122m Waimoku Falls can be seen ahead. We walked another 300 paces to a fork in the stream where it was joined by another stream on its left. We crossed the left hand stream and followed the right hand stream about 250 paces beyond this fork, to Waimoku Falls, its waters taking the long plunge down the face of a horseshoe-shaped cliff into a shallow pool at its base. Hikers are welcome to cool off, but are cautioned never to pollute the waters with soaps or shampoos. We spent a good hour in that rocky ampitheater, feeling the mists, wading in the stream, and just looking up to see the top of the fall bathed in brilliant sunlight from our cool refuge below. We soaked up every bit of this natural air conditioning knowing what kind of heat awaited us in the pasture below. Many more waterfalls exist above Waimoku Falls, but an unsupervised hike there is a death-defying one. Ken Schmitt's **Hike Maui** [see page 13] *sometimes* leads a hike to the next major cascade above Waimoku.

The Waimoku Falls hike is a 4 mile / 6km round trip; 2 hours up, and an hour and a half down. Bring water!

Photographs

For photo locations, see the map on page 104.

❺ Detail shot of the base of 400' / 122m Waimoku Falls.

❻ Waimoku Falls' height is put into perspective by including bathers in this shot.

❼ At the `Ohe`o Pools, commonly and erroneously known as the 7 Sacred Pools, early morning crowds are so sparse that each person you see here found both a pool and a fall to call his own. But do come early. It gets jammed by noon.

❻❼ →

❺

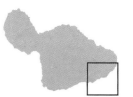

MAUI

The 'Ohe'o
Pools

❾

Kipahulu

*along an unpaved
section of the Hana Highway,
a horse hopes he can charm
the occupants of an
approaching car to stop and
feed him some fallen man-
goes which he cannot reach.
he does,
and they do.*

❸

❷

Kipahulu to Kaupo

MATCH THIS SYMBOL'S MAP NUMBER WITH THE CORRESPONDING PHOTO NUMBER TO LOCATE THE EXACT SPOT WHERE EACH PHOTOGRAPH WAS TAKEN.

The Hana Drive

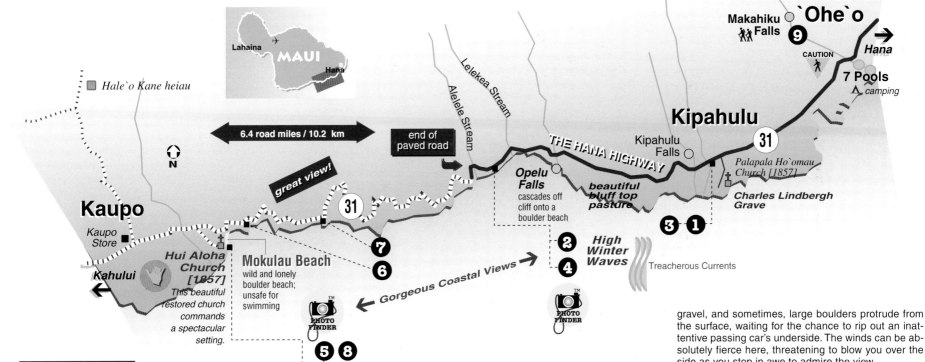

Photographs

9 These two shots of Makahiku Falls at `Ohe`o were taken less than a minute apart, yet you can see a significant difference in water volume between the two photos. Always be aware of the possibility of rapid water level changes in Hawaii's streams and pools. See Makahiku Falls location on maps on pages 104 & 109.

2 Near the border of Kipahulu and Kaupo, this view shows a section of the Hana Highway before and after paving and the addition of guardrails. Note Opelu Falls splashing onto the shore.

3 A hungry horse waits for a helping hand.

Perhaps if the Hana Drive to the 7 Pools frightened you, you may not want to drive any further than this, because now the real adventure begins.

Past the 7 Pools area, a number of people of means have made their homes in this lonely outpost named **Kipahulu**. One of the 20th century's greatest American heroes, **Charles A. Lindbergh**, chose to be buried here high on a bluff overlooking his beloved Pacific, at **Palapala Hoomau Congregational Church (c.1857)**. As he requested, he was laid to rest barefoot, dressed in khaki work clothes, in a plain eucalyptus wood casket. Against doctors' orders he left New York to die eight days later in Hana. He reportedly told the physicians, *"I'd rather live one day on Maui than one month in New York."*.

Uphill in the distance, the slopes and gullies of Mount Haleakala bleed white with dozens of waterfalls; horses graze peacefully atop glowing green cliff top pastures with mesmerizing Pacific views, and a little red-berried coffee plantation flourishes. Icy rushing streams

swiftly pass under the roadway one after another, only to spill over the rocky seacliffs and crash unappreciated on the boulder beaches below. The road hugs the very, very edge of the shore as breaking waves splash salty torrents over windshields, and signs caution drivers to blow their horns as they round the blind curves on this wild, ever-shrinking-as-we-go, single lane highway. And then suddenly, two and a half miles past 'Ohe'o, just when you thought it couldn't get any worse, the pavement ends.

The unpaved portion of the road is recommended for four wheel drive vehicles, and car rental agreements forbid driving off pavement, but, when conditions are dry, the passenger cars that local people drive don't seem to have any problems. The road is very rough, there's no doubt about that, and 5 mph in lowest gear seems like an optimum speed in many places. Road crews are ubiquitous in these parts, and their mammoth trucks can be frightening on narrow one lane roads. Pull over as soon as it is safe to do so to let them pass. We have found Maui's highway workers to be among Hawaii's most polite drivers, and they appreciate a cold drink if you have extra.

The road is composed of dirt stretches alternating with

gravel, and sometimes, large boulders protrude from the surface, waiting for the chance to rip out an inattentive passing car's underside. The winds can be absolutely fierce here, threatening to blow you over the side as you stop in awe to admire the view.

From the highway above, a blinding white apparition in the morning sun, **Hui Aloha Church**, surprises as it appears where one would least expect. The restored structure, built in **1857**, presides over a very isolated and solitary green finger of land that juts into the deep blue-violet sea, where waves crash onto a boulder beach and unfettered horses graze freely, friendly and grateful for the offering of a dog biscuit. The small entrance road, even rougher than the rutted unpaved highway itself, intersects it from the *makai* side at such a backward angle that its easy to miss. At the **HVB Warrior marker** (on the bluff overlooking the Bay) announcing Hui Aloha Church, set your odometer to 0. Then, **0.35 miles** down the road, look sharply *to the left* for the gravel road descending back toward Mokulau Bay and the church. A neat lava rock wall surrounds the little church and graveyard, where faces from the past stare back from the headstones. A tall freestanding lava rock ruin sits further out on the point where views encompass a wide-screen panorama of mountain slope, boundless ocean blue and wispy clouds brushing against the upper reaches of Haleakala. And way out there, far across Alenuihaha Channel, Mauna Loa towers, proudly snow capped, on the Big Island of Hawaii.

The **Hui Aloha Church** interior is spare and unadorned, and one wonders how the faithful can keep their minds on the service when there is so much wild and majestic beauty visible from every window.

On a table at the foot of the pulpit, a small cardboard box marked with a request for offerings from visitors lies violated, ripped open, and empty... a reminder that crime can exist in even the most isolated, unlikely and beautiful of places.

Photographs

4 Opelu Falls plunges from Kipahulu pasture lands into the deep azure sea.

5 Viewed from inside the Hui Aloha Church, windblown palm trees are framed by sunlit windowpanes.

6 A visitor stands on his car to get a better look at Hui Aloha Church (he can be seen at the right center edge of the photo). Hui Aloha must be among Hawaii's most spectacularly situated churches —and its most isolated.

7 In this area of wide open spaces, and unbridled wind and seas, the Hana Highway, as of this writing, remains unpaved.

8 Two horses find shade in the church's shadows.

5

4

Kaupo
the last outpost

❻

❽

❼

111

MATCH THIS SYMBOL'S **MAP NUMBER** WITH THE CORRESPONDING **PHOTO NUMBER** TO LOCATE THE EXACT SPOT WHERE EACH PHOTOGRAPH WAS TAKEN.

The road continues unpaved beyond Hui Aloha Church, where the surroundings become dryer and browner. At the profoundly isolated **Kaupo Store**, it might be a good idea to stop and pick up a snack or souvenir ...when its open. But don't count on it. The store operates on Maui time, meaning its open when its open and closed when its closed.

Beyond Kaupo, the Maui landscape takes on an otherworldly, desolate, Mars-like quality, with barren rusty colored slopes and deeply gouged gullies. It is stunning, awesome, and for some, disturbing. Beautiful in its own way, the road through this stark volcanic wonderland stretches for miles, and often you will not encounter another living soul, except for cows. Untamed winds blow unchecked over the barren landscape that is dotted in spring with wildflowers, and feral goats can be spotted climbing above.

This desolation, sadly, is of recent origin. Before man introduced goats and cattle, this entire area was covered with a native dry forest of halapepe and lama. About 15 miles after the Kaupo Store, the now-named

Kaupo Highway will enter the **Kanaio Natural Area Reserve** where the last remnants of this forest is now protected. The paved road resumes a few minutes before reaching Nu'u, more or less, and is now comparatively straight and fast, if bumpy, for the next 9 miles or so.

Seaside you will see old **Nu'u Landing**, and a mile beyond that, after crossing a dry riverbed, you can stop and walk up to a pool at the head of the gulch to see petroglyphs and caves. There are no swimmable beaches anywhere in this region, except perhaps at **Nu'u Beach** on a very calm day, but if its eerie isolation, wide open spaces and raw beauty you love, sit back and enjoy, for this is a wonderful place... totally unexpected... and quite the opposite of what many expect Maui to be like.

Photographs

1 The desolation of the Highway after passing Kaupo is very surprising, and in its own eerie way, quite beautiful.

2 Linda Domen poses for a portrait behind the counter at the Kaupo Store.

1

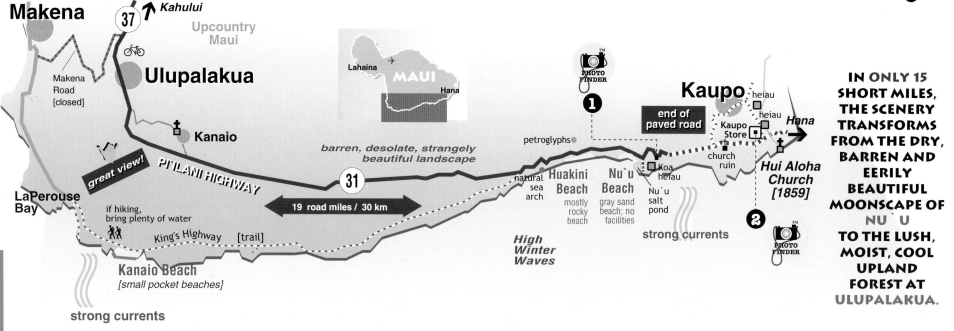

Makena

37 ↑ *Kahului*

Upcountry Maui

Ulupalakua

Makena Road [closed]

✝ **Kanaio**

LaPerouse Bay

if hiking, bring plenty of water

PI'ILANI HIGHWAY

great view!

King's Highway [trail]

Kanaio Beach [small pocket beaches]

strong currents

barren, desolate, strangely beautiful landscape

31

◄ 19 road miles / 30 km ►

natural sea arch

Huakini Beach mostly rocky beach

Nu'u Beach gray sand beach; no facilities

Nu'u salt pond

Koa heiau

High Winter Waves

strong currents

MAUI Lahaina / Hana

petroglyphs

end of paved road

Kaupo heiau / heiau

Kaupo Store

church ruin

Hui Aloha Church [1859]

Hana →

2

IN ONLY 15 SHORT MILES, THE SCENERY TRANSFORMS FROM THE DRY, BARREN AND EERILY BEAUTIFUL MOONSCAPE OF NU'U TO THE LUSH, MOIST, COOL UPLAND FOREST AT ULUPALAKUA.

MAUI

linda domen smiles from behind the counter at The Kaupo Store

Molokai The Most Hawaiian Island Of All

MOLOKAI

It is truly a challenge to keep up with the changes that take place among businesses on the island of Molokai. Since this book was first published in 1996, a dozen attractions, including the Hotel Molokai, Kaluakoi Resort, Kualapu`u Cookhouse, Molokai Mule Ride, Pau Hana Inn, the Halawa Falls Trail, Molokai Wildlife Park, and more, have opened, closed and *reopened*, some as many as three times. Just when we think we have to remove a closed business or attraction from this book, presto! Someone reopens it and life goes on as if nothing happened. We have had to accept that Molokai is forever in flux, and have decided to include these businesses even though one or more may not be operating at the time of your visit. We apologize for any confusion this may cause. But we hope we have partially solved this problem by providing current updates and additions on our website at <www.discoveringhawaii.com>.

Please write or email us if you encounter any changes we missed: <editor@discoveringhawaii.com>. When you arrive on Molokai, you can stop by the tourist information office in **Kaunakakai** with any questions you have. The staff loves meeting visitors. It is located in town at the **Kamoi Professional Building, Suite 700**. Call toll free from the US mainland, Canada, Alaska, US Virgin Islands and Puerto Rico ✆ **(800) 800-6367**. If you are in Hawaii as you read this, ✆ **553-3876** or **553-5221**. Or write to: **Moloka`i Visitors Association, Box 960, Kaunakakai HI 96748**.

Molokai is, without a doubt, the most underappreciated of all the Hawaiian Isles. Molokai's gifts to its visitors include unparalleled beauty, gracious and caring people, and a refreshing lack of tourists. Upon exploring this most Hawaiian of all the Hawaiian Islands, it is hard to understand how so much of its unique unspoiled majesty has thus far failed to capture the attention of the travel industry.

Molokai is as brim-full of awe inspiring beauty as its roads are devoid of traffic. Molokai is a motorist's dream and motorcyclists' heaven. Molokai's beaches are as fabulous as they are deserted. Molokai is nirvana for the stressed-out, heaven for golfers, bliss for privacy seekers, paradise found for explorers and adventurers...and sheer hell for party people. A popular local postcard shows nothing but a solid black rectangle on it with the caption "Molokai Nightlife".

Molokai's Western Shore is lined with superb beaches. It boasts Hawaii's widest, longest and most deserted public strand, **Papohaku Beach**, and the island's only true resort property, **Kaluakoi**. A short drive from this coast up toward the clouds reveals the plantation town of **Maunaloa**, whose isolation and tiny proportions belie the surprising sophistication of artwork and crafts found in its shops. On the western end of the north shore, **Mo'omomi Beach** caresses swimmers in the calm of summer, but sometimes swallows fishermen whole in stormy episodes when freak waves snatch them off their rocky perches. An extensive dune system at **Mo'omomi's Desert Strip** supports rare plant life found nowhere else. Along the western end's south shore, wondrously long and wide golden sandy beaches slumber, while often not a single footprint mars their wind-rippled surface.

At the Island's center, agricultural lands supporting macadamia and coffee trees surround the residential enclaves of Ho'olehua and Kualapu'u. An uphill turn on Hwy. 470 unfolds views of gorgeous pastures bathed in the golden light of late day rolling skyward to cool upland forests of pine, ironwood and eucalyptus. The road ends at **Pala'au State Park**, where just a one minute walk through the silent woods brings us to the lip of a sheer, seventeen hundred foot high rampart and a breathtaking view of beautiful **Kalaupapa Peninsula,** with its forlorn history as Hawaii's inhumane leper prison.

Molokai's South Shore for most of its eastern length is protected by reefs and decorated with a long necklace of fishponds. The principal town of **Kaunakakai** [pronounced *cow - nah - cock - eye*] is utilitarian rather than picturesque, but pleasant nonetheless. On Saturdays it bustles with activities surrounding a swap meet or a ball game, with locals lining up at the Kanemitsu Bakery for Molokai sweet bread and a few tourists buzzing around hunting for souvenirs. Startled, one sees purses, cassette players and other tempting valuables left unattended in the locals' cars parked on Ala Malama St., their windows wide open and doors unlocked. Just east of town, a string of lovely but narrow golden sand beaches begins, interrupted continually by rocky outcroppings and a multitude of fish ponds. At the 10 mile marker sleeps **Kamalo**, where a short dirt spur road leads to a little-used jetty. A walk out to the end of Kamalo Wharf rewards with a superb view back toward shore of the cloud shrouded blue valleys and gulches of Kamalo, dripping with a symphony of diaphanous waterfalls. As the Kamehameha Highway passes Kamalo, the road skirts the mountains and flashes tantalizing views deep into blue cathedral valleys to intrigue the motorist, but there is no access into their misty azure interiors, save for the penetration of a few faint and difficult ancient foot trails. The lovely and tiny white clapboard **St. Joseph's Church**, with a statue of its carpenter-builder Father Damien out front, awaits roadside.

The Kamehameha Highway winds and curves lazily as it skirts a number of pretty little palm-lined beaches, and the smooth, two lane highway soon shrinks to a narrower, undivided, heavily patched asphalt track. A few yards after this change, at mile marker 20, awaits the beautiful, classically tropical **Murphy's Beach**. Its golden sands are shaded in the afternoon by waving coconut palms and licked by becalmed, reef-protected turquoise waters that provide fine snorkeling grounds. Just around the next bend, the traditional ways of Hawaiians are still followed along **Honouli Wai Bay**, its taro fields fed by a stream with the same name. Near mile marker 21, surfers assemble to ride the best waves on this side of the island at **Pohakuloa Point**, known locally as **Rock Point**.

The scenery kicks into high gear as the road abandons the shore after passing little **Sandy Beach** and begins a winding climb into the vast pasture lands of the **Pu'u O Hoku (***Hill of Stars***) Ranch**, and through some of Hawaii's most unforgettable vistas. A couple of half-hidden dirt tracks on the seaward side of the road lead to superb coastal views reminiscent of California's Big Sur country. Pastures dotted with horses and cattle reach up to the cloud mists and roll down toward the sea, framing distant views of mysterious **Moku Ho'oniki** a mile offshore. The narrow road cuts a nasty gash in the hillsides as it passes under heavy canopies of pine-like Ironwood trees and over gurgling streams. A mile and a half before its terminus, at a hairpin turn, there is just enough room by the rail for a couple of cars to park and admire the expansive, inspiring view of **Halawa Valley**. Below, Halawa Beach is bisected by Halawa Stream as it empties into the bay, and when eyes search back into the valley for its source, majestic 500' **Hipuapua Falls** appears as a white thread in a vast fabric of green. The other pot of gold at the end of this rainbow is beautiful, two-stepped, 250' **Moa'ula Falls**. The one hour guided hike, conducted by local residents along the Moa'ula Falls Trail, ends at either of two of Hawaii's prettiest and most photogenic cascades. Enormous boulders in the stream bed furnish a perch for sunning. The chilly pools refresh the body, and the spirituality of this ancient place restores the soul, providing some of those rare moments when you realize just how lucky you are to be alive.

East Molokai Beaches

Traveling In A Counter-Clockwise Direction

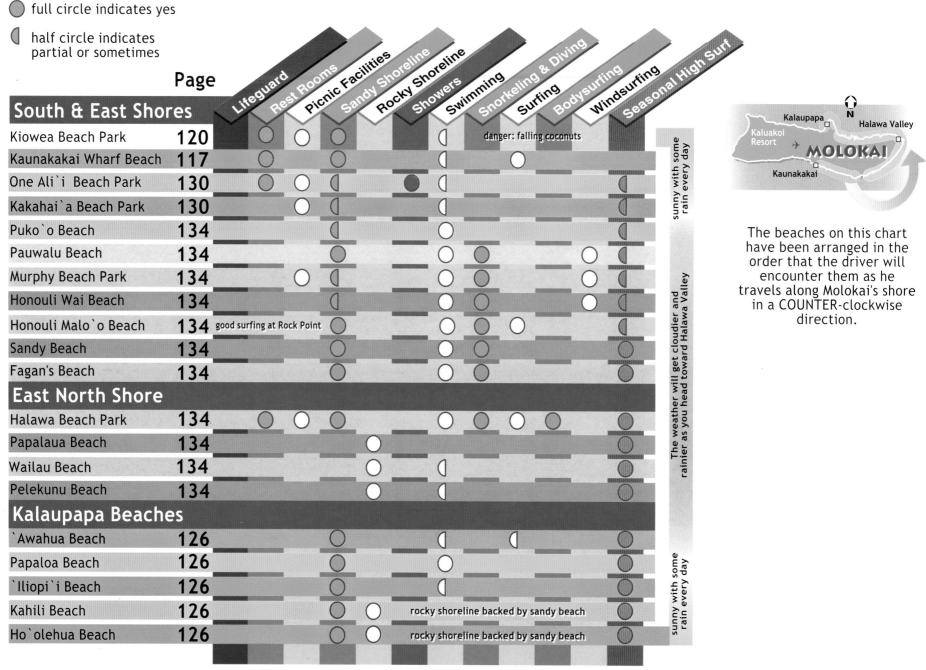

- ● full circle indicates yes
- ◐ half circle indicates partial or sometimes

	Page	Lifeguard	Rest Rooms	Picnic Facilities	Sandy Shoreline	Rocky Shoreline	Showers	Swimming	Snorkeling & Diving	Surfing	Bodysurfing	Windsurfing	Seasonal High Surf
South & East Shores													
Kiowea Beach Park	120		●	●			◐		danger: falling coconuts				
Kaunakakai Wharf Beach	117		●		●		◐		●				
One Ali`i Beach Park	130	●	●	◐		●	◐						◐
Kakahai`a Beach Park	130		●					●					◐
Puko`o Beach	134							●					◐
Pauwalu Beach	134			◐			●	●				●	◐
Murphy Beach Park	134		●				●	●				●	◐
Honouli Wai Beach	134			◐			●	●				●	◐
Honouli Malo`o Beach	134	good surfing at Rock Point	●				●	◐		●			◐
Sandy Beach	134			◐			●	●					◐
Fagan's Beach	134			◐			●	●					◐
East North Shore													
Halawa Beach Park	134	●	●	◐			●	●	●	●			◐
Papalaua Beach	134				●								◐
Wailau Beach	134				●		◐						◐
Pelekunu Beach	134				●								◐
Kalaupapa Beaches													
`Awahua Beach	126			◐			◐		◐				◐
Papaloa Beach	126			◐			●						◐
`Iliopi`i Beach	126			◐			◐						◐
Kahili Beach	126			◐	●	rocky shoreline backed by sandy beach							◐
Ho`olehua Beach	126			◐	●	rocky shoreline backed by sandy beach							◐

sunny with some rain every day

The weather will get cloudier and rainier as you head toward Halawa Valley

sunny with some rain every day

The beaches on this chart have been arranged in the order that the driver will encounter them as he travels along Molokai's shore in a COUNTER-clockwise direction.

Kalaupapa • Halawa Valley
Kaluakoi Resort
MOLOKAI
Kaunakakai

MOLOKAI

MATCH THIS SYMBOL'S MAP NUMBER WITH THE CORRESPONDING PHOTO NUMBER TO LOCATE THE EXACT SPOT WHERE EACH PHOTOGRAPH WAS TAKEN.

There is not one single traffic light on the island of Molokai, which gives you an idea of the size of its principal town, **Kaunakakai**, and the total volume of island traffic, which is practically nil. It does get a little busy in Kaunakakai on Saturdays when folks from all over the island come to town to shop or eat or take the ferry to visit family on Maui. Pick up a free copy of the **Molokai Advertiser News** or the **Molokai Dispatch** for all the latest local news and doings, and advertising by noteworthy new businesses that might not be included here.

As we stated previously, we have been caught off guard in the past by the unexpected closing of some long-time Molokai businesses. So please bear with us if some of the following are no longer around. A short walk down ALA MALAMA STREET will reveal whether any have closed or moved since this writing.

Beginning in town at Molokai's main crossroads with the Highway, ALA MALAMA STREET is Kaunakakai's main thoroughfare as it travels *mauka/toward the mountains*. At this intersection you will find the **tourist information office**, and behind it, a new mini mall with the popular **Molokai Pizza Cafe**. ALA MALAMA STREET passes the library, banks, and health food store before curving to the right where in a three block long grouping most of Molokai's shopping and eating places can be found.

Kanemitsu Bakery, on ALA MALAMA ST. *mauka*, is a magnet because of its 19 different breads, including the famous Molokai Sweet Bread, and cookies, but they also serve good meals at bargain prices. **Outpost Natural Foods**, 70 MAKAENA PL. *mauka*, specializes in making low- and nonfat taste great, and their take out counter serves a **bargain hot lunch** to enjoy on picnic tables outside until 3 p.m. **Molokai Fish & Dive** and **Molokai Island Creations**, ALA MALAMA ST. *mauka*, share a large space. Molokai Fish and Dive rents and sells sporting equipment, snorkeling gear, ice chests for your picnic, and boasts its own line of caps and T shirts. Molokai Island Creations is a fashion shop with many Molokai designs, and also sells jewelry and Hawaiian note cards, and **they have a large selection of books on Molokai and Hawaii**. Further down the street, **Molokai Surf** stocks surfing equipment, decals, and clothing, including "Nalu Molokai" T-shirts and sweats.

Friendly Market, **Takes Variety Store** and **Misaki's Groceries and Dry Goods** are all within a few steps of each other on the *makai* side of ALA MALAMA ST., and among the three you'll find just about everything you'll need in the way of food and general commodities. **Molokai Wines and Spirits** has a good selection of vintage wines as well as gourmet items. **Molokai Drugstore** is like a mini version of Long's drugs, carrying an impressive range of items, as well as **film and processing**, and has a **good selection of Hawaiiana books**.

Ask around about any **crafts fairs or flea markets** taking place during your stay, as they are great sources for unusual souvenirs. We always make it a point to check out **community bulletin boards** for goings-on we can attend or curious items for sale. Since Molokai is known as *"the most Hawaiian island"*, you might want to take part in local events, such as **Aloha Week** concerts at the community center, or the beginning of the **Molokai to Oahu outrigger canoe races** at Hale O Lono Harbor.

Kaunakakai residents are an interesting lot, ranging from a local cross dresser with kids in tow having lunch at the Molokai Pizza Cafe to the lady who fills your tank at the **Chevron Station** who's tickled pink to hear the Hawaiian music station playing on your car radio.

The station announces all the local gossip between songs, including weddings, births, visits by mainland relatives, and other important *'ohana* ("family") stuff. "That's what we call the *coconut wireless*", she says. "Its how we find out what's happening to our neighbors and friends all over Molokai and Maui". A testament to the high cost of living in paradise is the double takes you do, for example, upon recognizing that the guy who checked you in at your hotel desk is the same one who later, at the airport, also checks you in for your flight on Aloha Island Air. Many islanders hold two and three jobs in order to make ends meet.

One extraordinary sight we often see on our walks in Kaunakakai is valuable items, such as purses and electronic devices, left on the front seats of unattended, open-windowed, unlocked locals' cars parked along ALA MALAMA ST. Molokai certainly isn't crime free, but since in this small place just about everybody knows everybody else, the crime level is far below that of other islands.

The **Pau Hana Inn** is another integral Molokai business that has had its ups and downs over the years, and as of this writing, is rumored to be reopening yet again. Down the road, we like the Polynesian-style **Hotel Molokai**, local phone (808) **553-5347**, because it is close enough to, yet outside of town, about 2 miles east. The **Oceanfront Dining Room** [formerly named the *Holo Holo Kai*] at the Hotel Molokai has been our longtime personal favorite. We describe the Hotel Molokai fully in the **Halawa Valley Drive** section.

Traveling ALA MALAMA ST. *makai/toward the sea*, it changes names to WHARF ROAD after crossing the Highway. It then leads out to the end of **Kaunakakai Wharf**, where the ferry to Maui and commercial excursion boats dock, and the **Molokai Ice House** serves great plate lunches. In the evenings when we had to make phone calls we had a hard time finding a public phone where we were not eaten alive by mosquitoes. The phone booths on the wharf were a godsend...no mosquitoes there. Because the wharf extends very far into the harbor, it provides a great view of Kaunakakai town, Molokai's south coast, and the neighbor islands.

Traveling west from town on the highway, a large coconut grove known as **Kapuaiwa** promises some great classic Hawaii sunset shots, since the trees grow in tight profusion to the water's edge. The area is not well tended, which is a pity since a refurbishing would transform it into a really exceptional place. A WWII concrete bunker still sits at water's edge, and falling coconuts are a constant hazard to anyone walking among the trees (regard the signs). Sunset shots from the east end of **Kiowea Park** are best as this throws the trees and frond-littered ground into black silhouette against the brilliantly colored sky. Across the Highway from the coconut grove is Church Row, a grouping of interesting little churches of various architectural styles.

Photographs

See map on page 117 for these photo locations.

❶ The Molokai Public Library is located centertown on Ala Malama Street.

❷ Downtown Kaunakakai.

❸ At the end of the day, golden sunrays tint the Kapuaiwa Coconut grove.

❹ At Kiowea Beach Park, the Kapuaiwa Coconut Grove stands in silhouette against yet another wondrous Molokai Sunset. No filters were used for this shot.

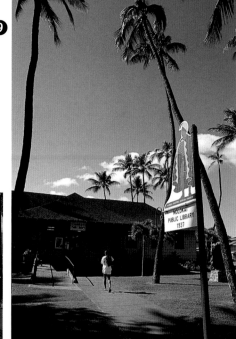

MOLOKAI

❹ *sunsets framed by molokai's* **Kapuaiwa** *coconut grove are among the prettiest in the world.*

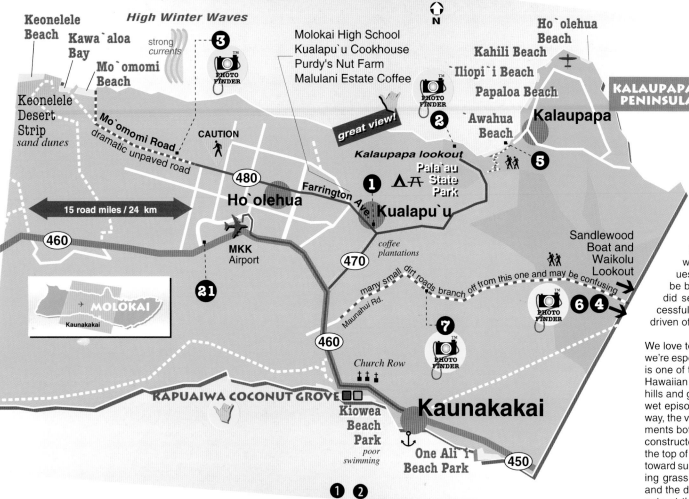

MOLOKAI

Keonelele Beach
Kawa`aloa Bay
Mo`omomi Beach

Keonelele Desert Strip
sand dunes

High Winter Waves
strong currents

Mo`omomi Road
dramatic unpaved road

CAUTION

Molokai High School
Kualapu`u Cookhouse
Purdy's Nut Farm
Malulani Estate Coffee

Ho`olehua Beach
Kahili Beach
`Iliopi`i Beach
Papaloa Beach
`Awahua Beach

KALAUPAPA PENINSULA

Kalaupapa

great view!

Kalaupapa lookout

Pala`au State Park

Ho`olehua

Farrington Ave.

480

460

15 road miles / 24 km

MKK Airport

MOLOKAI
Kaunakakai

Kualapu`u

coffee plantations

470

Maunahui Rd.

many small dirt roads branch off from this one and may be confusing

Sandlewood Boat and Waikolu Lookout

460

Church Row

KAPUAIWA COCONUT GROVE

Kiowea Beach Park
poor swimming

Kaunakakai

One Ali`i Beach Park

450

① ②

About 4.2 miles west of Kaunakakai, almost half way to the airport, HWY. 470 branches off from the main HWY 460, and **1.7 mile** later, across the road from beautiful coffee plantation and mountain views, FARRINGTON HIGHWAY intersects on the left. *Turn left on* FARRINGTON HWY. and drive through **Kualapu'u** town [we'll be coming back to visit later] **4.7 miles** to the end of the pavement. Although this road appears more residential neighborhood than rural, on a typical day quite a few horses will be tied up roadside, curiously watching us as we drive by. The road continues as a dirt jeep road, deeply rutted, which can be best handled by a 4WD vehicle, although we did see locals in small pick ups navigating successfully. Car rental agencies forbid their cars be driven off road.

We love to drive around and discover new things, and we're especially big suckers for picturesque roads. This is one of the prettiest in Hawaii: it passes through the Hawaiian Homelands, roller coastering through grassy hills and gulches that are colored emerald green after wet episodes or painted golden in dryer times. Either way, the vibrant rusty brilliance of the dirt road complements both hues beautifully. Handsome rustic fencing constructed from tree branches lines the way, and at the top of **Anahaki Gulch**, the winding road descends toward superb all-encompassing views of the surrounding grassland, the distant sand dunes at **Keonelele**, and the deep blue sea. When you come to the locked gate at the intersection, take the road *to the right* to visit **Mo'omomi Beach**. This even-more-deeply-rutted dirt road heads toward the water and a very popular fishing spot for locals. The beach here is not especially pretty in the winter, as its sands are carried away by the raging surf. But in summer the sands return, the seas calm down, and it becomes a popular swimming spot with locals. But because of strong currents and the inherent danger of the sea at this spot, we prefer to swim elsewhere. Walking along the shore toward the west will reveal a number of small isolated sandy pocket beaches. The rocks along shore are often strewn with unsightly flotsam and jetsam of every description, including litter left behind by the uncaring. The seas often rage along the north shore, and a number of locals who have spent many years of their lives fishing from these rocks have been swept to their deaths by

Moʻomomi Road

winds and roller-coasters its way through hawaiian homestead lands to the protected and unique moʻomomi dunes.

③

rogue waves. If it can happen to them, it can certainly happen to us, so we keep well away from the crashing surf.

West of Mo'omomi Beach are the **Mo'omomi (Keonelele) Dunes**, now under the protection of the Nature Conservancy. Monthly hikes are offered to this, one of Hawaii's last remaining intact coastal ecosystems, on one Sunday each month. The hike lasts about 5 hours, and although there is no charge to join the hike, donations to the Conservancy are welcomed. For details and reservations (hikes are often filled months in advance), write to **The Nature Conservancy, PO Box 220, Kualapu`u HI 96757. ✆ (808) 553-5236.**

Doubling back the way we came we stop for pictures and stare back at the horses and dogs along FARRINGTON HWY. who watch us with great interest. **Kualapu'u** was a plantation town when Del Monte was king, but now the surrounding lands grow coffee, macadamia nuts, corn and other crops. The road passes Molokai High School, where the students have decorated the exterior walls with epic undersea murals. The **Malulani Estate Coffee** [✆ 538-0080] warehouse sends heavenly scents of roasting Molokai-grown beans into the air, while the **Kualapu`u Cookhouse**, the "International Home of Slow Food" [✆ 567-6185] rustles up, in our opinion, **the best plate lunches in the state of Hawaii:** copious portions, with tons of fresh veggies and generous amounts of meat in the stir fry dishes. The menu is huge. They're open 'til 8pm weekdays. The Cookhouse is locally famous for its very dense, very chocolatey chocolate macadamia nut pie. Across the road from the restaurant the **Kualapu'u Market** is an after-school magnet for local kids who zoom around on their inline skates, talk on the pay phones, and socialize.

At the intersection with HWY. 470, *turn left uphill.* This is KALA'E HWY. The **R.W.Meyer Sugar Mill** [✆ 567-6436] is a star attraction here. The only surviving 19th century sugar mill in Hawaii has been restored to operating condition, and along with photographs, provides a vivid glimpse into the lives and times of those who worked Molokai's plantation.

The countryside as you ascend toward **Pala'au State Park** is exquisite, especially late in the afternoon. Undulating pasture lands rise toward forests of ironwood, pine, koa and eucalyptus and roll down toward distant views of Mo'omomi Dunes and West Molokai. Landscape photography opportunities abound here as the sun and clouds pattern the scene, and cattle and horses graze peacefully.

Entering the park, the **Molokai Mule Ride** barn will be on the left. The thrilling Mule Ride descends the steep, switchback Kalauapapa Trail to `Awahua Beach. ✆ **(800) 567-7550. You** can alternately check with the **Destination Molokai Association** ✆ **(800) 800-6367,**

toll free from the mainland, or if you are on Molokai, ✆ **553-3876,** or call one of the Kalaupapa Tour operators, such as **Damien Tours,** ✆ **567-6171.** At any rate, the top of the *newly restored trail* is on the right, just up ahead, but you cannot walk it without a permit. If its an unforgettable view of Kalaupapa you want, the best one is visible from the **Kalaupapa Lookout** a little further along the road. Drive to the end of the highway, past the picnic grounds, to the parking area. Signs direct you to a short, one-minute-long path through the woods to the overlook. The spectacle is lovely and gives little hint as to the horrors that once existed far below. Fresh winds blow up from the sea and the silence of the place is appropriate for contemplating the peninsula. Plaques at the overlook give a nutshell summation of the history of the leper colony at Kalaupapa.

Another longer uphill path leads to the infamous **phallic stone,** still a traditional place for women wishing to conceive a child to pay a visit, straddle the stone, and leave an offering. The surrounding forest is a little eerie and quite silent, and often times you'll see money offerings piled in a depression on the stone.

Photographs

Photo **21** on the map is located on page 160.
For the photo locations in this section, see map, page 120.

previous page:

1 The Kualapu`u Cookhouse.

2 The Phallic Stone, a ten minute hike through the forest at the end of Hwy. 470, is still visited today by women who wish to conceive. Offerings of money and other goods are left on the Stone by believers.

3 Unpaved Mo`omomi Rd., one of Hawaii's most dramatic, plunges in and out of gulches on its way to the sea.

this page:

4 Waikolu Lookout is so remote that at times even a 4WD can't get through the ten miles of uphill, muddy, rutted road. The clouds seen here disappeared just as quickly as they materialized.

5 Kalaupapa Lookout is just a one minute walk through the woods at the end of Hwy. 470. Story boards explain what you are viewing.

4

5

the **Kalaupapa overlook** *at molokai's pala`au state park*

Waikolu Lookout

On a clear day, for those with a private or 4WD vehicle, an adventurous and visually stunning trip awaits up MAUNAHUI ROAD. As we know from experience, not all Molokai roads are marked with street signs, and this is sometimes the case here. MAUNAHUI ROAD is also known as MAIN FOREST ROAD.

Coming from the airport *toward* the town of **Kaunakakai**, MAUNAHUI or MAIN FOREST ROAD is situated immediately after the bridge on the left hand side of the road, just after the **4 mile marker** —which at this point is located at the **left side of the road** facing oncoming traffic.

Coming from the town of Kaunakakai toward the **airport**, MAUNAHUI or MAIN FOREST ROAD is located on the **right**, immediately before the bridge, a little **before mile marker 4**, and just past the Seventh Day Adventist Church and School which are also on the right hand side of the road.

The paved road almost immediately turns into a dirt track after it passes the **Homelani Cemetery** and ascends into the mountains for 13 miles. This dirt road can become impassable for all vehicles after a heavy rainy episode, but at dry times we have seen locals' passenger cars driving it slowly with no problems. The **Sierra Club** schedules hikes through this area as well as other difficult-to-reach places elsewhere on Molokai and Maui, so call or write for dates and information. The tourist office in Kaunakakai will tell you if anyone is currently offering guided 4WD excursions into the area. The latest information for this area including road conditions is available from the **Dept. of Land and Natural Resources**, ✆ **(808) 567-6618, and from the Kamakou Preserve Manager, PO Box 40, Kualapu'u HI 96757.** ✆ **(808) 567-6680.**

Set your vehicle odometer to 0. The road climbs through handsome pasture lands (look behind you as you go for some nice views) for **3.7 miles** before trees start appearing. At **4.7 miles**, a young forest struggles to grow up, and at **5.1** or thereabouts, if it hasn't rained lately, you might see red dust covering all the trees, trunks and brush roadside. At **5.5**, you'll reach the forest boundary, plainly marked with a large sign. At **5.7**, you will come to a fork in the road. **Take the fork to the right.** You'll know you're on track when at **5.8** you pass the **Nature Conservancy Camp on the left.** You might want to stop to admire the woodcarver's art located at roadside, including the bearded portrait on the tree trunk, and a fanciful 3D hiking map of the trails that await up ahead. At **6.5**, towering Norfolk pine-shaded road embankments are carpeted in green fern. Ignore the many little side roads that branch off MAIN FOREST ROAD.

At approximately the **10 mile point** you will come to **Waikolu Overlook**, where *after heavy upland rains*, spectacular cascades of water numbering in the dozens tumble toward the valley floor almost 4000 feet / 1544 meters below. The Lookout is located at the 3600 foot / 1390 meters elevation and includes a magnificent panorama of **Waikolu Valley** from the verdant cliffs of the upper gorge. Red ohia blossoms on grizzled grey tree branches frame views of seacliffs, offshore islands, and the waterfalls and plunge pools that stairstep the vertical canyon walls. Even on clear days the view is often obscured in the afternoons when tradewind clouds envelop the upper canyon.

Competing with the views are some memorable sounds...the staccato flutter of a bird's wings as the flighted creature makes a breakneck direction change in the lifting currents, avian songs ricochetting off cliff sides, and the distant rush of waterfalls echoing through the valley. From the almost sheer pali walls, unreachable by humans, come the confident bleats of goats, mindlessly inflicting their irreversible damage on Hawaii's fragile environment. Often, there will be not a breeze, nor any sound, and then suddenly, the vast silence may be broken by the buzz of a solitary fly or bee.

Clouds erupt out of nothingness at the bottom of the valley right before your eyes, then waft up along the pali walls or through the center of the valley. Windows in the clouds reveal beautifully framed vignettes of waterfalls, hundreds of feet high, dripping down sheer rocky walls lined in the brightest of green growth. Is it moss? Ferns? Its so very far away, that even through a telephoto lens we can't discern. The red ohia blossoms that dot the twisted, gnarled and peeling silvery tree branches provide a colorful frame for the constantly changing scene. Looking far down to the sea at the mouth of the valley, lonely Okala Island stands sentinel just offshore. The waters of Waikolu Stream reflect silvery light and rush toward the ocean to embrace the incoming tide. The sun peeks through cloud windows and projects fast moving jigsaw puzzle pieces of light on the towering valley walls. The gorge suddenly becomes enveloped in a solid gray mass of clouds, the sun disappears, and yet from the depths of this opaque soup, birds zoom at warp speed out of the gloom, then immediately dive back in again, skillfully avoiding obstacles that we can't see even though we're standing still. Soon, the sun returns once again as the clouds disappear as quickly as they materialized.

Across the road from the Lookout there's an open sided pavilion with picnic tables and a very primitive restroom, which is made all the worse by the destruction wrought by vandals. No drinking water is available here; you must bring your own.

Past the Lookout, *the road worsens* still. A short walk along **Hanalilolio Trail**, which begins at a shoulder

turnout on the left, off the MAIN FOREST ROAD **0.2 mile** past Waikolu Lookout, will reveal other splendid views. This trail begins at 3500' / 1350m elevation, connecting with other trails that stretch on and on through the **Kamakou Reserve** to the delight of adventurers in search of strenuous, sweaty, challenging treks. One leads to an incredible view of neighboring **Pelekunu Valley**, whose sea cliffs are the highest in the world. The gates you will encounter along the way protect the area from destruction by *feral animals*. **Please make sure you close them securely behind you.**

The Kamakou Preserve contains excellent examples of cloud forests, bogs, mesic forests and shrublands which are prime habitat for many species of endangered plants and forest birds. The Preserve is part of the nationwide network of preserves set aside for the purpose of protecting America's unique environments.

A muddy three hour round trip from the Waikolu Lookout will take hikers through dense native cloud forest to **Pepeopae Bog**, where a wooden boardwalk keeps hikers from sinking deep in mud and protects the unique plant life from foot traffic damage. Ohia trees that grow to full height down slope, are here dwarfed to just a few inches in height. This precious piece of wilderness is one of the very last pockets of intact, unadulterated, pristine Hawaii left.

Photographs

For these photo locations, see map on page 120.

❻ This view from Waikolu Lookout was taken just a few minutes after the shot on page 122. What a difference a few minutes can make. When it comes to photography, it often pays to hang around a little while.

❼ On the way back down from Waikolu Lookout, this beautiful and unexpected tree carving greets travelers at the Nature Conservancy Camp on Maunahui Road.

Waikolu

MATCH THIS SYMBOL'S MAP NUMBER WITH THE CORRESPONDING PHOTO NUMBER TO LOCATE THE EXACT SPOT WHERE EACH PHOTOGRAPH WAS TAKEN.

Photographs

❶ The graveyard at St. Philomena's Church occupies a magnificent setting. Both Father Damien and Mother Marianne are buried here.

❷ Another stunner, this stormy view of Molokai's wild and wondrous North Shore was taken just east of the graveyard, at Judd Park in Kalawao.

Kalaupapa was chosen in 1866 as the dumping site for Hawaii's ailing, reviled and unwanted lepers. It was believed, due to its isolation and sheer 1600' cliffs, that banishing lepers to Kalaupapa would stop the spread of the disease.

The unfortunate were abandoned here with no shelter and only a ten day ration of provisions. Survival for the majority was measured in mere weeks. In 1873 a 33 year old Belgian Catholic Priest named Father Damien arrived on a two week mission, and was so taken with the lepers' horrific plight, that he stayed on for the rest of his life. He resettled the patients from blustery Kalawao to the less exposed Kalaupapa; he organized agriculture and water procurement, he built shelter and churches and motivated outsiders to join in aiding these hapless victims of man's inhumanity to man.

Flying into Kalaupapa's edge-of-the-planet airstrip is quite an adventure. Just a brief ten minute trip from Molokai's Ho'olehua airport, it has to be one of the world's most beautiful, and shortest, scheduled flights. The tiny Air Molokai or Aloha Island Air twin engine craft climbs up toward Pu'u Anoano after takeoff before veering a little left, and if you get to sit in the copilot's seat, the dizzying sensation of clearing the sea cliffs to abruptly see the cobalt Pacific 2000' even further below is better than any Disney ride. You fly along the cliffs and watch the dappled sun dance on their lush green walls as Makanalua Peninsula grows larger and details of Kalaupapa town's buildings become clearer. The plane touches down as huge waves crash on rocks at the end of the runway ahead, then taxis to the tiny terminal building, so small that it's fully shaded by a single tree.

Here you must wait for your tour guide, as unaccompanied visitors are not allowed to roam free on Kalaupapa. In our case, Richard Marks of **Damien Tours** was our steersman, and we were loaded onto the tour bus and immediately headed through town to meet other visitors who had hiked down the newly restored switchback mule trail from near the Kalaupapa Lookout in Pala'au State Park. Here we found **'Awahua Beach**, a beautiful dark sand beach, unsafe for swimming, its wide curve photogenically backed by an echoing of seacliffs plunging into the sea.

The tour proceeds through town, stopping at sites chosen by Richard or by popular demand, including an interesting visitors center and bookshop. The bookshop has an extraordinary exhibit that includes patient-invented gadgets which allowed them to accomplish normally simple tasks made difficult for those with missing fingers. After town, the bus proceeds across the peninsula, through the **Haunted Forest** to a lunch stop at **Judd Park** at road's end. From here, the views along the north shore seacliffs —their peaks usually shrouded in clouds, and rains often falling in their valleys— are wondrous. The distinctively shaped small offshore islands, Mokapu, furthest out, and Okala closer in, echo the contour of the cliffs, and great waves crash against both them and rocky Waikolu Beach in showy white display. We are at **Kalawao**, the original site of the leper colony, where patients were dumped unceremoniously into the terrifying sea for the next-to-impossible swim to shore...a shore providing no shelter, no food, no medicine. A shore from which there would be no leaving. A shore where friends and family would never be seen again.

As he drives his tour bus around the colony, Richard's stories of bureaucratic ineptitudes and stupidities at the expense of the residents' well being, as well as the pocketbooks of Hawaii's taxpayers, raise one's blood

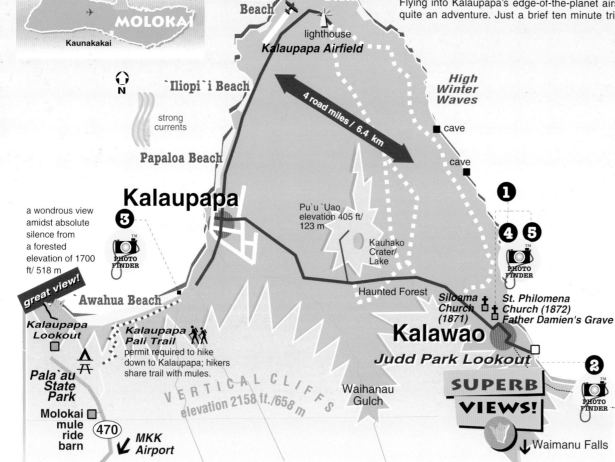

Kalaupapa

❷

pressure. His tales of the barbaric treatment the lepers received from those who transported them here are heartbreaking. They were literally kicked overboard, weak and desperately sick, into the roiling sea —expected somehow to make their way to shore. Uncounted numbers never did.

And after about two hours of intermittent horror stories as to the ways and whys of the lepers' subhuman treatment by others in their time, Richard skillfully draws a disturbing comparison to society's present day attitudes towards those with AIDS. And at that moment, as revealed in the newly enlightened faces of some of those on the tour, it seems that perhaps Mr. Marks has successfully planted the seeds of empathy in more than a few visitors' hearts.

Richard Marks' personal experience with Kalaupapa began at age 9 when he accompanied his own father to the commencement of his life sentence here after contracting leprosy. Richard stayed in the visitors quarters, while Kalaupapa's prisoners lined up outside upon his arrival. All were sheathed in bandages; most were horribly disfigured and crippled, and few of them could recall what a "clean" child looked like. And so they came to stare. And to remember. And to cry. Their bodies were covered in huge open sores, and the smell, Richard said, was appalling. As the years passed, Richard's nightmare wouldn't go away, as one by one, other family members exhibited manifestations of the disease, and were taken away. Then finally, in 1956, Richard himself tested positive for Hansen's disease, and was banished here.

Although the discovery of sulfone drugs in 1946 arrested the symptoms of the affliction, it wasn't until 1969 that other drugs terminated the danger of contagion, and the requirement of quarantine. After that, patients were allowed to leave Kalaupapa, but many were so disfigured that they preferred to stay, feeling more comfortable living here among their own. Today, only a few dozen remain.

After the Judd Park lunch stop, the bus rolls back to beautifully restored St. Philomena's Church, with its neat lava rock cemetery walls. Past the church a lovely country lane winds toward the lush, mist-enshrouded pali, and beyond the trees, to beautiful and poignant views. In the church graveyard rest some of **Father Damien's** bones —actually, just one of his hands— returned from Belgium in preparation for his canonization as a saint by the Catholic Church. Close by lies **Mother Marianne**, the Catholic nun who devoted her life to the lepers of Kalaupapa. She is also a candidate for sainthood. This setting remains the most heartbreakingly beautiful in all of Hawaii.

If you book ahead for the long tour (ask about it when you call), the bus will climb to the top of **Kauhako Crater** for panoramic views of the whole peninsula, and

will also tour the shoreline perimeter of the peninsula. After the tour's end, the bus returns to the airstrip for the return flight.

If you are flying into Kalaupapa from Honolulu, booking your flight through Damien Tours will save you money over other package tours. **Damien Tours** can be reached at ✆ **(808) 567-6171.**

If flying between Maui and Molokai, **Aloha Island Air** offers a spectacular Twin Otter flight via Kalaupapa that flies at the 3000' cliff level along Molokai's north shore —if the weather and visibility are good. You have to ask the pilot to do this. Otherwise he'll fly the normal instrument route which is much further out to sea.

Photographs

❸ `Awahua Beach, West Kalaupapa.

❹ Father Damien's grave marker at St. Philomena's Church in Kalawao.

❺ The newly restored exterior of St. Philomena's Church.

❸

Father Damien and Mother Marianne: Hawaii's Super Heroes

Father Damien de Veuster is Hawaii's first son to be designated by the Catholic Church for canonization as a saint. For this occa-sion, some of his bones were moved from their burial site in Belgium back to their original resting place among the lepers of Molokai. Buried near him in the beautiful graveyard of St. Philomena's Church at Kalaupapa is Mother Marianne, herself a candidate for sainthood. Both individuals demonstrated an almost unfathomable dedication to the lepers of Molokai, and in today's world —or even yesterday's, for that matter—their degree of self sacrifice cannot be easily understood.

Damien, the Hero of Molokai, came to Hawaii as a young deacon to replace his brother Pamphile, who had become ill after having been assigned by the Church to the islands. Damien was ordained a priest in downtown Honolulu, in the Cathedral of Our Lady of Peace, still located today at Bishop and Beretania Streets, in May of 1864. He was assigned to the Puna district on the Big Island until 1873, at which time he volunteered to care for the patients in the leper settlement at Kalaupapa. Originally the assignment was to last only a few months, but it stretched on to encompass the rest of his life.

His energy and untiring nature taxes the imagination. A carpenter and builder by trade, he constructed 2,000 coffins, numerous churches, dozens of homes, and a hospital; he planted orchards for food, constructed a water system to bring fresh water from the mountains above, moved the entire settlement to a more sheltered location and acted as sheriff and mayor to keep order. He truly acted as "Father" to the settlers. He gave hope and direction to the doomed and demoralized throngs by encouraging and incorporating their skills and their diminishing energies in the development of the settlement's master plan. He infused hope and purpose in people who felt they had lost everything.

He himself developed Hansen's disease in 1876 and subsequently suffered from its pestilence for thirteen years. Yet a year before his death, crippled and going blind, he could be seen working alongside the construction crew on the roof of St. Philomena's Church, supervising their labors.

At age 45, when most people start thinking about slowing down and living an easier life, Mother Marianne took a leave of absence from her sheltered and respected position as a Mother Superior in the Franciscan Order of nuns in Syracuse, N.Y. to join a group of missionaries heading to Hawaii. For five years she toiled among the afflicted and despairing in Honolulu at the Kaka'ako Branch Hospital for Lepers. Feeling that her true calling was service among the lepers and the dying Father Damien at Kalaupapa, she joined two other nuns on a journey to a place termed "unfit for white women".

She, along with Sister Leopolda Burns and Sister Vincent McCormick, arrived in Kalaupapa in November 1888 to bathe the open sores, bind the rotting stumps and attend to the physical and spiritual needs of the dying lepers. She was intrepid in the face of the lawlessness that marked Kalaupapa, suffering thievery and blatant threats to her well being. Like Damien, she found meaningful projects and goals for hopelessly idle hands, giving meaning to the lives of those who had little to exist for previous to meeting her. She routinely visited other outlying Franciscan missions, overseeing schools, hospitals and orphanages on three other islands.

Mother Marianne continued laboring until her 78th year, when she fell ill. She died in 1918, at age 80. In 1974, preliminary investigation was commenced for the process of beatification upon Mother Marianne of Molokai.

FATHER DAMIEN

❹

Kalaupapa

129

❺

MATCH THIS SYMBOL'S MAP NUMBER WITH THE CORRESPONDING PHOTO NUMBER TO LOCATE THE EXACT SPOT WHERE EACH PHOTOGRAPH WAS TAKEN.

PHOTO FINDER

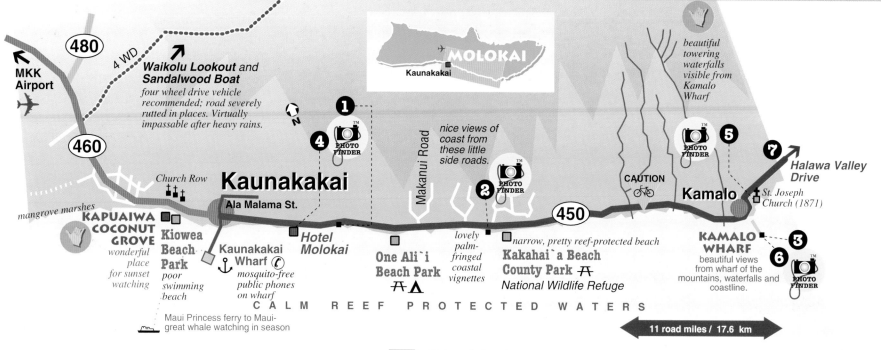

MOLOKAI
Kaunakakai

480

↖ MKK Airport

4 WD

↗ **Waikolu Lookout** and **Sandalwood Boat**
four wheel drive vehicle recommended; road severely rutted in places. Virtually impassable after heavy rains.

460

N

Church Row

Kaunakakai
Ala Malama St.

❶

❹ PHOTO FINDER

Makanui Road

nice views of coast from these little side roads.

❷ PHOTO FINDER

450

CAUTION 🚲

❺ PHOTO FINDER

Kamalo

St. Joseph Church (1871)

❼

beautiful towering waterfalls visible from Kamalo Wharf

↗ **Halawa Valley Drive**

mangrove marshes

KAPUAIWA COCONUT GROVE
wonderful place for sunset watching

Kiowea Beach Park
poor swimming beach

Kaunakakai Wharf ⚓
mosquito-free public phones on wharf

Hotel Molokai

One Ali`i Beach Park ⛩ ⛺

lovely palm-fringed coastal vignettes

narrow, pretty reef-protected beach

Kakahai`a Beach County Park ⛩
National Wildlife Refuge

KAMALO WHARF
beautiful views from wharf of the mountains, waterfalls and coastline.

❸

❻ PHOTO FINDER

C A L M   R E E F   P R O T E C T E D   W A T E R S

⛴ Maui Princess ferry to Maui- great whale watching in season

◄— 11 road miles / 17.6 km —►

❶

MOLOKAI

The Halawa Falls Drive was a complete surprise to us the first time we drove its length. All we were trying to do was get from the town of Kaunakakai to **Moa'ula Falls** in Halawa Valley, and assumed that not too much of interest lay between. Boy, were we wrong! No photo book or travel article had given us any idea of what to expect, or pictured what it was like, and in all the years that we've been hearing bits and pieces about Molokai, nobody had ever even mentioned it.

Combining the best of Maui's Hana Drive and its Rugged Northwest Coast Drive, but on a more compact scale, the Halawa Valley Drive rambles along Molokai's fishpond-scalloped south coast, past beautiful deserted golden sand beaches, misty blue valleys awash with numberless waterfalls, scores of handsome homes and neat farms, and primeval rocky headlands mercilessly pounded by the sea. It curves and winds along, disgorging beautiful dreamy views of Maui across the channel while laughing kids on their way to school stop a moment to pet horses tethered at roadside. Clinging to the very edge of the land, it meanders past an isolated settlement where the old Hawaiian way of life is nurtured still, and then inches past surfers' vans parked at Pohakuloa Point. It climbs up into 16,000 acres of green, manicured ranchland, where cattle rule over the unfolding green and gold spectacle and the road dips and gouges its way through hillsides shaded by little

forests of ironwood.

For a grand finale, before ending its journey, the highway glides into a valley so breathtaking —where glorious shafts of sunlight beam through rapidly moving clouds and towering waterfalls stand watch— that God must surely live there. Finally, the highway clings and hairpins along the edge of sheer precipices where an occasional stingy turnout provides just enough room to stop and capture snapshots of the unforgettable vistas of beautiful **Halawa Bay** and 500' **Hipuapua Falls**.

To begin, depart from the main crossroads in Kaunakaka. Drive *east* along KAMEHAMEHA HIGHWAY, which has changed numbers now from HWY. 460 to HWY. 450. The road is lined with residences, and passes both the **Pau Hana Inn** and the **Hotel Molokai**.

The **Hotel Molokai** is a great favorite of ours. It is reminiscent of the kind of colorful places that escapist South Seas novels of the 1940s and '50s introduced us to... a little eccentric, a little bohemian, with a thousand stories to tell and with wonderful characters working and staying there. The hotel is constructed in the style of a Polynesian village, its bungalows topped with pitched roofs slung in a distinctively South Seas style, and bas-

❷

❸

Photographs

For these photo locations, see the map on page 130.

❶ About 0.5 mile before/ west of One Ali`i Beach Park, a coconut grove serves as a tropical background to another Molokai sunrise.

❷ Kakaha`i Beach County Park.

❸ A beautiful early morning view photographed from the Kamalo Wharf highlights the local waterfalls.

❹ The Hotel Molokai feels, and looks, much more like a South Seas village than a hotel

❹

ket swings hang on the lanais. The property is set right on the reef-calmed waters, and the well tended landscaping encompasses a veritable tropical botanical garden on a compact scale, including creamy pink seashell ginger, breadfruit trees, brilliant red and yellow pendulums of heliconia suspended in the breeze, white plumeria, and red torch ginger. There is no TV or telephone at the Hotel Molokai to interrupt the mainland decompression process. Each room has a small refrigerator, and there is full maid service.

The staff is charming, accommodating and genuine. Running out of film one Friday, I was worried that a package of Kodachrome™ that I had sent to me at the hotel might not arrive in time, and I expressed my concern to Paula Murray, who was managing the Hotel Molokai's open air front desk. It had been sent via US Mail, and the post office was only going to be open for two hours on Saturday. I was starting to feel desperate. Molokai is a tiny place, and I soon discovered how quickly word can get around. I walked into the post office on Saturday morning to be greeted by name by a lady I had never seen before, and was presented my precious package with a big smile and a lot of friendly small talk and aloha. "Paula was really worried you wouldn't get this in time", she intoned concernedly as she handed it over. Back at the hotel, I proudly flashed my package to Paula, who sighed with relief and said, "I was so worried! I stopped by the post office last night on my way home to peek in the window, and when I saw a box there with the Priority Mail stickers, I knew it had to be yours. Now I'm happy."

The Hotel Molokai's open air bar, the **Oceanfront Lounge**, faces its open air **Oceanfront Dining Room**, which is right next to the pool. During the day a small cast of characters befitting a *Gilligan's Island* audition appears. The group during our stays have been entertaining, colorful and mysterious, hailing from Berlin and Tokyo, Tahiti and Quèbec. Offshore, a few fishermen wade relentlessly out toward the beckoning island of Lana`i until they are mere specks, yet the shallow waters never rise above their knees. If it's quiet, and it usually is, waves can be heard crashing far out on the barrier reef. Breakfast and lunch are delightfully lazy and laid back at the Oceanfront Dining Room, where you can dreamily sit and nurse your morning coffee forever if you'd like. At night, when the lights are low and the profile of Lana`i shines across the channel in the moonlight, and the soft romantic Hawaiian songs of local entertainers accompany dinner, the mood is uniquely Molokai's own. Call **(808) 553-5347** for information and reservations, or log on to their website at <www.hotelmolokai.com>

Five minutes after passing the Hotel Molokai, **One Ali`i Beach Park** appears with its playing fields, pavilions and picnic tables, but it has only a so-so beach, consisting of a mix of coral rubble and sand. A couple of minutes after One Ali`i Beach Park, a *left turn* on

MAKANUI ROAD will take you to uphill to an upscale neighborhood of handsome newer homes with pretty coastal views of the area's fishponds, the neighbor islands of Maui and Lana`i, and endless horizons.

Between **MM [mile marker] 5 and 6**, the lovely narrow sandy beach at **Kakahaia County Park and National Wildlife Refuge** provides some less than ideal reef sheltered water play, its shore bottom shallow and rocky. Around **MM 6**, trees and brush obscure the shore. A short walk *makai/seaward* reveals that these trees grow right up to the water's edge, making sunbathing impossible. If you're anxious to stretch out on a good beach, you'll have to wait until we get closer to the MM 15. Right after the **MM 9**, an open area with roadside shoulder parking provides your first good glimpse into the deep gorges and valleys of Kamalo.

At **MM 10** sleeps the settlement of **Kamalo**, where a short dirt spur road leads *makai/seaward* to a little-used jetty. A walk out to the end of **Kamalo Wharf** rewards with a **superb view** back toward shore of the cloud shrouded blue valleys and gulches of Kamalo, dripping with a symphony of translucent waterfalls. Here one may meet Uncle Larry Kalua, who lives across the highway but maintains a fishing camp on this shore, drying his squid in the sun and wind, playing with his dogs and the neighborhood kids and assorted family members, and enjoying life like no one we'd ever met before.

After having discovered this beautiful place the day before, we returned to the jetty at 7 a.m. for photographs, anticipating the glow of the early morning sun lighting the mountain tops. Larry, walking his dogs, stopped to introduce himself and talk story awhile. "I'll let you work now. But when you're done, you come over for some coffee", he said, pointing to his camp.

And so we did. The Hawaiian music station was playing on the radio, his shelter had all the comforts of home, and he insisted on cooking a live crab for breakfast. Larry opened a cooler where a half dozen of the angry monsters awaited their fate as they cleaned themselves. He popped the biggest into a waiting pot on the fire, and slammed on the lid. He gave us a choice between coffee or a beer. We chose the coffee. We had gotten busy talking when suddenly the lid flew off with a crash and the crab desperately tried to clamber out of the steaming pot. Larry dashed over and jammed the lid on again, this time placing a big rock on top of it to weigh it down. "Sorry buddy", said Uncle Larry to the crab, "but that's life in the fryin' pan."

As we ate the freshest and most delicious crab of our lives, Larry pulled out the family album to familiarize us with pictures of his five kids and ten siblings. One photo showed a brother, a huge and strikingly handsome bodybuilder, holding a child in each powerfully forged arm. "He's an artist, he made this", said Uncle

Halawa Falls Drive

❺

Larry, pointing to a beautifully carved koa wood sign strung in the tree above with the words *Aina Kamalo, "the land of Kamalo... my land"*. Alongside his camp, Larry cleverly grows eggplants, peppers and tomatoes in freestanding black plastic trash bags filled with potting soil, and trades his ocean catch locally for a cornucopia of other foodstuffs. "My dried octopus sells for $30 a pound in Honolulu", he proudly boasts. He shows me photos that some preceding breakfast guests have sent to him of his famous squid, tentacles outstretched like rays emanating from the sun, hanging in the wind to dry. "Everyone comes here, everyone is welcome, I share whatever I have", he says ingenuously. And truly, he does. We had to move on, but Larry told us to drop by "anytime, especially on weekends, when everybody's here".

After Kamalo, tiny, lovingly restored **St. Joseph's Church [1876]**, built by Father Damien, sits roadside to welcome visitors. Horses grazing along the shoulder of the road seem more plentiful here than other places in Hawaii and many of them have white cattle egrets riding on their backs, using the perch to scope out tasty snacks crawling through the grass.

Photographs

For the first two photo locations, see map on page 130.

❺ Detail of St. Joseph Church in Kamalo, built by Father Damien.

❻ 7:15 A.M.: Uncle Larry Kalua takes time from his fishing business to play with his dogs at the end of Kamalo Wharf.

㉔ Kids play basketball at Kilohana School. Look closely to see distant waterfalls in the mountains. For this photo location, see the map on page 134.

Kamalo

6

24

133

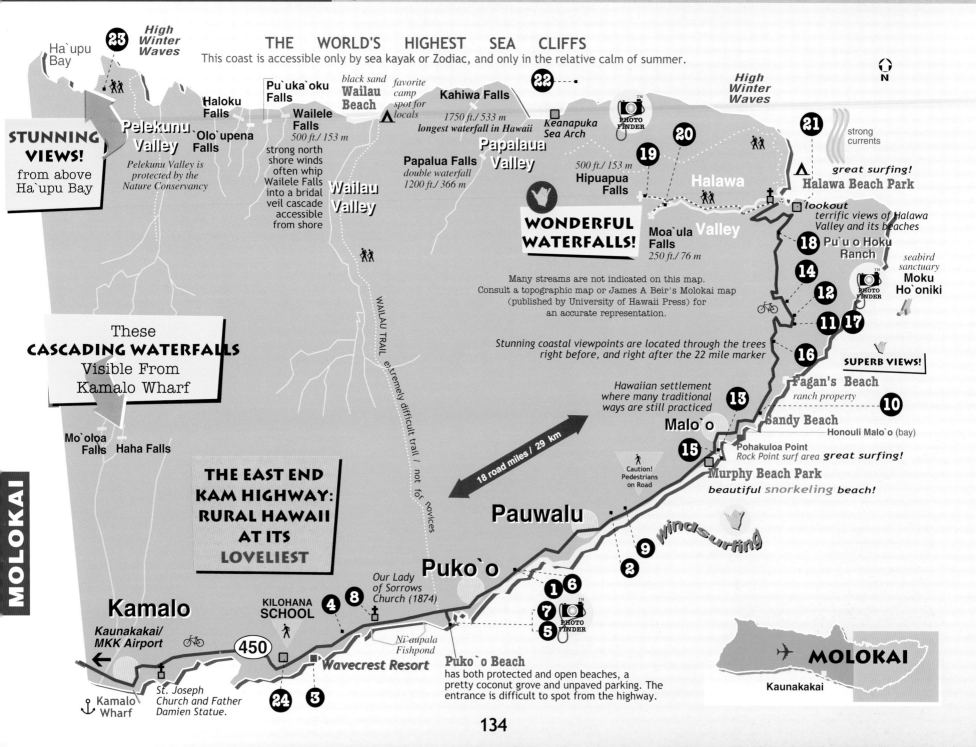

Molokai's East End

At mile marker 13 you will encounter a sign for the condo complex **Wavecrest Resort**, an ideal base for those who want accommodations with all the comforts of home. The Wavecrest is efficiently managed and offers large apartment units with color TV and kitchens fully equipped for meal preparation, with dishwashers and disposal. The bathrooms have tubs with shower. Parking is easy but not all units have in-room telephones. There is a fine swimming pool at the shoreline with pretty views of the mountains, the sea, and neighbor island Maui across the channel, and a pool pavilion with barbecues and an extensive library of paperbacks to get lost in. Fishermen bring their catch to the shore a few yards away and will sell you something wonderful and fresh out of the water to pop on one of the grills. A large and lovely palm-studded common lawn area with chaises makes a great place to pull up a lounge chair and have a glass of wine as the day wanes and the lights of Maui's Ka'anapali-Napili-Kapalua Resorts twinkle to life nine miles across the channel. Night-lit tennis courts round out the Wavecrest Resort's great appeal, and videos and VCRs are available for rent at the **Wavecrest Market**, but remember that this small but well stocked store **closes at 6 PM**. The Wavecrest Resort is wonderfully quiet, even during the day. Call toll-free from the mainland, ©
(800) 367-2980 or locally, © **558-8101.** The Wavecrest Market is your **last opportunity to stock up** on supplies and water before exploring further. There is no drinking water in Halawa Valley, the terminus of our journey and the home of the wonderful trail to Moa'ula and Hipuapua Falls.

A short way past the Wavecrest you will encounter another Father Damien-constructed jewel, pretty **Our Lady of Sorrows Church [1874]**. It is located on the *mauka* side of the road, and pictured here in the golden glow of late day. Right before **Puko'o**, about 0.7 mile past mile marker 15, there is a (sometimes unmarked) beach access road, *makai*. This short dirt track leads to a beautiful seaside area with two beaches. The little dirt road ends at a large grass parking area adjacent to a lovely little coconut grove. At the shore, a very protected brown sand beach awaits,

its silty shore bottom, home to thousands of crabs, a result of mud washing down the adjacent stream after heavy rains. Walk out along the jetty to find a beautiful little sandy white deserted beach with clear waters and a sandy-coral-rocky shore bottom, providing beautiful coastal views. A short walk to the left reveals nice views of this crescent white beach and the protected waters of handsome little Puko'o Harbor.

Back on the highway keep an eye on the rearview mirror for pretty little beaches that angle off behind you. They are not apparent unless you are driving in the opposite direction. Near mile **marker 19**, at **Pauwalu**, look for obvious places to pull onto the shoulder for handsome views of beaches and fishponds. This entire area is ideal for windsurfing, but as yet undiscovered. You may see a few riders out on the water.

Molokai Fish and Dive on Ala Malama St. in Kaunakakai © **553-5926** has information about equipment rentals. Right before **mile marker 20** the heretofore divided and excellent KAM HWY. narrows, making it necessary to use caution when rounding curves. **This is no place to speed** or be in any kind of hurry: children, dogs, cattle, surfers and fishermen all walk the road. Anyway, the most spectacular scenery now begins, and you don't want to miss a thing. Pull to the shoulder right before **MM 20** and walk out a little on the fishpond wall for a **great shot** of palm studded Murphy's Beach jutting into the channel, with imposing **Moku Ho'oniki** Island providing a picturesque counterpoint in the distance.

The highway rounds the point at beautiful Murphy's Beach, which is studded with coconut palms, making it very visually appealing. Believe it or not, this gorgeous place was once the *local dump* —until the Jaycees cleaned it up. Locals also know Murphy's Beach Park as **Murphy Beach** and as **Jaycees Park**. The shore bottom here is shallow with sandy areas between the rocks, providing protected swimming for children. **Snorkeling is super** —just look how clear the water is in the photographs— and they say it's even better outside the reef ....but strong currents are the rule out there on stormy days, so beware. After rounding the curve along Murphy's Beach Park, the road climbs a small rise. Immediately on the *makai/seaward* side is an unpaved parking area with great views of Murphy's, the island of Maui, and the rugged coast we are about to visit. The narrow road continues, tracing the coastline and jutting inward around **Honouli Wai Bay**. This small community incorporates old Hawaiian ways, the stream providing water for its taro patches. Drive very slowly through this area as children and pets are in the road. Around the next point, **Pohakuloa**, be cautious as you may encounter **surfers'** vans jutting into the road, tucked into any available nook or cranny they can find. When surf's up, this is a very popular surfing spot, known locally as **Rock Point**.

After he next bay, **Honouli Malo'o**, the road skirts pretty little **Sandy Beach**. Its golden sands are reef-protected and it offers a deeper shore bottom than Murphy's Beach. Its reported that there is a strong rip current at the right end of the beach. This is the last accessible sandy beach until we reach Halawa Valley. Right after Sandy Beach, the road begins its ascent into the **Pu'u O Hoku Ranchlands**. As it climbs and winds, keep an eye out soon for two little dirt tracks, *makai/seaward*. Park here, then walk out beyond the trees for wonderful, **dramatic coastal views** in both directions and **great photo opportunities**. This area is especially awesome on stormy

days when the wind is howling and great waves crash on the rocky headlands far below.

The highway will challenge with some very sharp curves, so please drive slowly. As you climb higher, wonderful views of grassland, rustic fences, and coastal vistas materialize. Cattle and horses are scattered on the hillsides, and below, **Kanaha Rock** and **Moku Ho'oniki** (moku means island in Hawaiian) lie undisturbed, their bird life protected about a mile offshore. The most notable place on Molokai for **diving**, Moku Ho'oniki also attracts snorkelers, but surface conditions are often very rough. Arrangements are normally made with Maui island dive companies to dive here as there are, as of this writing, no commercial dive outfits on Molokai. This former WWII bombing practice target is littered with artifacts from those episodes. There are many underwater pinnacles and drop-offs, and divers will encounter gray reef sharks, ulua, barracuda and long-nose hawkfish, as well as black coral. Depths range from 30-100 feet. There is a great view of Moku Ho'oniki from the *Aloha Island Air* Molokai-to-Kahului flight.

The road continues, gouged into the hillside in places and shaded by woods as it climbs higher. It passes the **Pu'u o Hoku Ranch headquarters** before winding around toward open sky at Alanuipuhipaka Ridge. There is a good-sized hairpin **turnout** here with **sensational views** of Halawa Valley, distant 500 foot tall **Hipuapua Falls**, and just a glimpse of the top of 250 foot **Moa'ula Falls**. **Halawa Bay Beach** lies directly below. The route from this point on takes on the look of a national park roadway as it winds downhill, bordered by neat low stone walls, hugging the precipices as it descends toward the valley. If there is no traffic, try to stop at each tiny turnout for different photo views.

Halawa Valley is one of Hawaii's loveliest valleys, and the first place on Molokai to have been settled by the ancient Hawaiians, early in the 7th century. Its rich soil nourished their crops for centuries, until two relatively recent tidal waves —in 1946 and 1957— covered the valley with an alluvium of plant killing salts. You will see many taro terraces, both abandoned restored, along the trail to Moa'ula Falls. The road passes a tiny **wooden church** on the *left* and some spooky tsunami building **ruins** on the *right*, just before the pavement ends. Halawa's beaches are straight ahead a hundred yards or so. **Kama'alaea Beach**, the curved beach on the *left*, and **Kawili Beach**, the more exposed beach to the *right* are safe for swimming when calm, mostly in summer. The shore bottoms slope gently to deeper waters and are somewhat rocky. These are some of the **best surfing beaches** on Molokai. Bring drinking water: none is available here.

Photographs

See map on page 134.
Photos, previous page:

❶❷ Two nearly identical beaches can be found located where the Kam Highway meets the shore in Puko`o (#1) near MM 16, and in Pauwalu (#2) at MM 18.3. See also photo #6, below.

This page:

❸ The Wavecrest Resort offers condo accommodations on Molokai's eastern shore.

❹ Between the 13 and 14 mile markers on the Kam Highway, a curious horse stands in the day's last rays of sunlight.

❺ Sunset at Puko`o. Graduated color filters were used to intensify the colors; a magenta on top and a red on the bottom.

❻ At MM 18.3, the Kam Hwy. again meets the shore at Pauwalu, and another officially unnamed beach appears.

❼ At Puko`o, its white sand beach lies at the open ocean end of the rock seawall.

❽ Just before sunset, the colors of nature intensify, such as in this shot taken at Our Lady of Sorrows Church. It is located about halfway between Kamalo and Puko`o. Across the Highway is Kopeahina Fishpond.

❾ Late afternoon rainbow at Pauwalu.

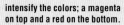

❸

❹

MOLOKAI

❻

❺

⑦ ⑧

❾

Halawa Falls Drive

Photographs

See map on page 134.

10 Sandy Beach is the last sandy beach having public access before the road climbs into Pu`u o Hoku ranchlands.

11 **12** Views from the road as the highway climbs through Pu`u o Hoku Ranch.

13 At Malo`o, just after Murphy Beach Park, the highway winds past two clear and pretty bays. This one is Honouli Wai.

14 Horses roadside sometimes strike the perfect pose just for you. Be camera-ready.

15 Murphy Beach Park has crystal clear waters, great snorkeling and fabulous wind surfing conditions. During the week, the place is deserted.

16 After the Highway leaves Sandy Beach and begins to climb, hard-to-see dirt parking areas, *makai*, provide dramatic views of the rugged coast. Drive slowly so you can keep an eye out for them.

138

Halawa Falls Drive

⑭

⑮
⑯

139

Photographs

See map on page 134.

17 Mokuo`oniki beckons from offshore, but the seas surrounding it can be treacherous.

18 The highway as it nears Halawa Valley gouges its way through the mountain side in a winter's foggy haze.

17

MOLOKAI

Halawa Falls Drive

Moaula Falls Hike

The first time we took the hike to Moa'ula Falls there were no guided treks available. We had to set out on a weekday by necessity, even though normally we try to take first-time hikes through unfamiliar territory on *weekends* when there are locals around to help us find our way, and more importantly, find our way *out*. We took our second and third hikes to Moa'ula Falls only a few months after the first, but by then radical changes had already taken place.

It seems that a visitor making the hike slipped somewhere along the way (surprise! –this *is* rainforest) and was injured, and then attempted to sue one of the elderly Halawa Valley residents for damages because he didn't attempt to stop the visitor from crossing his land! The urge for us to go into a tirade about personal responsibility is extremely tempting at this point, but we're not going to put you through *that* lecture. Instead, suffice it to say that visitors are solely responsible for their decisions and the outcome.

As a result of that legal action, local Halawa residents like Pilipo currently guide visitors to Moa'ula Falls. Pilipo, who was raised in Halawa Valley, gives more than just a guided hike. He recounts old tales, stories from his own childhood and the history of old Halawa. Tour prices are $25 per person and are scheduled Monday, Wednesday, Friday, and Saturday by reservation only. Hikers should be steady of foot and in good health, as the trail is rugged and slippery. Hikers should bring drinking water, a light meal, energy bars, trail mix or the like, and perhaps an extra pair of socks or watershoes if you have them, and wear good comfortable hiking shoes. All hikers will be required to sign a liability waiver. For more information and reservations call **(808) 553-4355**.

You can also ask at your hotel desk or in town about making hiking arrangements, in case the phone number or circumstances change.

Before arriving at Halawa, we make preparations by gathering everything we'll need for the trek and stowing everything that we don't. We usually stop at one of the lookouts to do this. We don't want to be seen placing things in the trunk at our final destination by any would-be thieves.

We bring an old pair sneakers and an extra pair of dry socks for crossing or walking in streams. Nothing is more uncomfortable than hiking in wet socks and shoes. The trail is bordered in places by brightly glowing impatiens, mangoes, Surinam cherries, tiny Hawaiian strawberries, ginger and liliko'i, elephant ear plants, ha'u trees and the remnants of old taro terraces.

The trail is lovely and extremely quiet. We expected to hear a cacophony of birds, but there was instead mostly silence, except for the sound of the gurgling stream.

At one point near our destination, there was a glimpse through the trees of both Moa'ula Falls, and its much taller neighbor, Hipuapua Falls. Soon after seeing this view, we crossed over Hipuapua Stream, hopping the giant dry boulders to the trail continuation on the other side. A water pipe crosses the stream here also. In less than five minutes from this point we were standing at the base of Moa'ula Falls, ready to take a soak in its plunge pool, which is much larger and deeper than we expected from the photos we'd seen of this lovely place.

Brown algae covers the rocks underwater, and although the water is very clear, the color of the algae makes it, at first glance, appear muddy. The algae also makes the rocks incredibly slippery, so we took great care easing ourselves into the cold water. We spent about two hours dry-boulder hopping up and down the stream, trying different vantage points for good photographs. Winds whipped up through the valley and caught the waters as they tipped over Moa'ula's two brinks, sending beautiful swirling ghostly mists into the air, backlit by the midday sun.

We find Moa'ula Falls to be among the prettiest in Hawaii, but we have sometimes heard this one-hour-long trail described as "very strenuous". We are in good shape, but we're not hikers really, more like wilderness walkers. We would describe this hike as tiring and somewhat challenging for non-hikers, especially if you go all the way to Hipuapua Falls. But we often saw overweight older people in their 50s and 60s at Moa'ula Falls looking happy and rested and none the worse for wear. We found the hike to Moa'ula Falls no more difficult, if a little longer, than the Manoa Falls Hike in Honolulu's Manoa Valley; muddy, slippery, sweaty, and all uphill. But as Pilipo remarked to me the first time we met, as he laughed and shook his head, "I don't know what some people expect. They think there's going to be a paved asphalt sidewalk all the way to the falls!".

To visit towering **Hipuapua Falls**, we took a detour 5 minutes before reaching Moa'ula Falls. When we initially reached Hipuapua Stream [where the water pipe crosses it], instead of crossing the stream to continue the trail to Moa'ula Falls on the other side, we began hopping upstream atop the stream bed's huge dry rocks and boulders, following Hipuapua Stream uphill to its source. There is no real foot trail that we could find, and we liked the aerobic challenge of quickly boulder-hopping our way along. We were hot, thirsty and a little tired, so it took us about 20 minutes after leaving the water pipe before we caught sight of Hipuapua Falls.

We were thrilled. Nobody else was around, there were no signs of humanity anywhere —no litter and no footprints. The waters of Hipuapua Falls drop 500' (that's the height indicated on maps, but some people doubt Hipuapua is that high) over the edge of a sheer cliff into a U-shaped pool. Again the water was very clear and cold, but we were so overheated that it felt like heaven. The water beneath the falls was neck-deep, but at the far edge of the U-shaped pool, it was much deeper.

The falls created a lovely rushing mist-cooled wind that kept mosquitoes away, and it was truly like every fantasy we've ever had of such a place. It was dramatic, loud, and beautiful, and in retrospect, almost unreal. What a world away it now seems... being pelted on the head by chilly virgin waters tumbling down a towering cliff, in an extremely isolated corner of Hawaii's least visited island, in a chain of islands located further away from land mass than any place on earth.

Now *that's* solitude.

Halawa Falls Drive

19

See map on page 134.

Photographs

19 Hipuapua Falls, according to maps, towers 500 feet / 152m, although it doesn't look that high.

20 Moaula Falls

MOLOKAI

double-decker Moa'ula Falls *splays its mists into the air.*

Halawa Falls Drive

㉒

Photographs

See map on page 134.

㉑ From the hairpin turnoff - lookout area above Halawa Valley, the sun streaks through the clouds. It almost obscures the view of Hipuapua Falls at the back of this scene but highlights the curve of the now very narrow Highway as it rounds a turn.

㉒ From a raft exploring Molokai's wild North Shore, a boy points out a waterfall to the other passengers.

㉓ In this superb shot, taken by author Peter Caldwell, Ha`upu Bay embodies the spirit and beauty, not only of Molokai, but Hawaii as a whole. As once featured in *National Geographic* magazine, one Hawaiian family, a single mother and her sons, lives here in stunning isolation. Their house can be seen in this shot at bottom left. The former leper colony of Kalaupapa Peninsula can be seen in the distance.

㉑

23

ethereal and beautiful, the north shore's Ha'upu Bay

◯ full circle indicates yes

◐ half circle indicates partial or sometimes

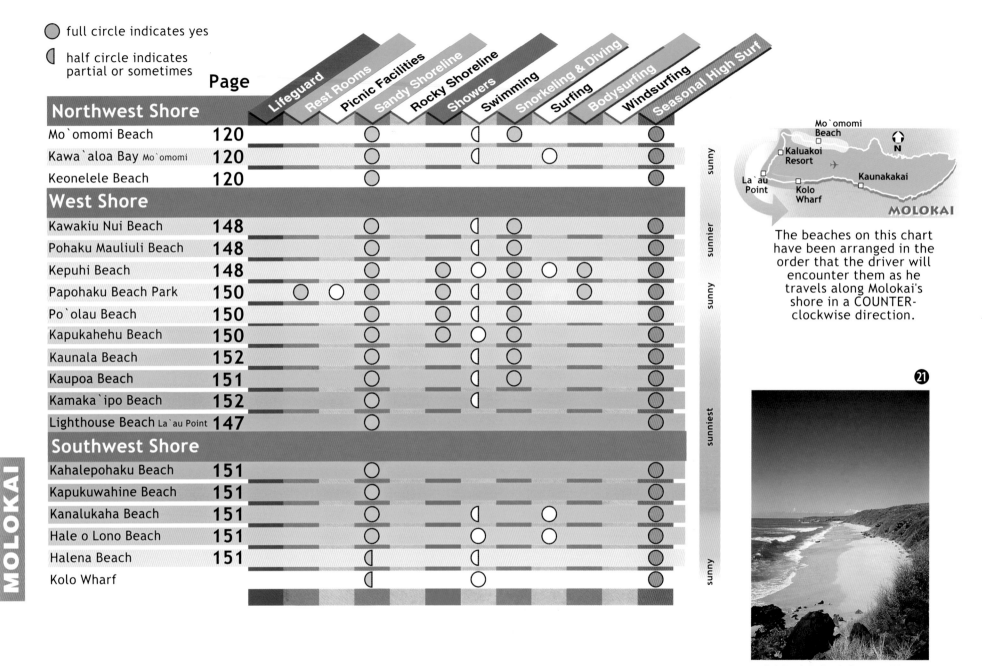

	Page	Lifeguard	Rest Rooms	Picnic Facilities	Sandy Shoreline	Rocky Shoreline	Showers	Swimming	Snorkeling & Diving	Surfing	Bodysurfing	Windsurfing	Seasonal High Surf
Northwest Shore													
Mo`omomi Beach	120				●			◐	●				●
Kawa`aloa Bay Mo`omomi	120				●			◐		●			●
Keonelele Beach	120				●								●
West Shore													
Kawakiu Nui Beach	148				●			◐	●				●
Pohaku Mauliuli Beach	148				●			◐	●				●
Kepuhi Beach	148				●		●	●	●	●	●		●
Papohaku Beach Park	150		●	●	●		●	◐	●		●		●
Po`olau Beach	150				●		●	◐	●				●
Kapukahehu Beach	150				●		●	●	●				●
Kaunala Beach	152				●			◐	●				●
Kaupoa Beach	151				●			◐	●				●
Kamaka`ipo Beach	152				●			◐					●
Lighthouse Beach La`au Point	147				●								●
Southwest Shore													
Kahalepohaku Beach	151				●								●
Kapukuwahine Beach	151				●								●
Kanalukaha Beach	151				●			◐		●			●
Hale o Lono Beach	151				●			●		●			●
Halena Beach	151				◐			◐					●
Kolo Wharf					◐			●					●

sunny · sunnier · sunny · sunniest · sunny

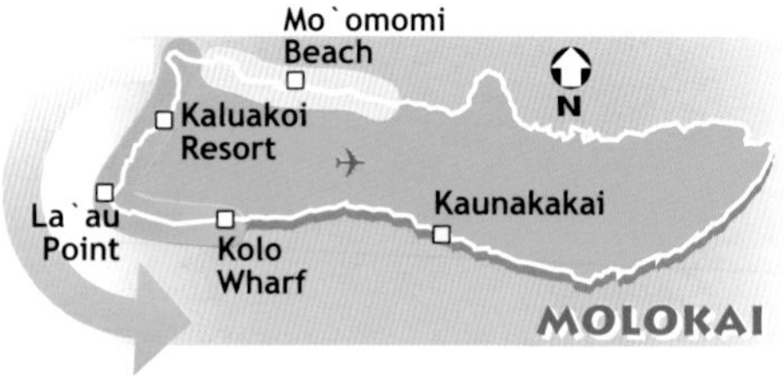

The beaches on this chart have been arranged in the order that the driver will encounter them as he travels along Molokai's shore in a COUNTER-clockwise direction.

21

Kahalepohaku Beach. See map, right.

MOLOKAI

Molokai's west end is this island's fun-in-the-sun paradise. The beaches are superb –beautiful, wide, golden and deserted. Few people live here, so houses are few and far between. A couple of loop roads have been built off the main highway, ostensibly for future housing development projects. But so far, Molokai's notorious water shortage problems, coupled with a stalled economy and a core of iron-willed citizens who want Molokai to stay the way it is, have obstructed those plans. Physically, West Molokai consists of seemingly endless acres of Molokai Ranchland and kiawe trees rolling down to the sea from 1400' / 540m Mauna Loa. The only town on west Molokai is **Maunaloa**, located at the top of Hwy. 460. There is precious little traffic on this side of Molokai, and even though the area's beach parks have paved parking, we've never seen their tiny parking lots full. **The photos of these beaches seen in Driving & Discovering Hawaii: Maui and Molokai *have not* been retouched to remove the people or the footprints.** Even on perfect, hot, blue-sky Sunday afternoons, when Oahu's Waikiki Beach is jammed blanket-to-blanket, there is often not a single soul to be seen on many West Molokai beaches.

The centerpiece of the western shore's Kaluakoi resort area is the **Kaluakoi Resort and Golf Club, currently closed as of this writing. We assume it will be up and running again in the near future as it has had three different owners since we first began publishing this book. Call the Molokai Visitors Association** [phone **(808) 553-3876**] for current news on the Kaluakoi Hotel. Private condominiums are open and still available as vacation rentals on property, however.

For beach lovers, the selection of strands in West Molokai is *superb*, and four are within a short hiking distance of the hotel. Directly in front of the hotel, split in two by the bluff that the swimming pool sits on, is **Kepuhi Beach**. Kepuhi, and all west Molokai beaches, is unsafe for swimming most if the time, except in the dead calm of summer. Kepuhi is boulder-strewn, making it hazardous and beautiful at the same time. The sand comes and goes with the seasons; it recedes somewhat in the stormy winter months and builds up again in the calm of summer. To the right, as you face the sea from the swimming pool area, the beach is more protected and sandier, and attracts small legions of Molokai surfers who have the **fabulous sets** all to themselves. Before doing any surfing yourself, check with the locals about hidden hazards.

If you hike along the edge of the golf course to the *right / north* of this beach, you will find the two **Pohaku Mauliuli Beaches**, the first one often having a sun-warmed tide pool at the rear and usually a large sized

untracked sand bank constantly washed over by incoming waves. Here, like at all exposed beaches in Hawaii, **never turn your back to the sea**. We can't emphasize strongly enough, that every year, a few locals who grew up in Hawaii and have walked these beaches a hundred times get dragged out to sea by unexpected rogue waves. If it can happen to them, it can certainly happen to us. Keep an eye out.

Climb over the bluff to view the second beautiful, primeval beach, where the sands climb up the headlands at the rear and seclusion is not hard to find. The offshore waters are deep, there are often strong currents, especially the alongshore kind, and the headlands are crumbling, so *you will not want to sunbathe near the base of the cliffs*. We met two male visitors here who had just emerged from the water with snorkeling gear. They had been **snorkeling** around the point and were *ecstatic* about the quantity and size of sea life, most notably giant sea turtles and sea anemones. We questioned their sanity, since the seas were extremely rough, and one of the men was bleeding from a number of places after being washed into the rocks. They seemed to think it was worth the risks. We don't. But on the other hand, they were also thrilled with their previous day's diving at **Murphy's Beach Park** on Molokai's East Shore —a far safer, calmer alternative.

Another beautiful and very secluded strand, **Kawakiu Beach**, lies further along the coast still, but it takes a 30 minute-plus rock hop to reach it from this point. The only way to drive there is via a **7 mile long unpaved 4WD road** that branches off Hwy. 460, beginning about 4 miles west of the airport. Check with your hotel's activities desk or with locals for current status of public access to KAWAKIU ROAD.

Back at the hotel, to the left of it as one faces the water at the SW end of the beach a trail can be seen climbing the edge of the crumbling bluff, promising some great views. Don't take this **dangerous** and slippery trail, because a **much easier**, safer and more rewarding pathway to the top of this bluff is located just around the back of the bluff. Our favorite time of day for this short hike is in the cool of the morning when the sunlight is soft and angled, the air is cool, and a stroll is a great way to walk off breakfast. At the far end of the beach you will see a stairway adjacent to the golf course lawn leading up to a paved public parking lot. (You can drive here by *turning makai* from KALUAKOI ROAD onto KAIAKA ROAD.) A dirt jeep road, sometimes with a chain across it to block cars (just walk around it) ascends from this lot to the top of the bluff. First it reaches a lookout point that surveys marvelous, nearly-three-mile-long **Papohaku Beach**. Then the red-dirt track winds prettily through a thicket of thorny kiawe trees, past an old WWII bunker to another lookout point that surveys **Kepuhi Beach** from whence we just came, the entire resort, and other coves and beaches that trail on up the coast.

After exploring the resort-adjacent beaches on foot, we're ready to hop in the car and head down KALUAKOI ROAD to check out long, wide and wondrous **Papohaku Beach** and the others that follow. Little roads branch off the highway *makai/seaward*. If you're not in a hurry, or if this is your first day and you're searching for the ideal beach, you may want to check out each turnoff that you pass.

A turn into **Papohaku Beach Park** surprises on weekdays, and often even on weekends, when you see that yours is the only car in the parking lot. This large, handsome tree-shaded park has **cooking grills, picnic tables, restrooms and showers**, and lots of blooming red hibiscus and seasonal wildflowers lining the pathway leading to the exquisite sands of Hawaii's third-longest beach [**Waimanalo Beach** on Oahu's Windward side is second longest, and **Polihale Beach** on Kauai is the champ]. *The crashing surf at Papohaku can be wild, so best keep children away from the shoreline.* The only safe time to swim might be in a dead summer calm. This beach is a wonder for its desertedness. Often, not one single human, —or even a footprint— will be seen on its very wide almost three-mile-long expanse. For those who revel in the freedom of open spaces, Papohaku will delight. Sand dunes guard the rear of the beach, which is backed by woods dotted with seasonal wildflowers. There are a few expensive homes along here, but they are unobtrusive for the most part.

The military used Papohaku Beach for landing exercises in the '40s and '50s. When these exercises were terminated, they buried their debris (!) at the shoreline toward the center of the beach. Here, abandoned vehicles and bales of wire and other sharp, rusted metal objects may be exposed by heavy seas, posing a serious hazard to you and yours. Be vigilant.

❶

❷

❸

Kaluakoi

❺

4

Photographs

See map on page 147 for photograph locations.

❶ A lone surfer, seen from the swimming pool area, revels in set after ideal set of perfectly shaped waves. Anywhere else in Hawaii, a surfing spot of this caliber would be crawling with wave riders.

❷ This morning view of the NE end of Papohaku Beach is from the first lookout atop Pu`u o Kaiaka's short and easy hiking trail/ jeep road.

❸ A surfer rides into Kepuhi Beach on a beautiful day.

❹ This view, of the unobtrusive hotel and SW end of Kepuhi Beach, was taken from the second lookout atop Pu`u o Kaiaka trail/ jeep road. The early morning rays of the sun selectively light different areas of the scene as a lone stroller finds the seclusion she's after.

❺ The Resort's rooms are housed in *hales* that dot the beautiful property.

The next p.r.o.w. (public right of way) from the Highway is at LAUHUE ST. The next one after that is at PAPAPA PLACE, which leads to a turnaround where KULUA ST. intersects. There is a shower here, but no restroom. A short walk to the beach reveals a fabulous panorama of the entire length of Papohaku Beach.

The following p.r.o.w. is hidden and little used. After PAPAPA PLACE, there will be a "T" intersection. To the left a sign says no outlet. Turn right, then turn right again on KULAWAI ST. Soon, you will reach another "T" intersection at KAULA ILI WAY. A right turn will soon dead end, but a left turn takes you to a little clifftop parking area, where there is an **open air shower** with a great view. When it's hot, we love to come here and take a shower at the edge of the cliff and delight in the wet, the wind and the views. We have been here a dozen times and have never seen another soul. There is a small beach here, to the left and hidden from view by thorny kiawe trees and brush. To the right, a path winds along the edge of a massive sand dune in the NE direction. This path soon reaches solid, flat ground soon, then rounds **Pu`u Koa`e Point** for a grand elevated vista of Papohaku Beach from its SW end. The remains of a sand mining operation have been left intact to somewhat spoil the view. Enormous amounts of sand were removed from unprotected Papohaku Beach in the '60s and '70s to supplement the dwindling sands at Waikiki. Similar removals were carried out at Waimea Beach on Oahu's north shore as well. One has to imagine what Papohaku and Waimea might look like today if they had been left alone.

Continuing in the SW direction, **Po'olau Beach** (shower, paved parking) has a rocky shore and less than ideal swimming conditions, which include a rocky shore bottom and treacherous inshore rip currents. It is however quite attractive and photogenic, especially when people remember to take their 'opala (garbage) away with them. Next, PAKA'A ST. leads to a boulder shore popular with fishermen. There is no beach here.

Finally, the paved road ends at **Kapukahehu Beach**, (shower, paved parking) also known locally as **Dixie Maru**, after a ship that was wrecked here in the 1920s. This sometimes lovely and photogenic crescent bay is popular with snorkelers and divers, but only when its been dry and the stream hasn't been running. Days after a rain, red mud can still color the waters. The shore bottom is rocky with sandy pockets, but despite its protected appearance, heavy surf can create dangerous inshore rip currents. The beach is backed by kiawe trees and beneath them seasonal wildflowers bloom. Although never crowded, there have usually been other people here when we have visited.

If you're in the mood for a 20-30 minute rock-hopping hike, follow the shore to the left/southward, as you face open ocean, to end up at a similar beach at **Kaunala Bay**. A lot of gorgeous big and little beach gems dot

this coast; ask at the Molokai Ranch offices about access.

Most visitors never get the chance to imprint Molokai's trackless virgin **Southwest Coast Beaches** with their footsteps because they are unaware that this Molokai Ranch-owned area is quite accessible from Maunaloa town. Also, the Molokai Ranch Outfitters Center offers a number of adventure activities on its vast property. Their horseback ride over the vast African-like landscape ends at an untrammeled beach, where kayaking, swimming or surfing is offered, along with a gourmet lunch. Mountain bike adventures allow visitors to explore the area at will, and if you make arrangements, they'll pick you up at the end of your day and drive you and your bike back to the Center...the return trip is all uphill. The Ranch's "tentalows", luxury tent cabin camps

with private baths, showers and real beds, overlook Kaupoa Beach. For information, phone toll-free from the mainland **(877) 726-4656.**

Even though Hawaii rental car contracts prohibit taking passenger vehicles off pavement, on Molokai more than any other Hawaiian island, unpaved roads lead to a lot of wonderful destinations. Most roads in West Molokai are very well maintained by the Ranch.

The main dirt road into the **Southwest** area, which originates in Maunaloa town, is usually in excellent repair unless there has been a major storm. During the annual **Molokai to Oahu Outrigger Canoe Races** in June and October, lots of older local passenger cars make the trip down this unpaved road to Hale O Lono Harbor without any problem. Just west of the harbor is

Photographs

See map on page 147.

6 Papohaku Beach is viewed here from its midpoint. This photo was not retouched to remove footprints, and it was indeed taken on a beautiful Sunday afternoon...amazing, considering that this is Molokai's most popular beach park!

MOLOKAI

150

Papohaku Beach

❻

Kanalukaha Beach. A very rough jeep road parallels the shore, but a (usually) locked gate will probably prevent you from driving it. Park your car in the shade and hike along this road or along Kanalukaha Beach. No beach along these **Southwest** shores is safe for swimming as all are exposed to the open sea. **Kanalukaha Beach** is a very long white sand beach backed by small sand dunes and kiawe trees. The beachcombing here is good, and is seasonally abundant in puka shells, for those who would like to string their own puka shell necklaces.

The jeep road rounds and climbs the rear of the bluff at the end of Kanalukaha Beach and a walk out onto the bluff reveals the expanse of enchanting **Kapukuwahine Beach**. This beautiful, secluded, pristine, untouched, wide, white sandy beach is backed by low sand dunes and kiawe trees for its full length.

A hike along Kapukuwahine Beach will mark its perfect sands with the only footsteps it's seen in a while. We have never been here when it seemed safe to swim. The jeep road ends at the bluff at its far end. A climb up and over this bluff reveals yet another, even more isolated wonder, **Kahalepohaku Beach**. Its location close to **Laʻau Point**'s treacherous currents make this beauty an even more unsuitable recreational swimming spot than any of the others. **Kahalepohaku** is backed by eroding seacliffs. The unchecked surf washes up very high onto the wide beach, so be careful where you choose to lie down. Don't snooze here!

Backtracking to POHAKULOA ROAD (the main dirt road) continue along the beach-lined coast to see **Hale o Lono Harbor** which becomes a sea of colorful outriggers at canoe race time, but is otherwise deserted. Past the harbor area, to the left as you face the water, more sandy beaches line the shore. The first one is within a protected cove which appears to have the only calmed waters in this harbor area. The dirt road veers away from the shore at this point and becomes deeply rutted in spots. It continues on to **Halena**, and then on to **Kolo Wharf**, where swimming possibilities are a little better than at other beaches along the way, but the Ranch office can advise you best.

Backtracking again to POHAKULOA ROAD, *drive uphill* about halfway back to the gate (see map page 147). On the *left*, a small dirt road leads *seaward*. This is the road which leads down to gorgeous **Kaupoa Beach** and Molokai Ranch's Kaupoa camp. The road's condition depends on the damage that recent storms might have done. In the past we've had to stop a few times to move boulders out of the way of our vehicle before we could proceed. The soil and road are colored brilliant red, and the trees and landscape quite unlike anyone's idea of what Hawaii should look like, resembling East Africa more than anything else.

The Molokai Ranch maintains their beautifully situated, luxury "tentalow" camp at **Kaupoa Beach**. They include all meals, real beds, private baths with showers, maid service and a wooden deck. Kaupoa Beach itself is shaped roughly like the letter W, with two cove-like areas divided by a rocky outcrop near beach center. The right cove as you face the water has the best swimming. The beach sand is brilliant white, the beach itself wide, steep and sandy; the waters are a crystalline turquoise in color, and in a summer calm the swimming is great. The water gets deep very quickly right off shore. Over the rocks to the right is another small white sand beach, but it has a very rocky shoreline. For those who love being as far away from civilization as possible, Kaupoa Beach is extremely isolated. The only thing that might spoil the illusion is the distant twinkling lights of Waikiki seen at night, far across the channel.

A rough road continues on along the shore north eastward to **Kaunala Bay** and **Kaunala Beach**. Kaunala Beach can alternately be reached by hiking around the point (it will take 20-30 minutes of rock hopping) to the *left / south* of Kapukahehu Beach (described on page 150), which is the last beach accessible to the public from paved KALUAKOI ROAD (see map page 147). **Kaunala Beach**'s waters, like those of its neighbor **Kapukahehu Beach**, can be quite murky after a rain due to mud carried in by running streams. In dry periods though, both places offer good snorkeling and swimming on calm days.

Even though we weren't riding bikes, the network of dirt roads that lead to all these beautiful pristine beaches, as well as to **Kamaka'ipo Beach** and its **Soda Pop Pool** (the pool being the only safe swimming spot in these parts) looked like mountain bike heaven to us. Unencumbered views, vibrating colors, surprising wildlife, clear waters and endless acres to explore make Molokai's Southwest Coast one of Hawaii's **premier mountain biking destinations**.

Photographs

See map on page 147.

7 Members of the California outrigger team ready their craft at Hale o Lono Harbor on the day before the big race in October.

8 This westward view of Kapukuwahine Beach was taken about a 20 minute walk west of unpaved Po'olau Road.

9 Kapukahehu Beach is the last beach in West Molokai that is accessible via paved public road. Its crescent shape makes it look protected, but under stormy conditions, a rip current exists.

next page:

10 Outriggers beached at Hale o Lono Harbor awaiting the big race form a colorful assemblage in this detail shot.

11 The Molokai Ranch maintains luxury tent cabins for rent at beautiful, blindingly white Kaupoa Beach. No one lives for miles around, so if its privacy you've been searching for, your quest ends here.

12 A weathered log lies bleached in the sun and the trackless sands at Papohaku Beach. We can't promise that you won't see anyone else's footprints here ...but we've visited more times when there weren't any tracks than when there were.

13 A pastel sunset ends a perfect day at Kepuhi Beach. No photo filters were used... this is exactly the way it looked.

7

8

9

⑩

⑪

⑬

⑫

nature rewards visitors to *MoLoKai* with some of hawaii's best beaches

Maunaloa

the tiny town of maunaloa offers a surprisingly generous number of photo opportunities, including sweeping views and humorous details.

Lost surfboards found washed up on the beach are transformed into a picket fence —molokai style

Mauanloa

At the end of Highway 460, perched on the slopes of the "*mountain*" named Mauna Loa, is the *town* of **Maunaloa**. This classic plantation village was the company town for Dole pineapple until 1975, when Dole began to wind down its operations on Molokai. At one time Maunaloa was connected to **Kaunakakai** and the rest of the island only by a dirt road, and those who resided here lived in relative isolation. What were at one time pineapple fields are now the pasture lands of **Molokai Ranch**, the largest land owner on the island, at about 60,000 acres. The views up here are wonderful, especially after a wet season when the landscape shines in a virtual sea of green waving grasses. The air is crisp and clear, refreshing breezes bounce along the rolling terrain, and red dirt roads radiate up, down, and along-slope to some of Molokai's least visited areas, including the untrammeled virgin beaches of the **Southwest Shore**.

In recent years, extraordinary physical changes have taken place in Maunaloa. The red fire station pictured here has been torn down, along with the surfboard fence and a few other structures. We decided to keep these photos in the book as they represent the spirit and the atmosphere of Maunaloa. Since we began publishing this book, almost half of the major businesses on Molokai have closed at least once, only to reopen some time later. This has made guidebook updating very difficult. It might be best to expect that one or more of the businesses mentioned herein might not be up and running during your visit.

As it approaches town, Highway 460 makes an abrupt curve upslope to the left, and immediately enters the tiny business district. Maunaloa has the best souvenir shopping on the island, and despite the town's minuscule size, businesses here can keep you busy for a couple of hours or more.

A number of former plantation buildings, located close to each other, have been converted to interesting shops selling the work of talented Molokai artisans. Made-on-Molokai treasures fill the eye as well as every spare inch of space at the **Plantation Gallery**. The gallery sells the work of dozens of Molokai artists and crafts people, and the wares include clothing, jewelry, baskets, Hawaiian quilts and pillow covers, watercolors, frames, items made from Molokai axis deer horn, and a whole range of things imported from Bali, including batiks, Balinese masks and crib angels. Laurie Cavanaugh's dolls are for sale here as well. Laurie used to operate the **Dolly Hale**, which is presently closed.

Our favorite Hawaii souvenirs are always those we can make use of in our daily lives, and there are plenty to choose from at the Plantation Gallery. Adjoining the Plantation Gallery is the **Big Wind Kite Factory** selling custom kites and windsocks, and offering free lessons in an open area nearby. Call **552-2364** for both the Kite Factory and Plantation Gallery. Hours are Monday through Saturday, 8:30 a.m. until 5 p.m., Sundays 10 a.m. until 2 p.m.

Located across the street is the **Maunaloa General Store**, which stays open until 6 PM. Here you can find just about whatever you need in the way of food and drink, as well as T shirts. Downhill from the store are the offices of the **Molokai Ranch** and its **Outfitters Center** [phone toll free from the mainland **877-726-4656**]. The Outfitters Center **gift shop** sells a terrific line of paniolo-themed T shirts and Molokai Ranch logo-embossed belt buckles and bandanas. You may also inquire about their horseback rides, mountain bike, and hunting adventures and their unique, sensitively designed wilderness luxury yurts, or "tentalows" scattered throughout the ranch property. These feature queen beds, private bath with shower, wood decks, maid service, all meals and snacks, with close access to Hawaii's most beautiful and deserted beaches.

Elegant accommodations are available at the 22 room **Molokai Ranch Lodge** [phone toll free from the mainland **877-726- 4656**] . All rooms include a wet bar, refrigerator, robes and slippers, cable television and private lanai. Eating choices at the Lodge include two options: the upscale Maunaloa Room, and the more casual Paniolo Lounge. Serving breakfast and dinner, the **Maunaloa Dining Room** is noted for its Molokai regional cuisine, romantic ambiance and spectacular views. Signature dishes include the fresh fish of the day prepared Mediterranean style, the paniolo New York steak and Caesar salad prepared tableside. For a lighter bite, sandwiches and pupus (appetizers) are available in the **Paniolo Lounge**, which also features spectacular views in addition to its cowboy and plantation décor.

Molokai Ranch has been a **working cattle ranch** for more than a hundred years, and its *paniolo* (Hawaiian cowboy) heritage spans five generations. The paniolos of Molokai Ranch are proud to share their heritage with you and hope to communicate an appreciation for their unique way of life. The 2000 seat Molokai Ranch Arena hosts many outdoor events. For information on any and all Molokai Ranch activities, call Molokai Ranch Information toll free at **877-726-4656**.

16

17

⑱

⑲

Photographs

Turn to map on page 147 for photograph locations.

⑭ Maunaloa's rolling pasture lands as seen from the rear of the tiny town.

⑮ A picket fence, Molokai style, made from lost surfboards washed up on the beach.

⑯ Molokai Ranch Outfitters leads horseback rides through the expansive and beautiful landscape.

⑰ The Maunaloa fire station gets a new coat of paint.

⑱ "Downtown" Maunaloa as seen from the terminus of Hwy. 460.

⑲ A Molokai Ranch employee engages in a loathesome backbiting episode after overhearing a particularly nasty remark.

㉑

㉒

6 pm: Molokai Rush Hour.

Molokai Weekend Surf Jam.

Molokai Weekend Beach Crowd.

Molokai Freeway.

SPEED LIMIT 15

㉔ For photo location 21 see map on page 120.
For photo locations 22, 23 and 24 see map on page 147.

㉓